Advance Pi

JOHN DEWEY'S IMAGINATI\ ... ...uu
Combining Theory and Practice

"*John Dewey's Imaginative Vision of Teaching* is a remarkable achievement. Here, a first-rate scholar deliberately and successfully writes a philosophical text for undergraduates and does so without compromising scholarly integrity. Dewey advocated teaching and curriculum that addresses not only the students' intellect, but their needs, desires, and interests in a demanding and disciplined manner. Deron Boyles enacts Dewey's philosophy of education rather than just writing about it. Established scholars will also find the book a rewarding read."

—JIM GARRISON
VIRGINIA TECH
PAST PRESIDENT, JOHN DEWEY SOCIETY, PHILOSOPHY OF EDUCATION
SOCIETY, AND SOCIETY OF PROFESSORS OF EDUCATION

"In the last twenty years, there has been a resurgence of Deweyan language in schools and teacher preparation programs without an analogous adoption of the central meanings driving Dewey's educational vision. In this insightful text, Boyles unravels the complex web of John Dewey's philosophy and weaves it into one of the most careful and accessible introductions to his philosophy of education in recent memory. This is an invaluable resource for anyone who wants to understand the richness of Dewey's ideas in the context of contemporary educational practice."

—AARON STOLLER
DIRECTOR OF THE OFFICE OF ACADEMIC PROGRAMS, COLORADO COLLEGE

"Deron Boyles is a wonderful writer and a powerful thinker. In this book, he brings together a lifetime of theory and practice in defense of public education. He addresses his undergraduate audience in a way that both challenges and instructs them— but, even more importantly, reassures them that they have the capacity to humanize schools through their intelligent action."

—KYLE GREENWALT
DEPARTMENT OF TEACHER EDUCATION, MICHIGAN STATE UNIVERSITY
PRESIDENT-ELECT, JOHN DEWEY SOCIETY

"For many undergraduates, John Dewey's ideas tend to disappear amidst dense philosophical texts. In this engaging book, Boyles brings Dewey's ideas to life, enabling his key ideas to jump off the page and into practice, while never divorcing them from their important theoretical contexts. Boyles demystifies Deweyan teaching by grounding it in helpful explanations and contemporary examples. Boyles provides an accessible way for preservice teachers to envision becoming the sort of imaginative, trusting, and risk-taking teachers that Dewey described and many of us hope to see in our schools today."

—SARAH STITZLEIN
PROFESSOR OF EDUCATION, UNIVERSITY OF CINCINNATI
PRESIDENT, JOHN DEWEY SOCIETY

"Deron Boyles knows Dewey's philosophy, he knows teaching, and he knows the reality of learning and working in schools. This makes him a particularly acute commentator about 'what the known demands,' as Dewey would put it. This book, drawing on previous work, but fully and carefully rethought for undergraduates, takes those undergraduates seriously. Boyles recognizes that these smart and good young people who are considering teaching already suspect what he—and Dewey— are trying to teach them: that the practices that made them successful in school are not the experiences needed for education. He invites them to try on, with Dewey, an 'imaginative view of teaching.' It's an invitation hard to resist."

—BARBARA S. STENGEL
PROFESSOR OF THE PRACTICE OF EDUCATION, EMERITA, VANDERBILT UNIVERSITY
PAST PRESIDENT, PHILOSOPHY OF EDUCATION SOCIETY

"Deron Boyles is one of the most knowledgeable and captivating Deweyan philosophers of education working today. In *John Dewey's Imaginative Vision of Teaching*, his compelling blend of philosophy and educational practice, as well as his thoroughly original voice, is on full display. A great teaching text, in every sense of the term."

—KATHLEEN KNIGHT ABOWITZ
PROFESSOR, MIAMI UNIVERSITY
PAST PRESIDENT, JOHN DEWEY SOCIETY

"Boyles's re-turn to a Deweyan Imagination by teachers with students offers a significant opportunity for the 'new normal' in schooling. The pandemic/post-era insistent focus on different technological processes must entail more. From this gifted scholar and reformer, there is attention to reconsider Dewey for new contextualized inquiry with new ideas, new meanings, a new future."

—LYNDA STONE, SAMUEL M. HOLTON DISTINGUISHED PROFESSOR
THE UNIVERSITY OF NORTH CAROLINA AT CHAPEL HILL
PAST PRESIDENT, AMERICAN EDUCATIONAL STUDIES ASSOCIATION
AND JOHN DEWEY SOCIETY

JOHN DEWEY'S IMAGINATIVE VISION OF TEACHING

Combining Theory and Practice

THE ACADEMY BOOK SERIES IN EDUCATION

Steven P. Jones and Eric C. Sheffield, *Editors*

The *Academy Book Series in Education* focuses serious attention on the often-missed nexus of educational theory and educational practice. The volumes in this series, both monographs and edited collections, consider theoretical, philosophical, historical, socio-logical, and other conceptual orientations in light of what those orientations can tell readers about successful classroom practice and sound educational policy. In this regard, the *Academy Series* aims to offer a wide array of themes including school reform, content specific practice, contemporary problems in higher education, the impact of technology on teaching and learning, matters of diversity, and other essential contemporary issues in educational thought and practice.

BOOKS IN THE SERIES

Why Kids Love (and Hate) School: Reflections on Difference
edited by Steven Jones and Eric Sheffield (2018)
Why Kids Love (and Hate) School: Reflections on Practice
edited by Steven Jones and Eric Sheffield (2018)
A Case for Kindness: A New Look at the Teaching Ethic
by Steve Broidy (2019)
Making Sense of Race in Education: Practices for Change in Difficult Times
edited by Jessica A. Heybach and Sheron Fraser-Burgess (2020)
John Dewey's Imaginative Vision of Teaching: Combining Theory and Practice
by Deron Boyles (2020)

Steven P. Jones is a professor in the College of Education at Missouri State University and Executive Director of the Academy for Educational Studies. He is author of *Blame Teachers: The Emotional Reasons for Educational Reform*—a book that investigates how and why so many people try to justify educational change by deriding the efforts and ef-fectiveness of our public school teachers. A former high school English teacher in Jefferson County, Colorado, Jones received his BA in English from the University of Denver, his MA in Educational Administration from the University of Colorado (Boulder), and his PhD in Curriculum and Instruction from the University of Chicago.

Eric C. Sheffield is Professor and Department Chair of Educational Studies at Western Illinois University in Macomb. He is also founding editor of the Academy for Educational Studies' peer reviewed journal, *Critical Questions in Education*. A former English teacher in Putman County Florida, Sheffield received his BA in Philosophy from Illinois College, and his MEd (English Education) & PhD (Philosophy of Education) from the University of Florida.

The editors of the *Academy Book Series in Education* are interested in reviewing man-uscripts and proposals for possible publication in the series. Scholars who wish to be considered should email their proposals, along with two sample chapters and current CVs, to the editors. For instructions and advice on preparing a prospectus, please refer to the Myers Education Press website at http://myersedpress.com/sites/stylus/MEP/Docs/Prospectus%20Guidelines%20MEP.pdf. You can send your material to:

Steven P. Jones
Eric C. Sheffield
academyedbooks@gmail.com

JOHN DEWEY'S IMAGINATIVE VISION OF TEACHING

Combining Theory and Practice

By Deron Boyles

Myers
Education
Press

GORHAM, MAINE

Published by Myers Education Press, LLC
P.O. Box 424 Gorham, ME 04038

Myers Education Press is an academic publisher specializing in books, e-books, and digital content in the field of education. All of our books are subjected to a rigorous peer-review process and produced in compliance with the standards of the Council on Library and Information Resources.

Library of Congress Cataloging-in-Publication Data available from Library of Congress.

13-digit ISBN 978-1-9755-0292-8 (paperback)
13-digit ISBN 978-1-9755-0291-1 (hard cover)
13-digit ISBN 978-1-9755-0293-5 (library networkable e-edition)
13-digit ISBN 978-1-9755-0294-2 (consumer e-edition)

Printed in the United States of America.

All first editions printed on acid-free paper that meets the American National Standards Institute Z39-48 standard.

Books published by Myers Education Press may be purchased at special quantity discount rates for groups, workshops, training organizations, and classroom usage. Please call our customer service department at 1-800-232-0223 for details.

Cover design by Sophie Appel

Visit us on the web at www.myersedpress.com to browse our complete list of titles.

TABLE OF CONTENTS

PREFACE

THIS BOOK IS THE culmination of thirty years of investigating John Dewey's philosophy and its possible application to classroom practice. In true Deweyan fashion, I still have a lot to learn. But this effort is one that has allowed me to revisit previous work, update it, and rethink it. I am grateful for this opportunity to combine theory and practice. I thank the publishers and journal editors who have granted me permission to use revised versions of the following:

Chapter 1 is derived from Deron Boyles, "From Transmission to Transaction: John Dewey's Imaginative Vision of Teaching," *Education 3-13: The International Journal of Primary, Elementary and Early Years Education* 46, no. 4 (2018): 393-401. Chapter 2 began as Leann Logsdon and Deron Boyles, "Reimagining Arts-Centered Inquiry in Schools as Pragmatic Instrumentalism." *Philosophy of Education 2012*, ed. Claudia W. Ruitenberg (Urbana: University of Illinois Press, 2012): 405-413. Chapter 3 is based on Deron R. Boyles, "Dewey's Epistemology: An Argument for Warranted Assertions, Knowing, and Meaningful Classroom Practice," *Educational Theory* 56, no. 1 (2006): 57-68. Part of chapter 4 was published as Deron Boyles, "Dewey, Ecology, and Education: Historical and Contemporary Debates over Dewey's Naturalism and (Transactional) Realism," *Educational Theory* 62, no. 2 (2012): 143-161. Finally, a section of chapter 6 appeared as Deron Boyles, "Would You Like Values with That? The Role of Chick-fil-A in Character Education," *JCT: The Journal of Curriculum Theorizing* (Summer, 2005): 43-60.

The cover art is John Dewey, studio portrait, ca. 1890, courtesy of University of Michigan Bentley Historical Library.

THIS BOOK EXPLORES THE merger between John Dewey's philosophy and the practice of teaching. My goal is to show the importance of applied theory by explaining Dewey's ideas in relation to meaningful classroom practice. Other books have been written that do the same thing or something similar.[1] If there's a difference between those books and this one it would be that this book is intended for undergraduates. So, instead of talking about undergraduates, I'm going to talk to them. When I write *you*, *your*, and *you're* in this work, I'm addressing undergraduates directly. The trick has been to merge philosophy with practice and not do damage to either. I try to be true to Dewey's philosophy while linking it to illustrations and examples that clarify how the theory links to real classrooms. It's not easy to take complex philosophical ideas and convey them in clear and accessible terms. Sometimes that process means losing some nuance in the translation. If the language is too abstract, it might not be understood. If it's too general, it might not accurately convey the meaning. This is the challenge and the project of this book: to take the density of Dewey's thinking and make it clear (well, clearer). The project is not without risk, but Dewey argued that we should take risks, so here it goes.

Much of Dewey's theoretical work focused on primary fields within philosophy, like aesthetics (beauty), ontology (existence), epistemology (knowledge), and ethics (moral principles). He was a bit of a rarity in his time, however, because he related those fields of philosophy to teacher practice and education policy. He believed that the more people understood the

---

1 See, for example, James Scott Johnston, *Deweyan Inquiry: From Education Theory to Practice* (Albany, NY: SUNY Press, 2008); Jeff Frank, *Teaching in the Now: John Dewey on the Educational Present* (West Lafayette, IN: Purdue University Press, 2019); Jim Garrison, Stefan Neubert, and Kersten Reich, *John Dewey's Philosophy of Education: An Introduction and Recontextualization for Our Times* (New York: Palgrave Macmillan, 2012); Katherine Camp Mayhew and Anna Camp Edwards, *The Dewey School: The Laboratory School of the University of Chicago, 1896-1903* (New York: D. Appleton-Century, 1936); Laurel Tanner, *Dewey's Lab School: Lessons for Today* (New York: Teachers College Press, 1997); and Stephen M. Fishman and Lucille McCarthy, *John Dewey and the Challenge of Classroom Practice* (New York: Teachers College Press, 1998).

integration of theory and practice the better they would be as citizens, parents, teachers, students, and the like. The problem we face in the US in 2020 is that you are successful in school. Read that again. The *problem* is that you have been successful navigating the drudgery of traditional schooling. Your success, sadly, means that you have learned how to play the game of school. This game is largely one of following instructions, aligning to rubrics, and basically gaming the system. But success in these areas means that you're not very critical or imaginative or willing to take risks. You are smart enough to figure out how to get good grades without having to put a lot of energy into your learning. In short, you don't read. What reading is done tends to be cursory and shallow. Too many of you, in other words, have figured out how to use the least amount of effort to get the maximum amount of points. School is about grades. It's about credits. To the degree that I'm correctly characterizing many or most of you as "successful" students in US public schools is the very degree to which this book is a tricky project. How do I explain Dewey's complex philosophy in ways that are clear and engaging? I answer that question in two ways: (1) generous reading; and (2) examples and illustrations.

To the first answer, a generous reading requires us to *desire* to understand Dewey's ideas. I suggest that readers of this book find a picture of Dewey in his later years. He looks like a gentle, kind man. He was. Consider him your grandfather. Think of him as someone who is worthy of your time. Think of him as someone you *want to understand*. I think that's half the battle.[2] To the second answer, I use a variety of illustrations and examples. Some are historical. Some are personal. All are intended to clarify and illustrate. None of them, however, is pure or perfect. They're not offered as "the model" to follow. That's part of the problem I identify in this book: Even well-intentioned teachers find it hard to understand what it means to enact Dewey's imaginative vision of teaching. Why? Because they, too, have been "successful" students. They want the lesson plan. They want the sixteen steps it takes to put Dewey into practice. They want the rubric. It's the wrong approach to understanding Dewey.

Before I outline the book, I want to highlight a few biographical details about Dewey so you get an initial sense of the man. He was interested in

---

2   A.G. Rud and Jim Garrison, "Reverence and Listening in Teaching and Leading." *Teachers College Record* 112, no. 11 (2010): 2777-2792.

education from a young age. After he graduated from the University of Vermont, in 1879, he was a teacher in Oil City, Pennsylvania for three years and in Charlotte, Vermont for a year.[3] I note this point because you often see pictures of Dewey and imagine him tapping away at his typewriter, writing book after book of abstract ideas. He was a teacher. Not a very good one, ironically. But he was, by all the accounts that I've read, among the most kind and gentle people you'd ever want to know. Unfortunately for us, his writing was often impenetrable, and his style often sounded like someone speaking in the 19th century. That makes sense, of course. He was born in 1859 (the same year Darwin's *Origin of Species* was published). He died in 1952. That span of time is long. Think about some of what happened during those years: Civil War, Spanish-American War, World War I, World War II, Korean conflict; the second Industrial Revolution, electricity, telephones; planes, trains, automobiles; evolution, theory of relativity, atom bomb. The arc of Dewey's development and the arc of his career is, to me, stunning in its scope and depth. At risk of overstating a comparison, I'm hoping this book follows a similar arc. I begin with more introductory information and explanations. Toward the middle of the book, there are more philosophical terms and ideas. The end of the book highlights case studies and provides more illustrations, with an uncommon approach to dealing with a few issues. Throughout the book, I draw connections between chapters so readers can see the interconnected elements in Dewey's thought and practice. In short, this book is an effort to convey Dewey's imaginative vision of teaching that's informed by his philosophy and philosophy of education.

Another thing to remember is that Dewey founded his laboratory school at the University of Chicago in 1894.[4] It lasted ten years before being merged with other organizations. He left Chicago in 1904 for Columbia University. At the beginning of the school, there was an enormous amount of trial-and-error. According to two of the teachers at the school, it was a major adjustment for the newly-hired teachers to shift from a more rote and

---

3 I'm severely limiting Dewey's biography in the interest of space. For biographies of Dewey, I suggest Robert B. Westbrook, *John Dewey and American Democracy* (Ithaca, NY: Cornell University Press, 1991); Jay Martin, *The Education of John Dewey* (New York: Columbia University Press, 2003); and, for a celebratory and firsthand account, Sidney Hook, *John Dewey: An Intellectual Portrait* (New York: John Day, 1939).

4 It didn't open to students until 1896, but two years' worth of planning went into the project.

compartmentalized approach to teaching and learning to what Dewey was still working out.[5] The basis of education, for Dewey, was recognizing that children are innately inquisitive. How to harness that inquiry and direct it toward ever-expanding topics and ideas was a central goal of the teachers in the school. Because the lab school was housed at the University of Chicago, there were other important elements to keep in mind. Most of the students were children of professors, so they were arguably already set to succeed in school. Another important point to note is that professors (who did not have children at the school) were also involved in mentoring and teaching at the school. Additionally, graduate students at the university were also part of the educational and social fabric. This is in keeping with Dewey's view that school is a small society with many moving parts. His goal, and the goal of lead teachers and supervisors, was to organize the moving parts so they would work together toward the aims of growth and educative experience.

Much of what we know about the early workings of the school come from archival information at the University of Chicago. Laurel Tanner's book, *Dewey's Laboratory School: Lessons for Today*, cites letters, reports, and teachers' plans to clarify what the school was like.[6] Add to Tanner's book the Mayhew and Edwards book and we have a pretty good insider's look into the running of the school. One point worth mentioning, I think, is that the Mayhew and Edwards book wasn't published until 1936—more than thirty years after the lab school was merged with other schools and Dewey had left Chicago for Columbia. I'll leave it to others to bicker over some of these details because my point is to focus on Dewey's imaginative vision of teaching. What teaching looked like and what elements were required for teaching at the lab school are important, no doubt. Important, too, is the experimental method Dewey and his teachers employed and why, philosophically, it should matter to teachers in 2020 and beyond.

It may also surprise some to know that Dewey was not only fine with lesson plans, he liked them. Vital to this point, however, is how these plans functioned. In current schools, lesson plans are used more for accountability and bureaucracy. Teachers draft plans in a formulaic way and their plans strictly adhere to centralized and standardized goals and objectives. Current lesson plans include sections like goals, objectives, strategies, etc. Again,

---

5   Mayhew and Edwards, *The Dewey School*.

6   Tanner, *Dewey's Lab School*.

Dewey didn't mind lesson plans. In fact, he encouraged them. They were used, however, as guiding features of a broader inquiry into central fields of study linked to student interests (not student whim). There were history classes and math classes and science classes in the lab school, to be sure. But they weren't functionally compartmentalized. Inquiry and projects were integrated across subjects. The fundamental differences between lab school lesson plans and contemporary lesson plans should be seen in at least two ways: (1) trust; and (2) risk. I'm asserting that both elements are necessary features for imaginative teaching, and you can't have (2) without (1). Here's why.

If we carefully consider the topic of teacher quality, we'll run into a few competing views. Some people think that you're born to be a good teacher and that the formal elements of certification limit teacher creativity. Others claim that good teachers are made through courses in teacher training: classroom management, scope and sequencing of curriculum, and methods of transmitting content. Still others argue that good teachers should have a liberal arts or other content-specialist degree and think that teacher education programs (or teacher training, depending on what courses and expectations exist) are intellectually shallow.[7] Additional views suggest that "life experience" matters most and that in an age of teacher shortages, people with corporate, military, or other career experience should be recruited as teachers without any certification at all. There are also those who claim that taking only online classes to gain course credit and certification are as good as or better than traditionally trained or educated teachers. Teach for America argues that having a bachelor's degree in a STEM field or in English or history and about a six-week summer course in "teaching" is good enough.[8] Pearson and edTPA require teacher-candidates to develop portfolios attesting to their ability, even though Pearson gets the copyright for every teacher-candidate's work submitted to it.[9] Charter schools like KIPP think that a

---

7   They're largely correct, unfortunately. Why? See David Labaree, *The Trouble with Ed Schools* (New Haven: Yale University Press, 2006); and David Labaree, *How to Succeed in School Without Really Learning: The Credentials Race in American Education* (New Haven: Yale University Press, 1999).

8   See Kathleen deMarrais and T. Jameson Brewer, eds., *Teach For America Counter-Narratives: Alumni Speak Up and Speak Out* (New York: Peter Lang, 2015).

9   Dennis Attick and Deron Boyles, "Pearson Learning and the Ongoing Corporatization of Public Education." *Journal of Thought* 50, nos. 1 and 2 (Spring-Summer 2016): 5-19; and Martha K. Donovan and Susan O. Cannon, "The University Supervisor, edTPA, and the New Making of the Teacher." *Education Policy Analysis Archives* 26, no. 28 (2018): 1-26.

business model is more important. They select students to be in the schools and also select those who leave it. They get to rig their stats to appear more successful than they are.[10]

There are mixtures of this sort of thinking, as well. I'm fine, for example, in asserting that a bachelor's degree in a specific field *should* mean that you know your content area. It's not a guarantee, however. There are plenty of people with degrees who are not particularly smart—just like there are plenty of teachers with degrees in education who can't teach well, either. I don't, therefore, think a bachelor's degree in a specific field is enough. We've all had the teacher who we knew was smart. They could've been an expert in their field, too. But they couldn't teach. We've also had the teacher who is really a coach but gets placed in a social studies class or a health class to make it appear that their primary role is to teach rather than to coach. With so many possibilities, then, do we continue with the mosaic of options and let the conditions of schools determine who teaches? Apparently, we do, perhaps with the veneer of expertise vested in professional standards commissions, accrediting agencies, and other bureaucracies that fight over what counts as the legitimate credentials for teachers. What's missing most, however, is trust and risk.

We are driven so much by accountability that trust is eroded and risk is a four-letter word. Risk *is* a four-letter word, but it isn't supposed to be rude or vulgar. Risk is where, granting obvious safety issues, learning occurs. Said differently, we learn from failing. We learn from making mistakes. We learn when something goes wrong, and we must fix it. It's called life and Dewey recognized that teaching requires risk and that risk requires trust. Here, then, might be an opening to explore not only what constitutes legitimate risk and appropriate trust, but also how current thinking tends to warp our thinking about risk and trust. I hope you'll trust me enough to take the risk to explore Dewey's imaginative vision of teaching. Let me explain how the book is organized.

Generally speaking, each chapter begins with theory and ends with practical implications. While there are many, many books on Dewey, there are relatively few that connect his philosophy of education to actual practice. By linking primary fields of philosophy with classroom teaching and

---

10   See Kristen L. Buras, *Charter Schools, Race, and Urban Space* (New York: Routledge, 2014).

education policy, this book suggests that splitting theory and practice apart sets up a false chasm. That split should be merged if teaching and learning are to change into dynamic, reflective, and creative interactions.

The first chapter sets out the primary title of the book and explores what Dewey means by teaching and learning. I highlight some of the key concepts in Dewey's more widely known works like *Democracy and Education and Experience and Education*.[11] But I also provide insights from practice.[12] Chapter 1 also links to teacher practice by calling on my experiences working with teachers and parents at a Deweyan school in Roswell, GA (Chrysalis Experiential Academy).[13] I served as the president of the Advisory Board from 2002-2014, before it closed in 2016. Those experiences provide insight into the limitations of teacher practice that are learned in colleges and schools of education that are not Deweyan. Indeed, one of the major problems in working with teachers at Chrysalis was the degree of *un*-learning that needed to take place. We had to re-think the role and function of teaching and learning before Deweyan practice could be understood and demonstrated by people who already claimed to be (or wanted to be) Deweyan in their teaching practice.

The second chapter includes a little bit more theory as part of a trajectory in the book that arcs in the middle (chapters 3 and 4) with a bit more philosophy than the first two or the last two chapters. Chapter 2 deals with arts-centered teaching and learning and how it has become at least partially corrupted by the STEM-STEAM (science, technology, engineering, arts, and mathematics) initiatives characterizing current talk about schools. Illustrations feature prominently in this chapter, too, in order to clarify the link between theory and practice and to make the case that good practice is made better when informed by theory. Dewey's view of art is not divorced from his theory of knowledge, theory of being/theory of reality, or ethics.[14] Chapter 2 continues the process of combining philosophy with policy and practice.

---

11   John Dewey, *Democracy and Education* (New York: The Free Press, 1916) and John Dewey *Experience and Education* (New York: Kappa Delta Pi and The Free Press, 1938).

12   Tanner, *Dewey's Lab School*; and Fishman and McCarthy, *John Dewey and the Challenge of Classroom Practice*.

13   If you're interested in seeing this interaction, there's a YouTube video of a parent-teacher session from Chrysalis. See https://www.youtube.com/watch?v=V_fzsNn A57I.

14   Nathan Crick, *Democracy & Rhetoric: John Dewey on the Arts of Becoming* (Columbia, SC: University of South Carolina Press, 2010).

Chapter 3 explores Dewey's epistemology—his theory of knowledge—by clarifying what it is versus what it has been mistakenly interpreted to be. Dewey was, in philosophical terms, a fallibilist. This means that ultimate truth and abstract universals were not his goal. Indeed, abstractions are meaningless in anything other than a thought experiment. The philosophical emphasis in this chapter is important because of the confusion often surrounding Dewey's commitments to knowledge and knowing. He is often dismissed as a relativist or otherwise put down as a base utilitarian. Some neopragmatists even think Dewey argued against epistemology as a legitimate field. They're wrong. This chapter details why he is neither a relativist nor a base utilitarian by clarifying what transactional realism is and what it means for classroom teaching and learning. Chapters 3 and 4 are the most philosophically "heavy" chapters. I suggest you read them, and the rest of the book, as follows: Approach it as a generous reading. If, at any point, the terms are too vague or the argument is too convoluted, stop. Turn the page. Keep going. Like most other philosophers, I'm going to repeat myself. You shouldn't get frustrated, in other words. Just skip a page or two and continue. The important points will be restated. I'm not suggesting that you skim, just that you not get too bothered if a section or two doesn't make perfect sense. Keep going. It's Deweyan to persevere.

Like the third chapter, Chapter 4 focuses on a specific area within philosophy and argues that Dewey's ecology requires interconnections between people and their surroundings—between teachers and students and the world outside of classrooms. The chapter claims that Dewey's theories of knowing, learning, and living are ultimately biocentric and transactive, not anthropocentric and unidirectional. This means that Dewey's ecology is not a one-way street where nature is used by humans solely for their controlling and exploitative interests. Anthropocentrism (literally, human-centered) situates humans as the ones who exploit nature for the benefit of humans. Biocentrism (life-centered) recognizes that humans are not the only living creatures on the planet. Biocentrism also means that humans have an ethical responsibility to care for the entire world, not just the survival of human beings. This view alters what it means to teach and to learn both in terms of Dewey's transactional theory of knowing (chapter 3) and his imaginative vision of teaching (chapter 1). While there is more theoretical material at the beginning of this chapter, extensive practical commentary is also added to the end of the chapter to clarify and link the major ideas together.

Chapter 5 picks up Dewey's naturalism and connects his naturalism to his ethics. The importance of Dewey's ethics for classroom interaction is in the generative and cooperative nature of democratic teaching and learning. Dewey's ethics, like his ontology, epistemology, aesthetics, etc., cannot be separated from each other. His ethics are practical actions in human connection, not rules or lists of behaviors. They are emergent, qualified, and varied. They also must navigate a US context that is saturated with business logic and corporate influences on and in schools. In the chapter, I provide a series of examples of how corporations exploit public schools. Part of the point is to show what teachers face when they are bombarded with advertising and other initiatives to promote business interests in schools. The way I explore ethical considerations should be useful in any situation teachers face in their classrooms. So, what this chapter does is approach the broad field of ethics through Dewey's business ethics. Those ethics are then used to explore a series of instances—lots of mini-illustrations—of ethical problems students and teachers face in actual classroom contexts. I ultimately propose that we use the illustrations of exploitation as object lessons to help bring about Dewey's imaginative vision of teaching. We are, in other words, still combining theory and practice. Illustrations from Chrysalis clarify the varied and variable ways ethics in learning alters both power and outcomes for the betterment of student understanding and human agency.

I address issues of diversity and the relationship between diversity and Dewey's view of imaginative teaching in chapter 6. I do so in what might seem like an odd way: I primarily focus on religious diversity. I begin this chapter with a case study that involves curriculum, character, diversity, and teacher autonomy. Each of these topics is rethought considering religion, specifically fundamentalist Christianity. But the topic of religious fundamentalism in the case study is also representative of the struggle between standardized expectations for teaching and learning, and the honoring of diversity and difference. The critical way I approach the case study might also be helpful in showing how criticism can be used to reveal otherwise hidden meaning and power. The goal is to show you where and how teacher and student power is subsumed under market forces—in this case with a character education program as the cover for religion. I then move to another, more personal illustration of Dewey's philosophy of education in practice that also raises further questions about diversity. I retell my experience as part of a fifth grade class and the Deweyan project we undertook involving Thanksgiving. I also problematize elements of my experience with the benefit of hindsight that does not regress or lessen itself to the kind of woke presentism I also question at the end of the chapter. I finish the chapter by highlighting debates about whether Dewey was racist, sexist, and ethnocentric. He wasn't any of these things, but I'm obliged to share with you some of the works that make such charges. I don't engage the complexity of every aspect of diversity, but I provide sources that can be read to figure out for yourselves what you think Dewey's view of diversity was.[15]

It's at this point that I'm reminded of James Scott Johnston's characterization of Dewey's theory of inquiry. I quote Johnston at length because I think he captures much of the focus of this book. He writes:

> What makes Dewey's theory of inquiry ideal for schools is, first, its sensitivity. Dewey's theory of inquiry is context-bound: it is not a method brought down from on high to bear on all educational practices or problems. Rather, it is a set of methods, built up in and through contexts which they serve, for the purposes of understanding, ordering, and controlling, our experiences of, and our relations with, the world. Second, Dewey's theory of inquiry is self-correcting: it is designed to adjust itself in light of anticipated and unanticipated changes in educational practice. This makes Dewey's theory of inquiry more user-friendly than might otherwise be imagined; it can be developed in and through a variety of contexts. Third, it is driven by problems. These problems are problems of the child, not the problems of the teacher, or the textbook, or the state, meaning it is the child's interests and effort guiding inquiry; inquiry is finished when there is no longer the unsettled situation that gave rise to inquiry in the first place.[16]

The chapters that follow are intended to capture Johnston's point by inviting inquiry and context that is grounded by philosophy. Just keep in mind that *philosophy* (*philo-sophia*) means "love of wisdom." As you read about the

---

15   In fact, I provide extensive sources in footnotes throughout the more philosophically-heavy chapters of the book. I do this because I want you to understand that there are more books and articles you can read if a specific idea or theme interests you.

16   Johnston, *Deweyan Inquiry*, 3.

combining of theory and practice, I invite you to imagine schools as places where students and teachers engage as co-learners in solving problems to make the world a smarter, better, safer, happier, and wiser place to be.

References

Attick, Dennis, and Deron Boyles. "Pearson Learning and the Ongoing Corporation of Education." *Journal of Thought* 50, nos. 1-2 (Spring-Summer, 2016): 5-19.

Boyles, Deron. "Experiential Education." Chrysalis Experiential Academy, Parent-Teacher Lecture. March 22, 2010. https://www.youtube.com/watch?v=V_fzsNnA57I.

Buras, Kristen L. *Charter Schools, Race, and Urban Space.* New York: Routledge, 2014.

Crick, Nathan. *Democracy & Rhetoric; John Dewey on the Arts of Becoming.* Columbia SC: University of South Carolina Press, 2010.

deMarrais, Kathleen, and T. Jameson Brewer, eds., *Teach for America Counter-Narratives: Alumni Speak Up and Speak Out.* New York: Peter Lang, 2015.

Donovan, Martha K., and Susan O. Cannon. "The University Supervisor, edTPA, and the New Making of the Teacher." *Education Policy Analysis Archives* 26, no. 28 (2018): 1-26.

Fishman, Steven M., and Lucille McCarthy. *John Dewey and the Challenge of Classroom Practice.* New York: Teachers College Press, 1998.

Frank, Jeff. *Teaching in the Now: John Dewey on the Educational Present.* West Lafayette, IN: Purdue University Press, 2019.

Garrison, Jim, Stefan Neubert, and Kersten Reich. *John Dewey's Philosophy of Education: An Introduction and Recontextualization for Our Times.* New York: Palgrave Macmillan, 2012.

Hook, Sidney. *John Dewey: An Intellectual Portrait.* New York: John Day, 1939.

Johnston, James Scott. *Deweyan Inquiry: From Education Theory to Practice.* Albany, NY: SUNY Press, 2008.

Labaree, David. *How to Succeed in School Without Really Learning: The Credentials Race in American Education.* New Haven: Yale University Press, 1999.

Labaree, David. *The Trouble with Ed Schools.* New Haven: Yale University Press, 2006.

Martin, Jay. *The Education of John Dewey.* New York: Columbia University Press, 2003.

Mayhew, Katherine Camp and Anna Camp Edwards. *The Dewey School: The Laboratory School of the University of Chicago, 1896-1903.* New York: J. Appleton-Century Company, Inc., 1936.

Rud, A.G. and Jim Garrison. "Reverence and Listening in Teaching and Leading." *Teachers College Record* 112, no. 11 (2010): 2777-2792.

Tanner, Laurel. *Dewey's Laboratory School: Lessons for Today.* New York: Teachers College Press, 1997.

Westbrook, Robert B. *John Dewey and American Democracy.* Ithaca, NY: Cornell University Press, 1991.

CHAPTER ONE

JOHN DEWEY'S IMAGINATIVE VISION OF TEACHING

JOHN DEWEY WROTE EXTENSIVELY about all sorts of philosophical and educational topics. I assert that his insights into imaginative teaching are best understood in relation to the works spanning some of the central fields in philosophy. Dewey wrote on everything from epistemology, the ontology of naturalism, ethics, and ecology to sociology, psychology, aesthetics, and ethics. Some of his work is limited to a few articles, other work includes multiple books and book revisions. I link his philosophical and theoretical points with practical experiences of my own in working with teachers and parents at the Dewey-inspired school, Chrysalis Experiential Academy.[1] My goal in this chapter is to clarify some of the central ideas necessary to understand Dewey's imaginative vision of teaching and learning. I begin with what's arguably Dewey's most popular work in philosophy and education, *Democracy and Education*, first published in 1916.

Dewey's *Democracy and Education* includes so many important concepts that it might be surprising to note that specific references to teaching are few.[2] Between "teacher" and "teaching," there are only four single pages (17, 71, 160, and 163) and one span of three pages (4–6) noted in the

---

1   https://www.youtube.com/watch?v=V_fzsNnA57I.

2   John Dewey, *Democracy and Education* (New York: The Free Press, 1916).

index. In a work that's 360 pages long, why did Dewey give so little explicit space to teaching? Beyond index issues, I argue that Dewey's imaginative vision of teaching is fully integrated throughout his book. It also provides an important alternative to traditional teaching—both from Dewey's time and what we generally understand teaching to mean 100 years later.[3] Like the rest of the chapters in this book, I provide parts or sections to clarify Dewey's thought. My goal is to explain his thinking so you can follow his argument and his logic. By breaking down some of the more complex ideas, it should be easier to understand what Dewey meant and how his ideas relate to teaching.

This chapter proceeds in three parts. First, I argue that Dewey's initial view of teaching-as-transmission is an intentional trick. He meant to make teaching-as-transmission a point and a theme he could attack. By making teaching-as-transmission so obvious and clear, Dewey then distinguishes traditional teaching from his view of authentic, good, and imaginative teaching. I also explore Dewey's distinction between maturity and immaturity, educative experiences, and interdisciplinary content to clarify the imaginative teaching he wanted. Second, I utilize what's known as Dewey's transactional realism to identify what Deweyan teaching requires. Transactional realism is just another way of talking about teachers and learners in a form of interaction that continually expands inquiry into the world around them (see chapters 3 and 4). Their mutual, dialogic exchanges about real problems that interest them is the process the phrase "transactional realism" tries to capture. Finally, I call on my experiences as the president of the advisory board of the Dewey-inspired Chrysalis Experiential Academy in Roswell, Georgia, to provide illustrations of the continuing struggles teachers confront in transforming teaching from transmission to transaction, from traditional teaching to imaginative teaching. Part of these struggles, as will be shown, include clarifying *with* (as opposed to *for*) teachers what Deweyan experiential education requires and what imaginative teaching both includes and excludes. I pay special attention to what elements of traditional schooling are maintained but transformed in imaginative teaching practice.

---

3   Ellen Lagemann, "Experimenting with Education: John Dewey and Ella Flagg Young at the University of Chicago," *American Journal of Education* 104, no. 3 (1996): 171–185; Laurel Tanner, *Dewey's Laboratory School: Lessons for Today* (New York: Teachers College Press, 1997); and Stephen M. Fishman and Lucille McCarthy, *John Dewey and the Challenge of Classroom Practice* (New York: Teachers College Press, 1998).

The Deweyan project of reforming teaching means getting rid of or altering almost everything we know teaching to include. Some traditional aspects of teaching are OK, but most are not. I identify the important elements of traditional teaching that should be kept and those elements of traditional teaching that should be transformed if we want to demonstrate Dewey's imaginative vision of teaching.

Section I: Teaching as Transmission

At the beginning of *Democracy and Education*, Dewey notes that the transmission and communication of values and the essential or characteristic customs and conventions of a community are basic for society. Parents and teachers tell students the way the world is. There are seven days in a week and twenty-four hours in a day. Like parents who teach their children manners and ways of behaving, teachers do something very similar. They transmit basic information, social conventions, and rules. This isn't a problem for Dewey. He specifically claims that "So obvious, indeed, is the necessity of teaching and learning for the continued existence of a society that we may seem to be dwelling unduly on a truism."[4] A truism is a truth that is so obviously true that it doesn't have to be highlighted or explained. I believe Dewey ultimately operates on this assumption of transmission as necessary in society but not enough to characterize teaching and learning. That is, though communicating values and rules are necessary for social groups, such communication is merely one facet of human interaction. More is required for the kind of transaction and inquiry that's better than transmission. In other words, transmission may be necessary, but it is not sufficient for good teaching. "Schools are, indeed," notes Dewey, "one important method of the transmission which forms the dispositions of the immature; but it is only one means, and, compared with other agencies, a relatively superficial means."[5] Of course, teachers establish rules of behavior. Of course, teachers tell students basic information they need to navigate the classroom, the school, and even the broader society. But there are limits to telling. There are dangers, too.

One of the limits to telling is that one teacher's view of the world or the way the classroom should be is not always shared by other teachers.

---

4   Dewey, *Democracy and Education*, 4.

5   Ibid.

A teacher's rules may not be shared by parents, either. Then what? What happens, for instance, when a teacher corrects a student's pronunciation of basic terms? A student asks to go to the "bafroom" or wants a drink of "wooder." Does the teacher correct the student and point out that the proper pronunciation is "bath-room" and "wa-ter"? Is the teacher demonstrating a form of bias against dialect or folkways of speaking? Or is it the responsibility of the teacher to correct pronunciation, so that pronunciation conforms to standard English? These may seem like minor issues. Alone they are. But taken together, they are a major part of what Dewey understood as the social role of education: building community.

To paraphrase Dewey, living close to one another is not the same as being in community. Efficiency and effectiveness in carrying out key functions of and for the community are also not important enough to determine or characterize what is meaningfully social. The teacher correcting pronunciation risks turning imaginative teaching into a rote or routine process. Here's where Dewey draws on machinery to make the point: "The parts of a machine work with a maximum of cooperativeness for a common result, but they do not form a community."[6] He goes on: "Individuals use one another so as to get desired results, without reference to the emotional and intellectual disposition and consent of those used."[7] How do teachers interact with their students in correcting pronunciation? Is the interaction a "because I said so" command to correct "bafroom" to "bath-room," or does the teacher understand what code-switching is and whether the meaning of the term is still conveyed and understood? What's the role of cultural sensitivity, understanding, and appreciation? There's a qualitative difference in these options of communication. One is dry and harsh, the other humane and empathetic.[8] The goal may still be to clarify standard or status quo pronunciation, but if in the process teachers destroy community, Dewey isn't happy. Neither are students.

---

6   Ibid., 5.

7   Ibid.

8   See, for instance, Lisa Delpit, *Other People's Children: Cultural Conflict in the Classroom* (New York: The New Press, 1993/2006). See also, Joyce E. King, et al., *Preparing Teachers for Cultural Diversity* (New York: Teachers College Press, 1997); Christopher Emdin, *For White Folks Who Teach in the Hood . . . and the Rest of Y'all Too: Reality Pedagogy and Urban Education* (Boston: Beacon Press, 2017); and Bettina Love, *We Want to Do More Than Survive: Abolitionist Teaching and the Pursuit of Educational Freedom* (Boston: Beacon Press, 2019).

More broadly, but related, Dewey's perceptive about issues in education like grading, tracking, school-to-school test score comparisons, and international rankings—all of which may indicate something about what goes on in the school. Teachers and students may participate in these rituals and restrictive habits, but they're effectively gutted of humanity and community in the process. Teachers and students become reduced to material ends, mere "resources," in a process called schooling that is overburdened by imposed and formulaic rules. Teachers and students also become pawns in the broader assumption about the purpose of schools: Teachers tell students what skills they will need to get a job in a global economy. Dewey warns us not to overemphasize capitalism, hyper-vocationalism, or some other assumed goal for schooling that dismisses teachers and students themselves (see chapter 5). Teachers and students already bring experiences and values into the classroom. But a class isn't a community until experiences are understood and values are shared. Understanding and sharing aren't always pleasant and lovely, either. We debate and argue about what the rules should be, whether they should change, and who gets to make the rules in the first place. One risk is seeing debate and argument as competitive and negative. Schools in general suffer from discussions about education that are mired in comparative-competitive modes of production. Schools suffer because the evaluative criteria for judging schools in the first place (i.e., in determining whether they are "failing" or "succeeding," "top 25" or "#1 in offering Advanced Placement courses," "innovative," "a school of excellence," etc.) are restricted to measurement standards that favor economic analyses and business rationales that alter what it means to be in community with one another. We're reduced to—and reduce each other to—merely human resources.

Teaching and learning, as a result, tend to be reduced to processes of production that must meet market goals of transfer efficiency and quality control. Cover the material and test it. Grade students, pass or fail them, and move on to the next class. Such forms of teaching and learning favor corporate interests and privatization efforts because the form of the measurements of knowledge (standardized, scientific, objective), is the same form of measurements used on durable goods and hard services. One problem is that teaching and learning are reduced to structures that are stand-ins for community, inquiry, imagination, and growth. Teachers and students in non-Deweyan schools tend to execute and perform roles that are predefined and imposed, thus transmitted and restrictive of potential. What I mean is that the structure of schools forces teachers and students into roles that may not reflect who the teachers and students actually are. The roles inhibit growth and Dewey was nothing if not a champion of growth. Dewey wants a very different understanding of teaching and learning.

Section II: Teaching as Transactional

Dewey's imaginative vision of teaching is centered on the transactional realism that is both his epistemology and his ontology, as chapters 3 and 4 show in more detail. That is, Dewey has a theory of knowledge (epistemology) and a theory of reality (ontology). These theories applied to classroom life inform what teaching and schooling mean. Transaction, as opposed to transmission, requires movement and change from contextual situations upward and outward. In classrooms, meaning emerges from student and teacher experiences and is not confined to an imposed view of what others think students should learn and teachers should teach. This point is significant because it highlights the dramatic difference between imposition and transaction. Most schools, most of the time, in most of the United States, are bounded by external learning objectives (think Common Core) that must be confined to lesson planning and, thus, conform to the assumption that, for example, "best practices" already exist and need only be adopted for good teaching and learning to take place. In the typical classroom, teachers talk and students listen, rules of order are followed, quizzes are taken, grades are noted, and students and teachers become habituated to routines that, in a circular fashion, reinforce more routines. Teachers are arguably more like data-entry clerks than engaged co-learners with their students. This reality is the opposite of Dewey's imaginative educational vision.

Classrooms are supposed to be places where transacting what he called "existing capacities" of children with the social setup of situations, including others (teachers too), leads to worthwhile experiences. Traditional schools, Dewey complained, provided an environment, but one that was so transmission-oriented, so stacked with inauthentic and contrived exercises that what was determined to be worthwhile was left to the teacher or, worse, to administrators and politicians: Students are primarily a source of problems to overcome or an unruly force to be subdued. Dewey partially blamed Johann Friedrich Herbart for what we now know as "scope and sequencing" in teaching. Bear with me as I include an extended quote. It's helpful for clarifying why teaching as transmission and traditional schooling are so problematic.

> The fundamental theoretical defect of [teaching as transmission] lies in ignoring the existence of a living being of active and specific functions which are developed in the redirection and combination which occur as they are occupied with their environment. The theory represents the Schoolmaster come to his [sic] own. This fact expresses at once its strength and weakness. The conception that the mind consists of what has been taught, and that the importance of what has been taught consists in its availability for further teaching, reflects the pedagogue's view of life. The philosophy is eloquent about the duty of the teacher in instructing pupils; it is almost silent regarding his [sic] privilege of learning. It emphasizes the influence of intellectual environment upon the mind; it slurs over the fact that the environment involves a personal sharing in common experiences . . . It insists upon the old, the past, and passes lightly over the operation of the genuinely novel and unforeseeable. It takes, in brief, everything educational into account save its essence,—vital energy seeking opportunity for effective exercise. All education forms character, mental and moral, but formation consists in the selection and coordination of native activities so that they may utilize the subject matter of the social environment. Moreover, the formation is not only a formation of native activities, but it takes place through them. It is a process of reconstruction, reorganization.[9]

Instead of "accidental" learning, classrooms should be environments that are extensions of nature. Classrooms should be ecological spaces for conjoint inquiry where that inquiry is neither canned nor prepackaged, in contrast to much of the curricula in the United States today. More is said about this in chapter 4, but just as Dewey denied that schools are separate from society, classrooms are not separate from the broader environment or culture either. The relevance of this point is pretty straightforward: We should see classrooms as reconstructed, organic spaces safe for and encouraging of

---

9   Dewey, *Democracy and Education*, 71-72.

transactions between and among students, teachers, and emergent content.

The problem, of course, is that in most schools the comfortable routines, traditional attitudes, and entrenched expectations of preparing kids for future jobs reinforces a contrived and imposed understanding of the nature of teaching and learning. The challenge may be huge in terms of changing the worst elements of traditional practices in schools, but this does not change the fact that Dewey's imaginative view of education significantly alters what it means to teach. As he notes, "what conscious, deliberate teaching can do is at most to free the capacities thus formed for fuller exercise, to purge them of some of their grossness, and to furnish objects which make their activity more productive of meaning."[10] What most traditional schools reinforce is the idea that producing productive workers is the singular goal of education. Schools, in this view, exist to transmit the necessary skills students will need to get a job. It's an economic view of the world. Teachers and children are exploited by such a view, if hegemonically so (see chapter 5). That is, by reinforcing teaching and learning in transmission-oriented, economistic, reductionist ways, teachers and students learn what their roles are supposed to be and, with perverse energy, enact or perform those roles willingly. Teachers come to believe that "best practices" exist and that formulaic lessons plans are necessary. Worse, arguably, they largely agree that the overall purpose of schooling is about preparation for a future life—a point Dewey directly challenges. In "My Pedagogic Creed," Dewey wrote the following: "I believe that education, therefore, is a process of living and not a preparation for future living."[11] You can't get much clearer than that, can you?

Let's also clarify three terms: training, schooling, and education. Training is teaching the steps and techniques necessary to complete tasks. Anything that follows "I want to learn *how to* _____" is training. I want to learn how to cook. I want to learn how to ski. I want to learn how to teach. These are all training-oriented topics. They're also OK. There's nothing wrong with learning how to sew or learning how to drive. Training may not result in a credential, although there are plenty of instances when successful training leads to some form of certificate or license. You can be trained or

---

10   Ibid., 17.

11   John Dewey, "My Pedagogic Creed," *School Journal* 54 (January 1897): 77-80, 78, Article II.

licensed to drive a bus or to be a surgeon. But you can also be trained and not receive a certificate or a diploma. You learn how to make soup or clean laundry without certification. Schooling, however, usually does result in a diploma or formal paper like a certificate. Schooling is the formal process of learning. High school, vocational school, vacation Bible school, graduate school—these are all places of learning that usually confer a formal document to commemorate your successful completion of the processes that make up schooling. You earn a degree or an endorsement of some sort. It's a formal achievement. Education, differently still, is the broadest of the three categories. You can be educated and not have graduated high school. Many of us have ancestors who had to drop out of school in the sixth grade or in high school because of family hardships, the Great Depression, a war, or any number of other reasons. They didn't earn a diploma or a degree. But not earning a certificate doesn't mean your great-grandfather was not educated. He may have been very wise, in fact, owing to life experiences, family traditions, or other means of knowing. The distinctions I'm drawing here are not new. They're important, however, because we tend to use the concepts training, schooling, and education interchangeably. We talk of schooling as though it's the broader category of education even when what goes on in most schools most of the time is training. By conflating training with education, we muddle our thinking. We conceptually confuse the terms and it's not a good idea to say one thing but mean another.

Although it's true that Dewey, as a pragmatist, is most interested in inquiry that solves problems and improves our futures, the point is to inquire now into ideas and topics that are interesting to the teachers and students who comprise actual communities of learners. As it stands, most schools in most of the United States are deeply, hegemonically dedicated to mistaking training for education and committing themselves to a form of transmission-preparation that will only get worse under capitalist educational priorities, where schools are viewed as competitive businesses themselves. Another challenge for schools is the growing view that education isn't for everybody and that you can do "better" foregoing college altogether and entering the workforce.[12] Bill Gates was a college dropout and he's a billionaire, so the thinking goes, a degree is not necessary to succeed. One problem

---

12   Peter Thiel is paying nearly a dozen students $100,000 *not* to go to college. See https://www.today.com/money/entrepreneur-whos-paying-kids-not-go-college-6C9677995.

with this logic is that it assumes that all of us can become billionaires, that becoming a billionaire is somehow a noble goal, and that being a billionaire means that you know more than other people. None of this is true. Bill and Melinda Gates influence thinking because of their money, especially in education, but they know nothing about the field.[13] Their money gives them power, but not knowledge. Dewey is in favor of more and more people becoming knowledgeable and understanding learning as hard, but worth the effort—not because there are dollars to be earned but because knowledge is something you can't lose in a tech bubble or stock market crash.

Section III: Teaching Teachers for Deweyan Teaching

To underscore the challenging task at hand, I'm going to draw upon my work with teachers at the Chrysalis Experiential Academy. Chrysalis was a Dewey-inspired independent school in Roswell, Georgia. It was founded in 2002 by Arlene Rotter and Richard Becker, was a 501(c)(3) (nonprofit) organization that was nonsectarian and offered instruction from grades 5 to 12. On average, there were sixty students and eight teachers in the school. Of the students 65 percent were male and 35 percent were female. Starting tuition was just under $10,000 per year, with 30 percent of students receiving financial assistance. Chrysalis was accredited by the Southern Association of Independent Schools and Southern Association of Colleges and Schools. It was in this school that I engaged in teaching seminars from 2002 to 2014 to clarify what it means to be a Deweyan teacher and a Deweyan student. What these encounters represent are instances in which even the most well-intentioned teachers operate on traditional assumptions about teaching and learning. That is, many of the teachers were adept at using Deweyan terms, but in decidedly un-Deweyan ways. My point is to highlight just how foreign Dewey's ideas are *even to those who want to be Deweyan*. If the task is so difficult with teachers who value the priorities of growth, emergence, and imagination, what possibility is there to effect wider changes for more and more teachers?

I'm suggesting that one of the largest barriers to Deweyan teaching in the United States is the degree to which teacher education programs have

---

13   See Philip E. Kovacs, ed., *The Gates Foundation and the Future of US "Public" Schools* (New York: Taylor and Francis, 2010).

been reduced to sites for teacher training, not sites for educative experiences, intellect, or imagination. Even for teachers interested in teaching in ways that are informed by and consistent with Dewey's views, there's a tension in Dewey's theory of teaching between the teacher's authority, the place of educative experiences, the role of content, and what the purpose of the transactions between teachers and students should yield. In chapter 12, "Thinking in Education," of *Democracy and Education*, Dewey specifies that "the educational moral" he is chiefly concerned to draw out is not "... that teachers would find their own work less of a grind and strain if school conditions favored learning in the sense of discovery and not in that of storing away what others pour into them; nor that it would be possible to give even children and youth the delights of personal intellectual productiveness—true and important as these things are. It is that no thought, no idea, can possibly be conveyed as an idea from one person to another."[14] The importance of this argument is central to understanding the tension between teacher authority and content, where content is dominated by externally imposed materials, facts, and details.

Teachers can, with their authority, prompt questions (best informed by students' background experiences), but they aren't the point of the interaction. It is the student who must engage and inquire. "If he [*sic*] cannot devise his own solution (not of course in isolation, but in correspondence [transaction] with the teacher and other pupils) and find his own way out he will not learn, not even if he can recite some correct answer with one hundred per cent accuracy."[15] There's a tension here: Dewey does not mean that the teacher is to stand off and look on; the alternative to furnishing ready-made subject matter and listening to the accuracy with which it is reproduced is not silence, but participation—sharing—in an activity. In such shared activity, the teacher is a learner, and the learner is, without knowing it, a teacher—and in the grand scheme of schooling, the less consciousness of these roles there is, on either side, the better. For Dewey, "the best type of teaching bears in mind the desirability of affecting . . . interaction. It puts the student in the habitual attitude of finding points of contact and mutual

---

14 Dewey, *Democracy and Education*, 159.

15 Ibid., 160.

bearings."[16] For teachers interested in this sort of teaching and learning, their success at becoming certified teachers often negates the very potential Dewey suggests. Far too often teacher training (vs. education) programs emphasize method, routine, and narrow habits unlike Dewey's. Remember the distinctions among training, schooling, and education from earlier. In general terms, teachers are trained to carry out edicts and already-decided-on content that is disconnected from both students and teachers.[17] Content is determined by bureaucrats and dumped on teachers who turn around and dump it on students. This problem of imposition and overtraining is compounded by structural requirements such as those enforced by Pearson's edTPA, where students have to pay to submit their work to prove they can successfully submit lesson plans.[18] It's training trainers to train more trainers. What a waste of human potential.

Such training was abundantly clear at Chrysalis. Extraordinarily smart and well-intentioned teachers struggled mightily with Dewey's imaginative concept of teaching. I'd use an icebreaker to get the conversation started. The icebreaker was essentially a brainstorming exercise in which teachers were asked to list the characteristics of a *good* teacher. People offered a variety of terms to characterize what they took good teaching to mean. Some of the terms included: *inspire, encourage, instruct, challenge, guide,* and *model*; but also *tell, lecture, discipline, control, manage,* and *test,* among many other terms and phrases. The icebreaker was not about determining the correct answers from the incorrect ones, although there was often a gap that opened between what has been experienced in the past (thus accurate) and what is proposed as new or Deweyan (thus alien). Most important, the brainstorming provided the opportunity to focus on meaning. The terms most consistently used were also the ones often least understood or clear. What does it mean to inspire a student? Does a teacher enter a classroom with inspiration as a conscious goal? Does inspiring suggest a kind of narcissism that masks transmission-oriented assumptions? That is, do teachers

---

16   Ibid., 163.

17   See Fishman and McCarthy, *John Dewey and the Challenge of Classroom Practice.*

18   See Dennis Attick and Deron Boyles, "Pearson Learning and the Ongoing Corporatization of Education," *Journal of Thought* 50, nos. 1-2 (Spring-Summer, 2016): 5-19; and Martha K. Donovan and Susan O. Cannon, "The University Supervisor, edTPA, and the New Making of the Teacher," *Education Policy Analysis Archives* 26, no. 28 (2018): 1-26.

want to be seen as inspiring, or actually *be* inspiring? Similarly, if teaching means instructing, what form does instruction take? If a teacher acts as a model, is this just another word for pretending? That is, if a teacher models for her students, is she genuine or is she fake?

Other concepts that teachers offered, such as discipline and control, raised questions about authority and order. The concern expressed is the same one learned in methods classes: Classroom management is everything, and you shouldn't smile until Thanksgiving. In no way does Dewey think that classroom management is insignificant. In many ways it's at the center of classroom practice. But, again, there are important questions to raise. What form of discipline and control is best? Do we want teachers as tyrants who threaten detention or other punishments? Is order something that is imposed? If so, what happens to community and inquiry in the process? As I repeat in other chapters, Dewey cared deeply about classroom management and the lab school has plenty of evidence of orderliness and discipline. Rarely, however, did discipline have to be imposed. Children who are engaged in learning are rarely discipline problems. They're too busy learning. So what was it that made the Chrysalis teachers so fearful? In addition to risk and trust from earlier, theirs was a typical reaction to democratic and free inquiry: Without traditional order, there will be chaos. If there aren't seventy-five rules posted at the front of the room, with corresponding penalties, of course, the school will break down into anarchy. The opposite of discipline and order was not unruly and disordered students but chaotic anarchists! This is the very extremity Dewey wants us to guard against. Topics and questions such as these were posed, and conversations were had to open communication and develop criticality. At least two consequences also followed from this interaction: (a) clarified meaning and (b) revealed biases supporting traditional understandings of teaching.

One theme that ran throughout discussions with teachers at Chrysalis was the degree to which a critique of traditional school practices was taken to mean that all elements of traditional schooling were bad. To be Deweyan meant throwing the baby out with the bathwater. It's simply not true that there's no order or discipline in Dewey's school, but understanding the shift to Deweyan thinking wasn't easy for teachers. I believe this was partly due to the problem of dualisms. A dualism only allows two options. Either x is right and y is wrong or y is right and x is wrong. I admit to contributing to this confusion in discussions with teachers because I tended to outline the differences between traditional schooling and Deweyan interaction. This sets up the very dualistic thinking that is part of the problem. Such either/or thinking allows teachers to become defensive about the elements of schooling that they successfully navigated and to look at any Deweyan suggestions as total replacements for authority and social conventions. Although I worked very hard to temper this sort of binary thinking, the remnants of certain habits are often too much to overcome. Consider a few illustrations: rules, habits, and educative experiences.

As noted earlier, teachers understand that classroom rules are fundamental. Parents expect that the teacher will be the authority in the classroom and will effectively manage the space. Dewey does not disagree with rules or authority, but the purpose of education is not, in his view, to reinforce external imposition. Instead, rules and authority are understood as mechanisms for potential growth and understanding. Rules, for instance, are not listed and posted by the teacher prior to students entering the room. They may already exist as part of a student handbook, for example, but the Deweyan point is that there will be much more self-control and social cohesion if the students are included in developing the rules—and the consequences for breaking those rules. Indeed, for Dewey, any preexisting rules in a student handbook are modifiable. The process of coming up with rules is a social and educational event that symbolizes Dewey's view of the community. There are rules, yes, but they come about in a way that demonstrates activity and learning that is largely agentic and authentic. The stipulation here is, of course, contingent on the teacher understanding the point of jointly constructing rules with students. The idea is for the students to be engaged in learning and self-control so that more and more learning happens. If the teacher only understands the practice as a prepackaged lesson or activity, the substantive point is lost and no matter how much "participation" is assumed to take place, it will not be educative in the sense that Dewey means.

Students (like their teachers and parents) are very good at routinization, but that is part of the problem, not part of the solution. When Dewey talks about developing habits, he means that there are at least two kinds of habits. The first habit is routine. It is an unthinking repetition. What do you do when you wake in the morning? Do you shower and dress before making tea? Do you let the dog out and check your Instagram? Do you brush your teeth and make your bed? Whatever the answer, whatever the routine, it is a habit of the first kind. This does not mean that the habit is necessarily bad, it simply means that the routine has become an unthinking part of your existence. Fine as far as it goes, the problem, for Dewey, is that schools promote these sorts of habits at the expense of better, more pragmatic ones. Walking in lines, raising hands, gathering worksheets, and so forth, are all fine habits until they become the majority of the day and the litmus tests for determining whether students are learning.

For Dewey, the better habit is the one that develops out of indeterminate situations. It is anticipatory and based on prior experiences to enable problem-solving. It is the unexpected situation that offers the most potential for growth, in other words. If my standard, routine habit of getting to work is to drive on the same roads every day, it becomes an unthinking situation to take a left turn, then a right, then another left, etc. When, however, the lights are out, or a tree has fallen across the road, I have to think and problem-solve the new, indeterminate situation. In a classroom, when the bell rings and everyone gets out their assignments, it's possible that we continue the first kind of habit. But what happens if a website is down or a current event overtakes everyone's thinking? It is in the indeterminate situation where flexibility, creativity, and imaginative teaching are found. They aren't scripted. They're not a routine. They arise from thinking in the moment and making connections that may never have been made before. The more rote, the more standardized, the more routine we become, the less likely we are to grow and learn outside of the limits of the first kind of habit. Take note: Having one imaginative moment in a week of routines is not enough. There must be a major shift in our understanding of what counts as good (Deweyan) teaching in the face of overwhelming drudgery and monotony. Take the following story as another way to explain the point.

In my work with teachers, I often used a well-worn illustration of two children, Johnny and Susie, walking to school. They find two pieces of a robin's eggshell on the sidewalk and each takes one of the pieces to their respective teacher. Susie goes to her teacher, Ms. Smith, and asks "What is this?" Ms. Smith replies that the object is a piece of a robin's eggshell and kindly asks Susie to take her seat and open her workbook to chapter 10. Johnny takes his piece of the shell to Ms. Jones and asks "What is this?" Ms. Jones replies with questions, not answers. "Where did you find it?" "Were there more pieces than the one in your hand?" "What color would you say the object is?" The class is then encouraged to view the object and consider what it is. Beyond that, Ms. Jones sets aside chapter 10 and, with input from the students, develops a lesson on birds, habitat, and environment. Ms. Smith was wedded to the first kind of habit, and Ms. Jones was open to the second kind of habit. Ms. Smith demonstrates excellent training and Ms. Jones demonstrates what a good teacher does. It's problem-posing for the purpose of expanding educative experiences. It's imaginative teaching. Ms. Smith may be said to be "more effective" by traditional administrators and parents but, in Dewey's view, Ms. Jones and her students are the better teachers and learners. Why? Because educative experiences are distinctive. In short, because they learned more. They experienced more. They know more.

Educative experiences, for Dewey, are one of three types of experiences—educative, miseducative, and noneducative. The distinctions are straightforward. Educative experiences are ones that boost students forward toward more learning. They represent growth and inquiry. They need not be positive experiences (i.e., I might spill birdseed when filling the feeder, but I learn not to hold the feeder a certain way or I learn to set the feeder on level bricks instead of on unlevel ground, etc.), but they add to understanding and provide the momentum for continuing investigation. Miseducative experiences, on the other hand, are experiences that stunt growth. They obstruct inquiry. When a student's question about the Spanish Inquisition, for instance, is deflected because the teacher is running out of time for the lesson, nothing comes of the inquiry. It's miseducative because it stopped the investigation. But miseducative experiences need not be "bad" experiences either. Much that goes on classrooms is so contrived as to make it appear that what's going on is educative, but it's not. When, for instance, science teachers use prepackaged experiments as activities to interest students, the students may be active in following the instructions. They may even enjoy moving around and mixing chemicals. But this is what Dewey worries about—using "fun activities" to cover over the continued imposition of transmission. Making a lesson appear engaging doesn't mean it's educative. If the teacher's lesson or the content is already laid out, what can students do other than react? Of course, it's possible that one of the prepackaged lessons spurs inquiry in students, but the locus of control and power is misplaced. The power is with the content, not the students. And if Dewey wants us to know anything about educating children it's that education is about them, not the adults, curriculum, politicians, or corporations.

The third kind of experience is noneducative. Noneducative experiences may be the rarest as they are experiences that achieve neither growth nor decay. They are static insofar as the experience "just is." Being stuck in traffic, learning nothing from it but not really being harmed by it either is a noneducative experience. These sorts of experiences are rare. For Dewey, the overall goal of distinguishing the three kinds of experiences was to link as many educative experiences together as one could to develop a web of understanding from which to gauge the indeterminate situations of the future. Think of an upward spiral. Put a few "x" marks randomly on the spiral. Those "x" marks indicate future problems. You don't know what they are because you're not in the future yet. But based on all your experiences, you're more likely to solve those future problems—those indeterminate situations—because you call on previous educative experiences to navigate the new issue or new problem. If there's anything close to "preparation" for Dewey, this would be it. This integrated notion of education is not, however, anything like "preparation for future living" that is the obsessive focus of current discussions about education (see chapters 2 and 5). Remember Dewey's quote: "I believe that education, therefore, is a process of living and not a preparation for future living."[19]

Art class had been, for a long time, a generator of Deweyan inquiry at Chrysalis. A student once brought in a military relic that developed into a temporary museum exhibition in the school. There was no course objective that stated, "Set up a museum exhibit about military families." The relic generated interest and grew through investigations. Getting to the exhibit, in other words, was central to demonstrating Dewey's imaginative vision of teaching and learning. Students explored family histories for military connections and sought out veterans' organizations from the surrounding community. They did so with prompts and guidance from teachers who were "thinking on their feet" and being creative—imaginative—regarding the directions of the inquiries. Some of the veterans the students interviewed were invited as guests of honor and shared more of their experiences in featured stories as part of the student-generated exhibit. Although the exhibit had all the markings of an art installation, it was artistic, yes, but it was far more than a traditional art project. The family history investigations,

---

19   Dewey, "My Pedagogic Creed," 78, Article II.

alone, were often eye-opening to visitors of the gallery. The point, however, is that they were eye-opening to the students. It was primarily the
students who learned and understood through the educative experience of
research into history and genealogy but without a course titled "History" or
"Genealogy." The content and the processes of learning were merged, not
artificially separated into themes or sections laid out by week and term and
then told to students. Their learning not only resulted in featuring family
members' specific military history; it yielded knowledge beyond and across
those boundaries, too. Military history contextualized history itself. Medals
were more than metal and ribbon hanging from a veteran's jacket; they
stood for something; they represented meaningful action that students better understood because of the educative experiences and growth resulting
from their inquiries.

In another instance, a donor contributed antique books to the school
that then turned into a project about publishing, monetary appraisals, and
the content of the manuscript itself. None of it was planned, which is much
of the point here. The books were donated as a kind gesture by a benefac-
tor. What the manuscripts were, where they came from, what they were
worth (an astonishing sum of about $10,000, as I recall), and what they
represented (as books, rare manuscripts, donations, antiques, etc.) are the
generative themes that evolve and emerge from authentic inquiry and educative experiences. The donation wasn't in any lesson plan. It wasn't even
part of the curriculum. Nobody had a clue what to do with the books. In
Deweyan fashion, an unexpected situation develops into another kind of
research project. Students became interested in finding out more about the
books and the inquiry grew in multiple directions.[20] Although nobody listed
"antique valuation" as a learning objective, not only was valuation learned,
but it was also understood because of the context of the inquiry and the relevance and relationship of the donation to the school itself. Once the research

---

20 Note that not every student in the school was involved in the veterans' exhibit or
the book donations. These are illustrations of how projects develop to include more and
more students but based on whether the students have an interest in the topic. This point
needs clarification, too. Students don't have to state "up front" that they are interested
in genealogy. That's too abstract and too esoteric. But it's sometimes by happenstance
that students who were not initially interested become interested because their friends
are constantly talking about what they are researching . . . and the research can evolve
to include more and more students, including students who may not have been interested
at the beginning of the project.

revealed how much the books were worth, more learning took place. What do we do with the books? Do we sell them? Do we preserve them? If we sell them, what process is best? Do we put them in a specialist auction, list them on Etsy, or something else? If we preserve them, what do we have to do? Will we need temperature-controlled rooms? What about light and how it damages paper and the binding?[21] Note how these questions flow. The more questions, the more inquiry. The more inquiry, the more growth. The more growth, the more knowing. These examples gesture toward Dewey's interdisciplinary understanding of school content. A project deriving from art class, or any class for that matter, represents an originating opportunity for multiple inquiries across subjects.[22]

In Dewey's lab school, there was an iconic story of the student who wanted to build a chair. This wasn't a project for a shop or industrial arts class, although it involved those areas. It was a project that illustrates the upward and expanding spiral of inquiry, connection, and educative experience. In making the chair, the student had to understand measurement, materials, and aesthetics. In other words, the student had to integrate math, science, and art. Add that, with guidance and problem-posing from teachers, the student was also encouraged to consider history, architectural style, and corresponding literature. What wood should be used? What tools are necessary? What size and scale should the chair be? How much sanding of the wood (and what grit is required of the sandpaper) is necessary to avoid splinters or snagging clothing? The result was a Victorian chair on which the student sat to read Victorian literature. The point I'm reinforcing is integration and educative experience, much like the examples of veterans and antique books. Instead of specialized and dedicated spaces for art, science, math, history, English, and so on, as separated, walled-off classes, Deweyan education still has the classes, but they are blended and centered on projects that cross boundaries and integrate rather than divide. They also originate largely (although not solely) from students' interests.

---

21   Also note that the students contacted experts in the auction business, the Roswell Historical Society, and others. This outreach meant that the learning community was much larger than one class in one school and also demonstrated the point that learning crosses multiple categories and disciplines.

22   Teachers also made links to the general curriculum, too. I return to this point shortly.

There are many more examples of this kind of Deweyan inquiry from Chrysalis, but it should also be pointed out that Chrysalis was not totally Deweyan. Given accreditation burdens, parental expectations for SAT exam scores, and the social pressures of getting a job, it might be that Deweyan theory was put into practice only occasionally. But here, too, there are important stipulations to be made. Chrysalis, as noted earlier, had a very small student population. The teacher-to-student ratio was 1:6. A typical classroom in the United States has approximately twenty-five to thirty students. Part of the dilemma, it seems to me, is that even in a small school that is interested in Deweyan philosophy and practice, navigating the outside pressures and assumptions placed on schools, teachers, and students to transmit "the basics" and learn "the skills" needed to get a job is difficult. In a more general sense, I fear that part of the problem is that teachers are relatively powerless, too. I don't mean that their unions and professional organizations have no power. I mean that their roles have become reinforced as marginal onlookers of prepackaged curricula that purportedly align content with testing.[23] Teachers have, effectively, become the unwitting pawns of corporate textbook publishers and testing companies that market their work as making teaching and learning easier because the hard work of alignment has already been done for them.[24] It is another instance of transmission that effectively celebrates the first kind of habit and advances the idea that teaching (as transmission) can be made easy or convenient.

Dewey's view understands teaching to be an entirely different enterprise. If you want to be a good teacher, demonstrate academic rigor and know your content areas well enough not to be the center of attention. Reread that point. You must be knowledgeable about your field to such a degree that you don't flaunt it. You must also be confident enough in your knowledge to say that you don't know the answer to a question—and then follow up the not-knowing with the very inquiry Dewey is talking about: Co-learning *with* students. Risk. Trust. You must also be interdisciplinary, curious, and willing to share power and control with your students. Reread

---

23 It might also be the case that the National Education Association and the American Federation of Teachers have become more like corporations and less like professional associations or unions.

24 See, for example, how different history books are written and marketed to different states: https://www.nytimes.com/interactive/2020/01/12/us/texas-vs-california-history-text books.html.

that point, too. You must ask more questions than you give answers and you must be comfortable with uncertainty. You must embrace failure in the sense that making mistakes often leads to the best educative experiences. Noise should not be a problem for Deweyan teachers because children make noise when they are actively involved in learning. Messes will be made—and they will be cleaned up, often in creative and inventive ways. This is not anarchy, in the typical use of that term. It is art. It is learning and knowing. It is, in short, life.

Given that most teachers are required to be experts in classroom management, teaching methods, and accountability systems, Deweyan teaching might seem to be a distant dream. In some ways, Deweyan teaching is more difficult because of teacher–student–content transactions. In other ways, however, getting rid of the restrictions of imposed expectations is freeing and opens the possibilities for student learning of a magnitude we can scarcely imagine. Remember the veterans? Remember the antique books? Remember the chair building? They illustrate how Deweyan teaching and learning are expansive, interconnected, and educative in the experiential ways that matter. The student didn't build the chair from a kit that listed steps 1, 2, and 3. The student built the chair through trial and error because it was of interest and use. That the project required information and elements from traditional content areas meant that those areas were used to solve a problem and were interrelated. The *experience* was an important part, but remember the distinction between educative and miseducative experiences. Not every experience is worthwhile or interesting. But this is where students and teachers transact problems and questions to advance inquiry as a genuine learning community. And, yet again, we might find ourselves caught in a bind. Even if we wanted to be Deweyan, would schools permit it? Would parents trust teachers enough to take what would likely appear to them to be a risk? Perhaps. But knowing more about Dewey's philosophy might mean the difference between thinking about changing what it means to teach and to learn and actually changing it.

To help that project, I turn, in the next chapter, to the arts, aesthetics, and school policy to both expand and clarify a larger point: Deweyan teaching requires knowing the content of courses being taught. It also requires knowing what Deweyan teaching, itself, is. This initial glimpse into Dewey's imaginative teaching is expanded in the next chapter, and the chapters that follow, to establish the philosophical justification and theoretical basis on which to build the practical and useful change required to bring about educative experiences for teachers and students in US public schools. It's a big task, but I argue that children's lives are worth it.

References

Attick, Dennis, and Deron Boyles. "Pearson Learning and the Ongoing Corporatization of Education." *Journal of Thought* 50, nos. 1-2 (2016): 5-19.

Boyles, Deron. "Experiential Education," Chrysalis Experiential Academy, Parent-Teacher Lecture. 2010. https://www.youtube.com/watch?v=V_fzsNnA57I.

Delpit, Lisa. *Other People's Children: Cultural Conflict in the Classroom*. New York: The New Press, 1993.

Dewey, John. *Democracy and Education*. New York: The Free Press, 1916.

Dewey, John. "My Pedagogic Creed," *School Journal* 54 (1897): 77-80.

Donovan, Martha K., and Susan O. Cannon. "The University Supervisor, edTPA, and the New Making of the Teacher." *Education Policy Analysis Archives* 26, no. 28 (2018):1-26.

Emdin, Christopher. *For White Folks Who Teach in the Hood . . . and the Rest of Y'all Too: Reality Pedagogy and Urban Education*. Boston: Beacon Press. 2017.

Fishman, Steven M., and Lucille McCarthy. *John Dewey and the Challenge of Classroom Practice*. New York: Teachers College Press, 1998.

Goldstein, Dana. "Two States. Eight Textbooks. Two American Stories," January 20, 2020. *The New York Times*: https://www.nytimes.com/interactive/2020/01/12/us/texas-vs-california-history-textbooks.html.

King, Joyce E., Etta R. Hollins, and Warren C. Hayman. *Preparing Teachers for Cultural Diversity*. New York: Teachers College Press, 1997.

Kovacs, Philip E. ed. *The Gates Foundation and the Future of US "Public" Schools*. New York: Taylor and Francis, 2010.

Lagemann, Ellen. "Experimenting with Education: John Dewey and Ella Flagg Young at the University of Chicago." *American Journal of Education* 104, no. 3 (1996): 171–185.

Linn, Allison. "The Entrepreneur Who's Paying Kids Not to Go to College," May 25, 2011. *Today*: https://www.today.com/money/entrepreneur-whos-paying-kids-not-go-college-6C9677995.

Love, Bettina. *We Want to Do More Than Survive: Abolitionist Teaching and the Pursuit of Educational Freedom*. Boston: Beacon Press, 2019.

Tanner, Laurel. *Dewey's Laboratory School: Lessons for Today*. New York: Teachers College Press, 1997.

CHAPTER TWO

DEWEY AND THE ARTS:

Everyday Experience, Advocacy, Policy, and Critical Problems for Imaginative Teaching

A S WE BEGIN THIS chapter, it's important to understand just how broadly Dewey understood the arts and what the relationship is between the arts and his view of imaginative teaching. We explored, in the last chapter, some examples of Deweyan learning and imaginative teaching. Whether it's chair-building, a veterans' exhibit, robin's eggs, or antique books, art is evident in each of the illustrations. To suggest that art is everywhere is not to say that everything is art. For Dewey, creativity and imagination are elements in everyday life to the degree that they represent meaning. I'll return to this point throughout the book but pay attention to the concept *meaning*. The meanings you glean from activities, lessons, and life are a central part of who you are and who you will become. "What does this mean?" should be a question you ask in order to grow and learn. It's not a question to ask in ways that are dismissive or that undermine continued inquiry.

I divide this chapter into two sections. The first, shorter section clarifies Dewey's view of the arts and aesthetics in relation to everyday life. The second section illustrates how debates about the arts in schools continue to misunderstand Dewey's view of art as experience. There are clear links between the theory and the practice, but to make them, we first need to understand the relationship between art and living our daily lives. What is art? What do we do with it? Why should we care about it?

What Constitutes Art?

For Dewey, primarily in his *Art as Experience*,[1] art isn't remote. It's also not formulaic. Art is a function in human existence. Writing, painting, playing music, making crafts, etc., are instances of artistry that are not separate from our daily lives. We may agree that Georgia O'Keeffe's *Black Iris III* is an inspiring interpretation of still life, Michelangelo's *David* is a brilliant sculpture, Frida Kahlo's *The Two Fridas* is a moving self-portrait, and Leonardo DaVinci's *Mona Lisa* is iconic "high art," but these, and a million other examples, are artistic artifacts. They're important, but they should not confine the meaning of art. Decorating your bedroom is art. What you put on your walls requires aesthetic decision-making. Deciding what your room looks like may be restricted or altered by "bed-in-a-bag" merchandising, but you still make aesthetic decisions about what you want your room to look like and how it might convey your tastes and who you are at the time. Similarly, how you dress for school or for the weekend involves art and aesthetics. Clothing decisions, like the "bed-in-a-bag" problem, are often influenced by peer pressure or commercial trends, but this only clarifies Dewey's point:

> the trouble with existing theories [of aesthetics] is that they start from a ready-made compartmentalization, or from a conception of art that "spiritualizes" it out of connection with the objects of concrete experience. The alternative, however, to such spiritualization is not a degrading and Philistinish materialization of works of fine art, but a conception that discloses the way in which these works idealize qualities found in common experience . . . A conception of fine art that sets out from its connection with discovered qualities of ordinary experience will be able to indicate the factors and forces that favor the normal development of common human activities into matters of artistic value.[2]

---

1   John Dewey, *Art as Experience* (New York: Perigee Books, 1934/1980).

2   Ibid., 11.

Art is not confined to museums, in other words, but we should not let com-mercialism decide *for us* what is aesthetically valuable, either. Here, again, is the active role of humans. We mediate and interpret what art *is* based on val-ues that are informed by parents, friends, social groups, online communities, etc., that nonetheless should not restrict our thinking.[3] If we allow limiting or narrowing of thought, we conform. We reinforce the status quo when we sell out to trends and fads, unless their adoption is a form of irony or com-mentary or some other conscious and deliberate action. Refusing the status quo is also true for living our lives generally and living our lives as teachers and students in schools, specifically. But here, obviously, is a major problem.

Schools tend to reinforce conformity. They operate on a long list of rules and regulations meant to keep order. This is true for both students *and* teachers. Think dress codes. Hall passes. Bell schedules. Homework. Per-mission slips. The busy-work that occupies most teachers' time is useful for order and control—of students, yes—but also to control teachers. Teachers who are focused on entering grade data or filling out standardized rubrics are preoccupied and therefore not considering why the drudgery of teaching is so exhausting in the first place. The problem all this poses for imaginative teaching should be clear: There is little to no time for thinking creatively. Indeed, given the sheer amount of standardized content, goals, objectives, outcomes, testing, and so forth, suggests that there isn't any meaningful space for imagination. The thinking has already been done for teachers. Why? There are too many reasons to explore but let me outline two: 1) trust (again); and 2) credibility.

For trust, we should think carefully about the degree to which it exists or does not exist in most public schools. By trust, I mean, again, the degree to which parents, administrators, other teachers, and students grant you leeway in doing your job. If I trust you, you have the freedom to experiment.

---

3   I happen to think that what most people call "modern art" isn't aesthetically pleasing at all. A blank canvas or a toilet hung on a wall may be provocative, but I don't think it's especially artistic. Works by Thomas Eakins and Henry Scott Tuke are far more to my liking and what I consider great art—and this is part of the point. My views do not con-form to most of the art world, but I have reasons and justifications as to why Eakins and Tuke are outstanding artists. You should develop your own reasons and justifications for why you think *x* or *y* counts as aesthetically pleasing art, regardless of what experts or the masses may say. It's called independent thought and it's rare in the US in 2020—ironic for a country that prides itself on its rugged individualism. Be careful, however, not to mistake your opinion as truth. It's your view, but it isn't necessarily right *because* it's your view.

I regard you as knowledgeable, thoughtful, and resourceful. You, in turn, continue to demonstrate your teaching prowess by earning the respect of your students, their parents, other faculty, etc. At Chrysalis, we trusted that students would learn from veterans, the historical society, and antique book dealers. We trusted teachers to mediate complications or misunderstandings so exhibits could be shown and learning could take place. If I don't trust you, you have to submit lesson plans to specify the goals and objectives you will "cover" in the time that you have in class (around forty-five minutes or so, unless you have block scheduling). You constantly must prove yourself and figure out how to navigate parent-teacher conferences, administrator observations of your classroom teaching, grading, and standardized testing. Most teachers must balance what they know is good teaching with what they also know is expected of them by parents and administrators. This repeatedly puts teachers in an awkward position. Parents who don't trust teachers may not trust them because they represent an unfair system where their children get lost in the shuffle. Teachers, in that unfair system, must navigate the requirements of keeping their jobs with the knowledge they have of what good teaching is and means. It's not easy. Formulaic teaching—following a scripted curriculum or state standards—may make it easier to keep your job, but often does not yield aesthetic, imaginative teaching and learning. As a result, teacher credibility suffers, and we find ourselves constantly on the defensive.

Credibility is related to trust and might be a precondition for it. That is, to be a credible teacher means that you must know your field. Yes, even (especially?) elementary school teachers must know content in ways that make them experts beyond what 6-year-olds perceive. Credibility is built over time. Think of credibility as your reputation. It takes a while to establish and the process of establishing a good reputation means that you must take calculated risks. Dewey called these "ends in view." You have a goal in mind, and you consider the possible consequences of the action you are taking. The more thoughtful you are about the process of achieving those ends, the more likely you are to build a good reputation and establish credibility. This is not, however, a perfect process. Mistakes, as I note throughout this book, are important episodes for learning. And mistakes can only be made in productive ways if you are trusted by your students and others. If this sounds a bit like the "chicken and the egg" dilemma, it is. For Dewey, the processes of establishing trust and credibility are not formulaic and "proven." They are, like the rest of life, merging activity, thought, content, purpose, and context in a constant process of inquiry and betterment . . . and all of this together is aesthetic and artistic. It also characterizes imaginative teaching because it requires a philosophical depth of understanding to recognize why so much effort is necessary to be a good teacher. This isn't a problem. It's the joy of teaching. The misery of teaching is getting rid of the interesting-but-constant attention necessary for good teaching and replacing it with the perfunctory patterns of teaching-as-telling that fit nicely together with externally imposed rules, rituals, and routines.

When I noted, in chapter 1, that teachers at Chrysalis had to "unlearn" what they thought teaching was, art and aesthetics were front and center in the discussions. They committed the "compartmental error" in thinking that art was done in "art class." They also thought art was represented only in the projects and artifacts produced. Remember the example of veterans' stories that became a much bigger project at the school (a mini museum, in fact). It started when students asked questions about war and terrorism, grew to include interviews with their grandparents and, as a result, a wider veteran community. Those interviews yielded artifacts that told the stories of veterans of wars, in this case World War II, the Korean War, the Vietnam War, and the so-called War on Terror.

Not only was art represented in the storytelling, the uniforms, the posters encouraging people to buy war bonds and enlist in the military, and the like, but art was also represented in the actions of interviewing, understanding, and putting together the installation itself. Decisions had to be made about whether to include war protest literature and, if so, how to include it. Historically male-dominated, straight, and white, what would the "museum installation" include regarding gender, the "don't ask don't tell" policy, and integration? Perhaps more importantly, *who* makes these decisions? The answer at Chrysalis was that it was a joint effort requiring, at times, adult-led decision-making that nonetheless was carried out in respectful discourse and debate. The art teacher was vital, not only because of his expertise in art; but his flexibility and acumen in seeing links to other classes. The decisions were informed by conversations that were, at times, tense. But because there was trust, the conversations not only could be had, they yielded better understanding of the role of the school, the purpose of learning (beyond veterans and wars), and what inquiry produces.

Chrysalis is only one example, of course, but it illustrates how the arts are intrinsic to school projects as life projects. The learning that took place, the educative experiences in putting together the exhibit, was not restricted to school. It was school, of course, but it wasn't limited to the school walls and it wasn't limited to one class of the same-aged students who had one art teacher. The interviews, the search for memorabilia, the distribution of chores and assignments to make the exhibit possible, the direction of the art teacher with other teachers, the involvement of parents, and the multi-aged groups that worked together to make the exhibit possible all indicate the degree to which inquiry merges intellect and abstraction with practical, social realities. It's what's supposed to happen in schools that recognize the importance of aesthetics. Unfortunately, larger economic forces often change the realities of school. I now turn to a broader examination of policy and the risks associated with advocating for the arts that are not understood in Dewey's terms.

Contemporary Debates about the Arts

When school district budgets are tight, art classes get bundled such that art teachers find themselves rolling carts around buildings and commuting from school to school so students are exposed to art at least once a week. If budgets are really tight, art classes go away. After art, music and theater become the targets. In larger school districts decisions are made about whether x, y, or z ensemble is "critical" to music education. Is choir more important than symphony? Is theater more important than marching band?

As noted earlier, Dewey believed the arts were integral to schooling and also believed that they were integrated in classes that didn't necessarily call themselves art. Science projects are also art. Reports in geography often use maps or other images that require at least some artistic manipulation and understanding. Tik Tok and YouTube videos. Homecoming floats. Backpacks and clothing. The cars you drive or the bikes you ride. All of these are art. As Aaron Stoller explains, "art is a naturalized form of making which is continuous with all other forms of knowing and understanding."[4] Where the disciplines of the arts may benefit from their own fields of expertise (music, art, dance, etc.), Dewey's point is that art and aesthetics span those fields of expertise and must be seen in practical, daily life, too. Politically

---

4   Aaron Stoller, *Knowing and Learning as Creative Action: A Reexamination of the Epistemological Foundations of Education* (New York: Palgrave Macmillan, 2016), 70.

and socially, however, this may set up a big problem. If art is "everywhere," its value is lessened because anything can be art. This isn't what Dewey was arguing, but it is a consequence of not reading Dewey carefully. One result for schools has been the minimizing and marginalizing of the arts in times of economic crisis and even after the crisis passes. In this section of the chapter, I explore how arts advocates may be doing themselves a disservice when they think of the arts in narrow and un-Deweyan ways.

Arts education advocates have argued for years that the arts deserve a place in the public school curriculum alongside other disciplines. Here I'm talking about art, music, theater, and dance in their various forms. Some schools have symphonies. Other schools have step. Some schools have chorus. Other schools have show choir. Some schools have a drama club. Other schools are known for their marching bands. The justification for these ensembles tends to reinforce a problem. The rationales to support the place of the arts suffer from the kind of career logic that minimizes inquiry to goals and objectives that are aligned with efficiency, production, and employment. The arts are put on the chopping block with other disciplines that then need to justify themselves in terms of student preparation and relevancy to the job market. The arts, on this view, are useful because they produce students with skills that will benefit their future lives in the work force. If you have a show choir, in other words, you ought to have graduates appearing on Broadway. Orchestra? Only if graduates go on to a conservatory or work in a symphony. At least two related moves are important to understand here: 1) that the meaning of the arts gets changed when it's evaluated in terms of job preparation; and 2) that the meaning of the arts gets changed when those advocating *for* the arts begin justifying them in the language of economics and job preparation. The first move is an assault on the arts by the career and corporate logic that characterizes the broader society. The second move is arguably worse because it has arts advocates caving-in to the career and corporate logic instead of confronting it.[5]

I'm suggesting that the discourse of utility is an important problem to challenge and I offer that Dewey's pragmatic instrumentalism is a better way to advocate for the arts. This is so, in part, because the practice of pragmatic instrumentalism differs from utilitarianism. Here's the philosophy, but don't

---

5   This is the problem called hegemony, explained in chapter 1: people willingly agreeing to arguments and policies that come back to hurt them.

turn the page yet. Utilitarian rationales offered by arts advocates not only lack empirical support but represent narrow and dualistic thinking inadequate to the task of understanding students' meaning-making when engaged in arts-centered inquiry. We need to rethink how we defend the arts.

I begin with Dewey's view that "knowing is not self-enclosed and final but is instrumental to reconstruction of situations"[6] to propose an expanded vision of arts-centered inquiry as pragmatic instrumentalism. Stick with me as I interrogate the current advocacy claim that arts education develops the creativity and innovation necessary to maintain the nation's global competitiveness. I draw a distinction between the use of the term *instrumental* in denoting structural, *utilitarian* justifications for the arts and the broader application of the term to encompass benefits the arts provide individual students in mediating complex and connected learning. The difference has to do with the center of power. Structural, *utilitarian* instrumentality has as its intended outcome efficient management of human behavior. Think classroom management strategies. By contrast, *pragmatic* instrumentalism looks at transformative consequences for people engaged in practical, everyday transactions. By reclaiming the *pragmatic* term *instrumental* for arts-centered inquiry, we can restore the notion of student and teacher engagement in arts inquiry grounded in Dewey's philosophy and connected to an imaginative vision of teaching and learning.

Reconceptualizing Instrumentalism in Arts Education

Dewey's work in reconstructing the concept of instrumentalism pragmatically reflects his time and place. Noting the industrial accomplishments and scientific achievements of his day, Dewey nevertheless considers industry and science inadequate in addressing the challenges confronting the world. He writes:

> What is the matter? It lies, I think, with our lack of *imagination* in generating leading ideas. Because we are afraid of speculative ideas, we do, and do over and over again, an immense amount of dead, specialized work in the region of "facts." We forget that

---

6 John Dewey, *Reconstruction in Philosophy* (Mineola, NY: Dover Publications, 1920/2004), 84.

such facts are only data; that is, are only fragmentary, uncompleted meanings, and unless they are rounded out into complete ideas—a work which can only be done by hypotheses, by a free *imagination* of intellectual possibilities—they are as helpless as are all maimed things and as repellent as are needlessly thwarted ones.[7]

Dewey's calling for a renewed commitment to the constructively instrumental work of producing imaginative and generative ideas to meet social needs. Arts education is ideally positioned to play a leading role in fostering just the kind of creativity and imagination needed to respond to today's pressing social concerns, but I question the utilitarian justifications associated with business- and government-sponsored efforts to place the arts in the service of developing skills "that enable businesses to compete successfully in the 21st century workplace."[8]

Karen Hamblen reminds us that over the years, advocates for the inclusion of art instruction in the school curriculum have offered a variety of philosophical perspectives. A century ago, some arts advocates argued that drawing lessons developed technical skills that were directly transferable to industry jobs. While others claimed that the arts contributed to social refinement. In both cases, however, the (utilitarian) benefits were to be seen in the future. More recently, arts advocates promote the study of art for its purported (utilitarian) connections to creativity, critical thinking, self-awareness, social adjustment, increased motivation, and higher test scores.[9] In

---

7   John Dewey, *Philosophy and Civilization* (New York: Minton, Balch, 1931), excerpted in *The American Pragmatists*, eds. Milton R. Konvitz and Gail Kennedy (New York: Meridian Books, 1960), 182. Emphasis added. See, also, John Dewey, *Freedom and Culture* (New York: Prometheus, 1989).

8   Thomas L. Birch, "Tough Times: Advocacy Strategies in an Economic Downturn," *The NASAA Advocate* 12, no. 1 (2009): 1-7: 2. Downloaded from the National Assembly of State Arts Agencies (NASAA) website, http://www.nasaa-arts.org. The advocacy trope of creativity and innovation for US global competitiveness is also evident on a number of other websites, including those of the Arts Education Partnership (http://www.aep-arts. org), the California Alliance for Arts Education (http://artsed411.org), BigThought, an arts partnership based in Dallas (http://bigthought.org), the College Board (http://advocacy.collegeboard.org), and Partnership for 21st Century Skills (http://www.p21.org).

9   Karen A. Hamblen, "Theories and Research that Support Art Instruction for Instrumental Outcomes," *Arts Education Policy Review* 98, no. 3 (January/February 1997): 27-33, 27.

place of the utilitarians' "overstated, unsubstantiated, and politically moti-
vated assumptions,"[10] a pragmatic instrumentalist approach to art instruction provides a philosophically sound alternative. On Hamblen's view, and
mine, arts study offers students experiences very different from those found
in other areas of the curriculum. Hamblen cites Susanne Langer's idea that
thinking includes many ways of knowing and experiencing: qualitative, relational, connotative, and affective.[11] Hamblen also argues that arts education
extends opportunities for students to engage in critical inquiry, examining
"hypotheses, statements of value, and the ambiguities of artistic meanings
and designations."[12] The engagement she's referring to is organic. It origi-
nates in student inquiry pragmatically, instrumentally, and authentically, i.e.,
from innate, natural curiosity and the transactions that organically follow.
These transactions are not as preparation for a distant future where living
will take place. They're enacted and mediated in the students' contexts such
that understanding and inquiring are in the present. Future problems may
well be solved by having such arts-rich educative experiences, but the focus is
on the aesthetic inquiry *in* the present and *for* the present, not as preparation
for a future job or career. Dewey, again: "I believe that education . . . is a
process of living and not a preparation for future living."[13]

Still, as Liora Bresler argues, although utilitarian, humanistic and instrumental research orientations differ with respect to the role of the arts in the
curriculum, they needn't be considered mutually exclusive, depending on
how broadly *instrumental* is defined.[14] Like Hamblen, Bresler points out that
the arts fulfill both economic and democratic functions within the education
system. She writes:

> The attempt to ground the arts in a pragmatic, instrumentalist
> framework has characterized arts education since its introduction

---

10   Ibid.

11   Ibid., 28. See, also, Susanne K. Langer, *Feeling and Form: A Theory of Art* (New
York: Charles Scribner's Sons, 1953), 240-241.

12   Hamblen, "Theories and Research that Support Art Instruction," 29.

13   John Dewey, "My Pedagogic Creed," *School Journal* 54 (January 1897): 77-80, 78,
Article II.

14   Liora Bresler, "Research, Policy, and Practice in Arts Education: Meeting Points for
Conversation," *Arts Education Policy Review* 99, no. 5 (May/June 1998): 9-15, 13.

to formal schooling in the nineteenth century, when advocates emphasized the arts' contributions to the world of work (for example, in drawing skills) and to good citizenship. "School arts" is a hybrid genre, existing between the educational and the artistic. Artistic forms and values are transformed or created as they enter the embrace of the school institution, assuming the look, practices, and goals of academic subject matters.[15]

Bresler draws a clear distinction between instrumentalist and utilitarian approaches to education. She argues: "A utilitarian approach to education is promoted by the voices of businesses and community members that associate education primarily with jobs, the economy, and the production of good citizens."[16] Warning that since education involves initiating the young into the norms and beliefs of the society they inhabit, it's necessary to consider *whose* values are being advocated in research, policy, and practice. Said differently, arts inquiry as pragmatic instrumentalism may lead to future benefits in a world of work and career. The problem is the knowability of that transfer as being specifically caused by particular types, methods, or models of arts inquiry. In advance of chapter 3, dealing with Dewey's theory of knowing, we cannot "know" so far ahead of time what, specifically, will be *utilized* from arts inquiry in future work. We didn't know antique books would be donated to Chrysalis and we didn't know our students' interests in veterans would turn into an exhibit and research study. Indeed, admitting that inquiry might—or even likely does—influence decisions and understandings about the world in the future does not free that future from the pragmatic present. To Bresler, the tensions within arts education resulting from narrowly conceived reasons for its educational value "reflect the problematic nature of a field that is not critical of itself."[17] This may be especially true of arts educators who are worried that their classes will be cut if budgets are underfunded. The concern goes like this: My chorus classes are at risk of being cut, so let me argue that chorus develops "teamwork." "Teamwork" is almost always cited as what businesses want, so chorus =

---

15   Ibid.

16   Ibid.

17   Ibid., 14.

teamwork = productive workers. The value of chorus, in other words, gets slanted (by you, the teacher) toward careers and away from chorus as valuable itself.

We should be skeptical of educators and politicians who use job skills as the primary justification for schooling. It reminds me of the adage "never trust anyone who wears a lapel pin." I'm similarly skeptical of advocacy efforts to market the arts as sellers of creativity and innovation. I think, instead, that arts-centered inquiry itself opens up inherently creative possibilities for individual students living connected lives. In critiquing the current arts advocacy discourse, pay attention to the theme "21st Century Skills" which saturates arguments justifying the inclusion of the arts in the curriculum. Phrases like "essential skills for success in today's world"[18] are philosophically at odds with the sensory immediacy and open-ended experimentation of aesthetic inquiry. Dewey's pragmatic instrumentalism connects continuous student growth to actions which support imaginative teaching and learning. The utilitarian view defines student success in terms of *projected economic indicators* that simply are not knowable. So why do it? It's my view that defining teaching and learning in terms of jobs, careers, and economics reinforces the idea that we are merely workers for an owning class and that we should not consider the value of a fulfilling, creative, happy life outside material comforts. As I detail in chapter 5, Dewey was also concerned that teaching and learning would be reduced to mere preparation for thankless (and meaningless?) jobs. Before then, consider the policy environment in which arts advocacy and teachers must navigate.

Philosophical Analysis in a Market-Driven Policy Environment

Over the past two decades, at least, arts advocacy claims of positive outcomes for students who study the arts have included improved overall academic performance and standardized test scores, enhanced personal identity and social skills, increased problem-solving skills, reasoning skills, communication skills, expanded creativity, and greater self-discipline.[19] The problem

---

18   Partnership for 21st Century Skills, "Framework for 21st Century Learning," http://www.p21.org/overview.

19   Constance Bumgarner Gee, "The 'Use and Abuse' of Arts Advocacy and Consequences for Music Education," *Arts Education Policy Review* 103, no. 4 (March/April 2002): 3-21, 5.

DEWEY AND THE ARTS 47

is that such specific claims are not justified.[20] While it's been demonstrated as true that students engaged in the arts generally do better in school and on their SATs, compared to students who are not involved in the arts, correlation is not the same as causation. As Ellen Winner and Lois Hetland revealed, there's no evidence to support the claim that arts training actually causes scores to rise.[21] Similarly, Elliot Eisner criticizes advocacy strategies that draw links between participation in the arts and non-arts outcomes: "To use the arts *primarily* to teach what is not truly distinctive about the arts is to undermine, in the long run, the justifying conditions for the arts in our schools."[22] We study drawing, painting, singing, etc., to know more about ourselves than about the supposed traits needed to get a job. Fifth graders don't play trumpet in the concert band so they can become another Wynton Marsalis, Clora Bryant, Louis Armstrong, or Maurice André. They play trumpet because their grandfather played it, they were fascinated to see three fingers move so quickly, they like the sound, or any number of a thousand reasons that have nothing whatsoever to do with getting a job after high school or college. But we force the logic of "preparation" and careers as though they should matter to a fifth grader. *They shouldn't*. Fifth graders should focus on fifth grade and the transactions between their lives inside and outside of school and should not be forced to think about the drudgery of a career so early in their young lives.

Still, the idea persists that arts education can reinvigorate the nation's schools and, thus, stimulate the economy. In May 2011, the President's Committee on the Arts and the Humanities (PCAH) released a report that referred to "decades of research show[ing] strong and consistent links between high-quality arts education and a wide range of impressive

---

20   Ellen Winner and Lois Hetland, "Art for Our Sake: School Arts Classes Matter More Than Ever—But Not for the Reasons You Think," *Arts Education Policy Review* 109, no. 5 (May/June 2008): 29-31. See also, Morgan Anderson, "The Case against 'Critical Thinking Skills': In Pursuit of a Humanizing Pedagogy," *Philosophical Studies in Education*, 46 (2015): 83-89.

21   Winner and Hetland, 30.

22   Elliot W. Eisner, "Does Experience in the Arts Boost Academic Achievement?" *Art Education* 51, no. 1 (January 1998): 7-15, 12.

educational outcomes."[23] In particular, the committee focused on "the need for federal and state education leaders to provide policy guidance for employing the arts to increase the rigor of curriculum, strengthen teacher quality, and improve low-performing schools. Building capacity to create and innovate in our students is central to guaranteeing the nation's competitiveness."[24] Notice the language that characterizes the policy. In opposition to Dewey, it exploits students. Adults are urged to "build capacity" to create and innovate *in our* students. Such policy language is not interested in the arts or the students. It is interested in reducing the field of teaching, and teachers and students themselves, to mere resources to be exploited.

By contrast, an expanded view of the term *instrumental* that pragmatically connects arts-centered inquiry with its consequences for student growth means valuing learners and the unforeseen possibilities that imaginative teaching and learning generates. A student's painstaking working out of a melodic phrase, a heated class debate over a painter's symbolic vocabulary, or a comedic improvisation on a political issue may all contribute to the development of "life skills," but the value of the arts in schools lies in the continuity and generativity of the human transactions taking place there each and every day. Indeed, phrases often repeated in the advocacy discourse to justify arts education such as "intrinsic value" and "art for art's sake" ring hollow unless students have opportunities to engage with the arts in ways that enable them, as Maxine Greene writes, "to notice what is there to be noticed, and to lend works of art their lives in such a way that they can achieve them as variously meaningful. When this happens, new connections are made in experience: new patterns are formed, new vistas are opened."[25] Arts-advocacy arguments which conceptualize "intrinsic" and "instrumental" in opposition to one another retain a pure/practical dualism or binary that limits understanding of student growth taking place *in the arts*. Remember that a dualism sets up

23   President's Committee on the Arts and the Humanities, *Reinvesting in Arts Education: Winning America's Future Through Creative Schools* (Washington, DC: President's Committee on the Arts and the Humanities, 2011), vi. Downloaded from the National Art Education Association website, "Research & Knowledge," http://www.arteducators.org/research/research. See, also, https://www.federalregister.gov/documents/2016/09/07/2016-21437/presidents-committee-on-the-arts-and-the-humanities-meeting-72 and note that the committee disbanded in 2017 because of President Donald Trump's stance toward funding the arts.

24   Ibid., viii.

25   Maxine Greene, *Variations on a Blue Guitar: The Lincoln Center Institute Lectures on Aesthetic Education* (New York: Teachers College Press, 2001), 6.

either-or thinking. The continued use of the terms *creativity* and *innovation* reflect the same dualist perspective within the arts advocacy discourse, even when the terms are taken to mean the same thing.[26] Let's look at how this actually works in policy and practice.

Arts-advocacy texts produced by Partnership for 21st Century Skills (P21) underscore the need to provide philosophically grounded opposition to arts advocacy claims that reinforce career and corporate-motivated practice, research, and policy expectations. Formed in 2002, P21 is a public-private "partnership" whose Strategic Council members include the National Education Association, major technology companies, and education publishers, as well as Crayola and the Walt Disney Company.[27] I'm using the P21 Skills Map for the Arts, one of five skills maps, to probe its assumption that creativity and innovation are commodities that can be traded across domains. I worry that arts educators risk undermining their primary responsibility to their students—rich and generative arts-centered inquiry—when the voices of corporate interests promoting utilitarian student outcomes provide the central themes for the arts advocacy discourse. Drama teachers are not responsible for career-focused jobs. If they were, to take this point to an absurd conclusion, their job (and the entire drama department) would be at risk if they didn't produce X-number of Tony- or Oscar-winning actors in a given span of time (no matter how random and arbitrary the time line might be). Great if they do, but, again, that's not the point of imaginative teaching. It's not about some job in the distant future (award-winning or not). It's about the value of the arts in the lives of students *now*, in the present *for* the present. And yet the problem remains.

The Skills Map for the Arts defines creativity as demonstrating originality and inventiveness in work. In the same framework, innovation is defined as "acting on creative ideas to make a tangible and useful contribution to the domain in which innovation occurs."[28] The inclusion of the sections on

---

26   For a discussion of the role of metaphor and synecdoche in educational policy discourse, see F. Tony Carusi, "The Persistence of Policy: A Tropological Analysis of Contemporary Education Policy Discourse in the United States" (PhD dissertation, Georgia State University, 2011).

27   Partnership for 21st Century Skills, "About Us," http://www.p21.org/about-us.

28   Partnership for 21st Century Skills, "21st Century Skills Map: The Arts," 6-7: http://p21.org. See, also, National Art Education Association. "Position Statement on 21st Century Skills and Visual Arts Education," https://www.arteducators.org/advocacy/articles/496-naeaposition-statement-on-21st-century-skills-and-visual- arts-education.

creativity and innovation in the Skills Map for the Arts has ironic implications. First, their inclusion is unnecessary. Based on the sample activities
offered by the arts educators invited to collaborate on the project, creativity
in the arts *is* arts-centered inquiry. It is what the arts do. For example, in an
eighth-grade performance task demonstrating creativity, students "identify
a topic, research, explore options, select and develop ideas, get feedback,
revise, refine, perform."[29] The Skills Map for the Arts *artificially manufac-
tures* creativity in schools. Dewey's course of action would be to promote
students' engagement in substantive arts-centered inquiry over the course of
several years and in varying—and variable—artistic ways. Put in Deweyan
language, the Skills Map for the Arts sees the arts as means to an end; imaginative teaching sees means and ends as combined and inseparable.[30]

The second philosophical irony is that whereas the Skills Map for the
Arts defines innovation in terms of tangible and useful contributions, P-12
students learn and develop in variable and idiosyncratic ways.[31] Engagement with the arts very often has consequences for students that are intan-
gible and yet powerfully instrumental to their growth. Learning activities
in which students use technology to manipulate sound, text, and graphics
to produce novel artifacts may be innovative, but they are not necessarily
educative.[32] As Dewey reminds us,

> The belief that all genuine education comes about through expe-
> rience does not mean that all experiences are genuinely or equally

---

29   Ibid., 6.

30   For more on means and ends as inseparable, see Dewey, *Democracy and Education*,
323. See, also, Jim Garrison, *Dewey and Eros: Wisdom and Desire in the Art of Teaching*
(Charlotte, NC: Information Age Press, 2010); David A. Granger, *John Dewey, Robert
Pirsig, and the Art of Living: Revisioning Aesthetic Education* (New York: Palgrave Macmillan, 2006); Scott R. Stroud, "Dewey on Art as Evocative Communication," *Education
and Culture* 23, no. 2 (2007): 6-26; Thomas Alexander, "Dewey's Philosophy of Art and
Aesthetic Experience," *Artizein: Arts and Teaching Journal* 2, no. 1 (2016): 59-67; and
Kathleen Knight Abowitz, "Moral Perception Through Aesthetics: Engaging Imaginations in Educational Ethics," *Journal of Teacher Education* 58, no. 4 (2007): 287-298.

31   See Samuel Hope, "Creativity, Content, and Policy," *Arts Education Policy Review* 111, no. 2 (2010): 39-47, 40-43.

32   See the sample activities listed on the Partnership for 21st Century Skills Map: The
Arts, "Innovation," 7.

educative . . . Hence the central problem of an education based upon experience is to select the kind of present experiences that live fruitfully and creatively in subsequent experiences.[33]

Dewey's vision of imaginative teaching means that identifying educative experiences is a dual project including both the teacher and the student. Educative experiences, recall from chapter 1, are those experiences that increase growth. They encourage continued inquiry. These experiences, therefore, are not necessarily happy or easy ones. But they must be authentic and connected to students' lives. Educative experiences sometimes come about from a formal lesson or activity. But the biggest mistake that teachers make is in thinking that *they* are the ones to develop the activities (or, worse, follow ones supplied to them by curriculum companies) *for* students. Educative experiences are rarely scripted, contrived, or imposed. There must be freedom in imagination—and the entailing risks associated with such freedom—if authentic growth and inquiry are to come about.

What I think follows from all of this is that educators and business leaders should acknowledge the complex kinds of thinking that students who are engaged in arts-centered inquiry demonstrate. They should also figure out ways to value such inquiry in schools. Noting that the curriculum often determines the kinds of thinking that takes place in schools and criticizing those who would privilege the intelligence exercised in the use of language and mathematics over the kinds of thinking demonstrated in artistic production, Dewey writes:

Any idea that ignores the necessary rôle of intelligence in production of works of art is based upon identification of thinking with use of one special kind of material, verbal signs and words. To think effectively in terms of relations of qualities is as severe a demand upon thought as to think in terms of symbols, verbal and mathematical.[34]

---

33   John Dewey, *Experience and Education* (New York: Collier Books, 1938).

34   Dewey, *Art as Experience*, 46.

Dewey emphasizes making sense of the whole situation, that is, understanding meaning in "relations of qualities." The Skills Map for the Arts, by contrast, largely focuses on discrete work habits, presumably important for future success in work settings. This is an example of the separation between imposed techniques and authentic inquiry. Skills maps are miseducative rather than educative because they're divorced from the lives of teachers and students.

To be sure, many have adopted a Deweyan philosophical stance when critiquing education policy and practice and have argued for a pragmatist approach to organizing subjects in schools such that they become, as Dewey writes in *How We Think*, "instruments for forming alert, persistent, and fruitful intellectual habits."[35] What has changed, however, is the context in which advocacy efforts—including those focusing on the arts—are enacted. In contrast to past arts advocacy campaigns which brought together supporters within a particular school district, the Partnership for 21st Century Skills mobilizes professional organizations of arts educators and corporate partners on a national scale around the idea that "the arts promote work habits that cultivate curiosity, imagination, creativity, and evaluation skills"[36] that are needed for a global work force. This is misdirected energy that harms the arts more than it helps.

Arts-centered inquiry, though not sufficient for carrying out the entire imaginative work of a comprehensive curriculum, nevertheless contributes to fostering growth and continuity within it. Recalling Dewey's philosophical commitment to connecting values with human needs,[37] I adopt Jim Garrison's definition of inquiry as "the creative activity of transforming needful situations into more desirable circumstances."[38] According to Garrison, inquiry is as much a moral task as an aesthetic adventure because imagining possibilities that expand freedom requires practical wisdom and practical reasoning to ensure that consequences of action are morally desirable, not merely desired.[39]

---

35   John Dewey, *How We Think* (Mineola, NY: Dover Publications, 1910/1997), 168.

36   Partnership for 21st Century Skills, "21st Century Skills Map: The Arts," Introduction. http://www.p21.org.

37   Monroe C. Beardsley, "Intrinsic Value," *Philosophy and Phenomenological Research* 26, no. 1 (September 1965): 1-17, 17.

38   Garrison, *Dewey and Eros*, xv.

39   Ibid., 22, 51. I also make this link in chapter 5.

Toward Hopeful Possibilities?

Pragmatically instrumentalist arts-centered inquiry fosters just the kind of creativity and imagination needed to respond to today's pressing social concerns. From a Deweyan perspective, connecting arts-centered inquiry with social change means students engaging in a playful open-mindedness with serious attention to the demands of the subject matter. Yet Dewey adds an important note of caution: "The child forced into premature concern with economic remote results may develop a surprising sharpening of wits in a particular direction, but this precocious specialization is always paid for by later apathy and dullness."[40] Pick your job based on a "Career Day" all you want or believe that career aptitude tests are legitimate (they're not),[41] but you'll regret not growing and learning as much as you would have without such restrictions and blinders. Here, again, is the importance of authenticity and imagination. By relying on the arbitrary collection of "careers" featured at career days or trusting that a standardized battery of tests will predict your future means that you at least partly give up free will and agency. Free will and agency are taken over by a world view that says you don't matter as much as rankings and graduation rates. Consequently, you get subsumed under external commands and find your identity and worth tied to a vision of humanity where what you do and how much you make defines who you are. Dewey thinks this is stupid—and you should, too.

Dewey argues that in designing the conditions for learning experiences, educators must exercise imagination and wisdom in judging which attitudes and habits are being developed that are conducive to students' continued growth. Imaginative teachers also work with students in figuring out which attitudes and habits are detrimental.[42] Consistent with the naturalistic stance that sees the live creature in transaction with the environment (see chapter 4) is also Dewey's philosophy of art. The primary task

---

40 Dewey, *How We Think*, 218-219.

41 There are lots of these kinds of tests and, tragically, many are administered by school counselors as part of their professional obligations. They each assert a kind of Myers-Briggs aptitude scaling that is supposed to tell you what job you are good at doing. Divorced from reality, these are the very illustrations of what is wrong with imposed assumptions and the perversion of schooling. Some of the tests include the following: 123 Career Test, Princeton Review Career Quiz, MAPP Career Test, Career Strengths Test, and PathSource.

42 Dewey, *Experience and Education*, 38-39.

is restoring continuity between aesthetic experience and everyday living.[43] This means knowing your students, developing understanding *with* them, and inquiring *with* them into all manner of topics and subjects connected to art, or any other content area that links to artistic inquiry. What imaginative teaching does *not* do is use art to "cover up obviously brutal features."[44] What Dewey means by "cover up" is the trickery that often masquerades as teaching. Enthusiastically leading "say and repeat" slogans, turning memorizing multiplication tables into rap songs, or jumping up and down on tables to "get kids excited about learning," are all tricks for imposing traditional curriculum. Teachers use "devices of art" like a spoon full of sugar to make horrible schooling palatable. That you might *sometimes* have to act in this way is understandable. Schools are terrible bureaucracies mostly interested in external control and compliance with standardized material. But, to demonstrate Dewey's imaginative vision of teaching you must do far more than follow scripts, lesson plans, and teaching-to-the-test techniques. You have to know content, process, and transaction. That's where the next chapter should be helpful. I turn to the question of what counts as knowledge and how Dewey differed from traditional theories of knowledge. In short, Dewey argues for knowing over knowledge to emphasize action and inquiry. The implication for imaginative teaching should be clear: It's in the doing, not preparing to do.

---

43   Dewey, *Art as Experience*, 2.

44   Dewey, *Experience and Education*, 19.

References

Abowitz, Kathleen Knight. "Moral Perception through Aesthetics: Engaging Imaginations in Educational Ethics." *Journal of Teacher Education* 58 (4) 2007: 287–98.

Alexander, Thomas. "Dewey's Philosophy of Art and Aesthetic Experience." *Artizein: Arts and Teaching Journal* 2 (1) 2016: 59–67.

Anderson, Morgan. "The Case against 'Critical Thinking Skills': In Pursuit of a Humanizing Pedagogy." *Philosophical Studies in Education* 46 (1) 2015: 83–89.

Beardsley, Monroe C. "Intrinsic Value." *Philosophy and Phenomenological Research* 26 (1) 1965: 1–17.

Birch, Thomas L. "Tough Times: Advocacy Strategies in an Economic Downturn." *The NASAA Advocate* 12 (1) 2009: 1-7.

Bresler, Liora. "Research, Policy, and Practice in Arts Education: Meeting Points for Conversation." *Arts Education Policy Review* 99 (5) 1998: 9–15.

Carusi, F. Tony. "The Persistence of Policy: A Tropological Analysis of Contemporary Education Policy Discourse in the United States." Ph.D. dissertation, Georgia State University, 2011.

Dewey, John. "My Pedagogic Creed." *School Journal* 54 (January, 1897): 77–80.

Dewey, John. *Democracy and Education*. New York: The Free Press, 1916.

Dewey, John. *Reconstruction in Philosophy*. New York: Henry Holt, 1920.

Dewey, John. *Philosophy and Civilization*. New York: Minton, Balch, 1931.

Dewey, John. *Art as Experience*. New York: Perigee Books, 1934.

Dewey, John. *Experience and Education*. New York: Collier Books, 1938.

Dewey, John. *How We Think*. Mineola, NY: Dover Publications, 1938.

Dewey, John. *Freedom and Culture*. New York: Prometheus, 1989.

Eisner, Elliot W. "Does Experience in the Arts Boost Academic Achievement?" *Art Education* 51 (1) 1998: 7–15.

Garrison, Jim. *Dewey and Eros: Wisdom and Desire in the Art of Teaching*. Charlotte, NC: Information Age Press, 2010.

Gee, Constance Bumgarner. "The 'Use and Abuse' of Arts Advocacy and Consequences for Music Education." *Arts Education Policy Review* 103 (4) 2002: 3–21.

Granger, David A. *John Dewey, Robert Pirsig, and the Art of Living: Revisioning Aesthetic Education*. New York: Palgrave Macmillan, 2006.

Greene, Maxine. *Variations on a Blue Guitar: The Lincoln Center Institute Lectures on Aesthetic Education*. New York: Teachers College Press, 2001.

Hamblen, Karen A. "Theories and Research that Support Art Instruction for Instrumental Outcomes." *Arts Education Policy Review* 98 (3) 1997: 27–33.

Hope, Samuel. "Creativity, Content, and Policy." *Arts Education Policy Review* 111 (2) 2010: 39–47.

Langer, Susanne K. *Feeling and Form: A Theory of Art*. New York: Charles Scribner's Sons, 1953.

National Art Education Association. "Position Statement on 21st Century Skills and Visual Arts Education." May 15, 2019. https://www.arteducators.org/advocacy/articles/496-naeaposition-statement-on-21st-century-skills-and-visual-arts-education.

Partnership for 21st Century Skills. 2019. "21st Century Skills Map: The Arts."
     http://p21.org.

Partnership for 21st Century Skills. 2019. "About Us." http://www.p21.org/
     about-us.

Partnership for 21st Century Skills. 2019. "Framework for 21st Century Learning."
     http://www.p21.org/overview.

President's Committee on the Arts and the Humanities. 2011. *Reinvesting in Arts
     Education: Winning America's Future through Creative Schools*. Washington,
     DC: President's Committee on the Arts and the Humanities. https://www.
     federalregister.gov/documents/2016/09/07/2016-21437/presidents-committee-
     on-the-arts-and-the-humanities-meeting-72.

Stoller, Aaron. *Knowing and Learning as Creative Action: A Reexamination of the
     Epistemological Foundations of Education*. New York: Palgrave Macmillan,
     2014.

Stroud, Scott R. "Dewey on Art as Evocative Communication." *Education and
     Culture* 23 (2) 2007: 6–26.

Winner, Ellen, and Lois Hetland. "Art for our Sake: School Arts Classes Matter
     More than Ever—But Not for the Reasons You Think." *Arts Education Policy
     Review* 109 (5) 2008: 29–31.

CHAPTER THREE

DEWEY'S THEORY OF KNOWLEDGE:

Knowing as Meaningful Classroom Practice

ONE OF DEWEY'S LIFE-LONG projects was to challenge what he called traditional epistemology and what it takes for us to say we know something. Epistemology is the study of knowledge and, since at least as far back as Plato's dialogues *Meno* and *Theaetetus*, has occupied an important place in most philosophers' thinking.[1] Part of Plato's goal was to identify what philosophers call the necessary and sufficient conditions for knowledge. These are the parts you must have both individually and collectively to say that you know something. If knowledge requires the conditions truth, belief, and justification, then you must have each of these elements and you also must have all of them together. You can't know, for Plato, with only a true belief because that's just a lucky guess. You can't have belief alone because that's just an opinion. What you know, again for Plato, must be

---

1 Plato, "Meno," in *The Dialogues of Plato, Vol. 1* trans. R.E. Allen (New Haven, CT: Yale University Press, 1984); and Myles Burnyeat, *The Theaetetus of Plato* trans. M.J. Levett (Indianapolis: Hackett Publishing Company, Inc., 1990).

true, you must believe it to be true, and you must justify that it's true. Each element and all of them together are the "necessary and sufficient conditions" you need to say that you know something.[2]

Dewey wasn't impressed with Plato's definitions. He wasn't impressed with philosophy's preoccupation defining the necessary and sufficient conditions as part of a syllogism, either. A syllogism is a structural argument in which a conclusion is drawn from given or assumed propositions. The traditional syllogism of knowledge goes like this: S knows something if, and only if, S has a justified true belief. Let's spell it out: A person (S) must have three things (justified true belief) to say that they know something. Among other issues, Dewey disliked the syllogism because it put S, or the person knowing, as somehow outside of or above context. He called it the spectator theory of knowledge (STK) because the person, S, appears to be sitting apart from the world, looking down on the world as a spectator would observe a baseball game. On this view, you're watching a ball game. You're not playing it. Dewey wants you in the game.

Being in the game means we shift our words and our meaning a bit, if we're going to distance ourselves from Plato and be consistent with Dewey: The goal is knowing and knowing is an active term. Knowledge, on the other hand, is static. It's an achievement. Once accomplished or gained, we're done. Traditionally, knowledge is equated with information or data and, for teachers, means that our role is to transmit, to instill, to give knowledge to students they will use in the future. We turn students, who are otherwise innately inquisitive, into mere spectators. There are several problems with treating knowledge as though it can be passed on or transferred in a simple

---

2   Plato ultimately questions whether truth, belief, and justification *actually are* the necessary and sufficient conditions for knowledge. Look at the end of his dialogue *Theaetetus* to see how his inquiry intentionally ends in confusion. Also note that epistemologists made a distinction between propositional knowledge (I know *that* I parked my car in the garage) and non-propositional knowledge (I know *how* to park a car). This difference is important. If we conflate one kind of knowing (propositional) with a different kind of knowing (non-propositional), we confuse the whole project. It might be important to learn *how to* cook, *how to* ride a bike, and *how to* teach. This knowing is different from knowing *that* cooking influences our health, *that* riding a bike cuts down on pollution, and *that* teaching is more than covering the material in a curriculum or a textbook. See John M. Cooper and D.S. Hutchinson, eds., *Plato: Complete Works* (Indianapolis, IN: Hackett Publishing Company, Inc., 1997).

exchange from teachers to students.[3] Let's look at two interrelated points to illustrate the problem and how Dewey's theory of knowing is a better approach for both students and teachers: 1) Knowledge transfer modifies teaching methods; and 2) knowledge transfer restricts student inquiry and emphasizes pre-existing external decisions about what counts as knowledge. As I do throughout the book, let's take each point in turn.

How does knowledge transfer modify teaching methods? It puts procedure above meaning and routine over thinking. The more we assume that knowledge resides in textbooks, lesson plans, and standardized curricula the more un-Deweyan we become. Knowledge transfer is like Paulo Freire's concept of banking: teachers talk and students listen; facts are written out by teachers and students take down the facts in notes; websites are referenced and students follow the links to what are essentially more repositories of more data.[4] Banking is the process of depositing information into the empty vaults called students' heads. Teachers withdraw information in the form of quizzes and tests and the process reinforces a problem for Dewey. There's little to no imagination in banking. It's primarily a one-way process of depositing and it's a process that's enacted repeatedly, from the earliest grades in elementary school to the upper grades in high school. Now, you might argue that students are "active" when they take notes and follow directions. They are, technically. But what is the quality of their activity? It's mundane. It's largely rote. It's perfunctory.

Think, again, of habits (chapter 1). Freire and Dewey both argue that banking reinforces unthinking habits that are not productive of empowerment. Students following directions is ok for basic order and control, but

---

3 Please note that I'm not saying that knowledge can never be transmitted. It can. The problem is when we think that transmission is the primary function of teaching. For Dewey, it isn't. The primary function is inquiry and the growth that results. See John Dewey, *The Quest for Certainty: A Study of the Relation of Knowledge and Action* (New York: Capricorn, 1960). Also see chapter 2; and Katherine Camp Mayhew and Anna Camp Edwards, *The Dewey School: The Laboratory School of the University of Chicago, 1896-1903* (New York: D. Appleton-Century, 1936). There was plenty of transmission going on in the lab school, but the purpose and origination of it was not to overload students with dry facts and random data to prepare them for future jobs.

4 See Paulo Freire, *Pedagogy of the Oppressed* (New York: Continuum, 1970); and Paulo Freire, *Pedagogy of Freedom: Ethics, Democracy, and Civic Education* (Lanham, MD: Rowman & Littlefield Publishers, Inc., 1998/2001).

horrible for enabling inquiry and questioning outside the parameters that banking sets up. Because the methods are largely the same routinized procedures, what counts as knowledge is restricted by the form of interaction. Note that it's interaction and not transaction (see chapter 4). Again, the difference is qualitative. Determining whether the teaching and learning are *meaningful* becomes the point for Dewey (and Freire). And this point raises questions about power. Who determines whether learning is meaningful and what criteria are used to make such a determination? Again, for Dewey, the answer does not reside in some magical space above and outside the classroom. Knowing isn't spectating. But saying that the determination of what is meaningful resides inside the classroom must consider just how deeply engrained traditional methods are in schools (see chapter 1 again). To be Deweyan means shifting from knowledge transfer to knowing as a creative, imaginative process. The former is easier in terms of procedural control. The latter is more difficult, but only when compared to how easy traditional methods are. To be Deweyan requires a pretty big shift from a focus on knowledge transfer and knowledge acquisition to a focus on *knowing*. And this leads to the second point.

How does knowledge transfer restrict inquiry? Because traditional methods are reinforced in knowledge transfer, the options for inquiry are, therefore, also necessarily limited. If we adopt a knowledge transfer approach to schooling, we reinforce the idea that knowing is a simple process of shifting information from the teacher to the student. As noted before, we do a lot of telling in schools. We tell students what they need to know. We tell them the skills they'll need for the future job market. What all this telling does is reinforce order, control, and power in ways Dewey didn't like. Instead, as Aaron Stoller explains Dewey's criticism of the link between traditional theories of knowledge and schooling:

> The major educational implication is that learning is neither linear, nor personally distant, nor efficient—nor is it an additive process as imagined by SP [STK] thinking, which functions like the compiling of data in cold, psychical storage. Education is a constant entering and returning into situations of alienation, confusion, and unknown which reconstruct the entirety of the student's horizon of understanding.[5]

---

5   Aaron Stoller, *Knowing and Learning as Creative Action: A Reexamination of the Epistemological Foundations of Education* (New York: Palgrave Macmillan, 2014), 25.

It may sound odd to argue for messiness. It's strange to think that classrooms are *not* efficient. But unpack Stoller's point. He's saying that classrooms, traditionally, *are* efficient. They are cold, calculating places where the life is sucked out of learning in order to adhere to procedures that make testing thinkable and possible in the way we know it. Get a stopwatch or a clock ready. Announce the start of the test. Have students break the seals to their testing pamphlets and feverishly bubble-in scantron sheets. Call it learning. Make teachers' salaries based on how well students answer standardized questions and call all of it "merit-based" in terms of knowledge and ability. Some learning takes place in this kind of teaching and learning, surely—but it's not imaginative and it doesn't yield much knowing.

Logic, Truth, and the Confusion over Propositions and Judgements

Remember that traditional theories of knowledge extend back at least to Plato, but the content or structural elements of syllogisms concerning knowledge found, say, in Plato's *Theaetetus*, only provide a starting point for understanding the development (or lack thereof) of traditional theories of knowledge. I'm saying that the high point of traditional epistemology is found in the analytic philosophy of thinkers like Gottlob Frege, Bertrand Russell, the early Ludwig Wittgenstein, etc. With those philosophers, the point was to achieve correspondence between uttered claims and extra-linguistic fact. This means that what you say must match the reality outside of your claim. You say that the capitol of Austria is Vienna. True. But if you spoke German, the capitol of Austria is Wien. It's the same place. It's the same truth. The Austrian capitol is the same thing, regardless of the language we use to name it. Philosophers call this an extra-linguistic fact. The truth is beyond the words we use to identify or name the fact. The point is that the claim corresponds to the fact of the matter. The truth condition in the traditional syllogism of epistemology, in other words, was the point. The belief and justification conditions served the truth condition. Let me say it another way, and more broadly: Traditional debates about the study of knowledge largely relied on a correspondence theory of truth. This point is important because key terms used most prominently by Russell distort Dewey's theory of knowledge and this has implications for how Dewey's imaginative vision of teaching is understood. We need to delve a bit deeper here, so let's focus on some philosophy and then link it back to the main point of classroom practice. I recommend a cup of coffee for the next section of this chapter.

Specifically, as Tom Burke notes, Russell misapplied the term *proposition* when considering Dewey's theory of logic and his theory of knowing.[6] Russell could not divorce propositions from a theory of truth, but Dewey's logic and epistemology relied on *judgements* and their warranted assertions. As a result, Dewey rejected the theories of reality that were so important for Plato, Russell, and others, even if Dewey rejected them in sometimes confusing ways. Bear with me as I point out the details so we can get a better and clearer picture of how all this theory of knowledge talk has direct implications for imaginative teaching.

Dewey is arguing for inquiry into things "lived" by people.[7] He means experimenting with solving problems such that the action taken in the solving of problems is inquiry itself. This may sound like "the process is more important than the product," but that's not Dewey's point. We make a mistake in thinking "it's the journey not the destination," because there is no destination that isn't connected to the journey. The process and product are the same thing. Dewey calls this means/ends thinking (recall chapter 2 where the means and ends are combined). His point is that the means, the journey, is not divorced from the end, the destination. Remember when Johnny took his piece of the robin's eggshell to Ms. Jones (chapter 1)? The process of presenting the shell and asking questions merged with the follow-up questions Ms. Jones posed. By asking where he found the shell, what the color was, and whether the shell was complete, Ms. Jones and Johnny were then engaged in the process of knowing. Within that process, understanding happens and more learning occurs. The questioning, answering, and learning are all part of the process *and* the product. Means and ends are the same thing. Learning and knowing are enmeshed and happen together, often in awkward and alien ways like Stoller mentioned above. Traditional teaching would have Ms. Jones lecturing Johnny on what the shell was and moving on with the prescribed lesson of the day. In Dewey's words, traditional teaching occurs when we "think in ways [we] should not when [we] follow methods of inquiry that experience of past inquiries shows are not competent to reach the intended end of the inquiries in question."[8] On the traditional

---

6   Tom Burke, *Dewey's New Logic: A Reply to Russell* (Chicago: University of Chicago Press, 1998).

7   I specifically and intentionally do not use the well-worn phrase "lived experience." Why? Because it's redundant. If you have or undergo an experience, of course you've lived it.

8   John Dewey, *Logic: The Theory of Inquiry* (New York: Henry Holt and Company, 1938), 103-104.

view, the only connection between the means and the ends are lectures to be noted and (afterward) tests to be taken. This separation of means from ends is a major problem for Dewey's project of knowing because it makes it much harder for students to understand. When means and ends are merged, students know more. They have, to use Dewey's phrase, warranted assertibility. The phrase may be awkward, but it's important to understand, so be patient with me as I explain. In traditional terms, the process of learning yields the products "belief," "truth," and "knowledge." Dewey didn't like these terms because they were too often associated with universalism, that is, a belief, truth, or knowledge that is settled and never changes. Instead of belief, truth, and knowledge, Dewey came up with the idea of warranted assertions.

In the living of life, problems will be faced and solved—often in serendipitous ways—such that achieving "justified true belief" (as traditional epistemology expects) is not useful. What are useful, instead, are warranted assertions. Dewey puts it this way:

> [Warranted assertion] is preferred to the terms *belief* and *knowledge* [because] it is free from the ambiguity of these latter terms, and it involves reference to inquiry as that which warrants assertion. When knowledge is taken as a general abstract term related to inquiry in the abstract, it means "warranted assertibility." The use of a term that designates potentiality rather than an actuality involves recognition that all special conclusions of special inquiries are parts of an enterprise that is continually renewed, or is a going concern.[9]

At least two important points follow from Dewey's claims: 1) Knowing is not an abstract, semantic enterprise—rather, it is experience rooted in problems faced by people in context. Dewey is arguing for teachers and students who defend their claims to knowing by making, inquiring, imagining, and contesting knowledge claims linked to their experiences. 2) One *can* know, but fallibly so. *Fallibly* means that I can know something even when that something isn't universal. I can know Pluto is a planet until it's demoted to a dwarf planet. Think about science, itself, as a process of inquiry that

---

9 Ibid., 9. Emphasis in original. See, also, John Dewey and Arthur F. Bentley, *Knowing and the Known* (Boston: Beacon Hill, 1949).

continually yields new knowledge. That's what Dewey wants all of us to understand and demonstrate—continual inquiry as expanded knowing. Dewey as a fallibilist, then, means that he is open to continued questioning. In this sense, being "fallible" is a good thing. To know that we don't know everything is freeing, as long as it doesn't yield apathy or complacency. Knowledge exists for fallibilists because, according to Dewey, there is no use or meaning that is derived without living. Language is a tool to make sense of our experiences, but it derives its meaning and utility from our lives. Here's how Dewey put it in *Logic*. Our lives should be guided, on Dewey's view, by inquiry: "the controlled or directed transformation of an indeterminate situation into one that is so determinate in its constituent distinctions and relations as to convert the elements of the original situation into a unified whole."[10] Knowing comes about when inquiry leads to understanding that goes beyond mere recognition. One might "understand," i.e., "apprehend" the ideas of veterans, donated books, or chairs, but knowing requires the "warrant" for asserting their existence and their meaning.[11] This is a key point I'll return to a bit later in discussing warranted assertions and classroom practice. Before then, consider how traditional notions like "truth" and "proposition" in the history of epistemology differ from elements within Dewey's theory of inquiry. I'll frame this discussion in terms of teaching and learning, too, to show the link between philosophy and classroom practice. Let's go just a bit more into the philosophy and then link it all to practical life in classrooms. Time to refill your coffee mug.

Logic, Truth, and the Confusion over Propositions and Judgements

In Dewey's view, as Tom Burke points out, "it is judgments, not propositions, which are warrantably assertible or not; and judgments are essentially rooted in concrete actions in the world insofar as the consequences of such actions serve to decide their warrantability."[12] This does not provide us with a correspondence theory of truth, but Dewey argued, instead, that warranted assertibility (rather than truth) should be a primary consideration in a theory of inference. What is true and what is false are conclusions, not the necessary factors of inquiry. In *Knowing and the Known*, Dewey and Arthur Bentley put it this way:

---

10   Dewey, *Logic*, 104-105.

11   Burke, 143.

12   Ibid., 238.

It is frequently said that no matter what form of inquiry one under-takes into life and mind one involves himself [sic] always in meta-physics and can never escape it. In contrast with this hoary adage, our position is that if one seeks with enough earnestness to identify his attitude of workmanship and the directions of his orientation, he can by-pass the metaphysics by the simple act of keeping ob-servation and postulation hand-in-hand; *the varied "ultimates" of metaphysics become chips that lie where they fall.*[13]

What Dewey means is that the inquiry is the focus, not ultimate or universal truth. As Burke notes, "The truth or falsity of a given judgment is character-ized in terms of relations and correspondence among expectation and actual result of actions formulated in the course of the respective inquiry, but, strict-ly speaking, it is the assertion of the judgment which is true or not, not the information involved in ascertaining the judgment . . ."[14] Claiming Vienna or Wien is the capitol of Austria means the assertion of the judgment is true. To say all of this somewhat differently, the warranted assertibility of your judgment is demonstrated through your concrete actions in the world. Edu-cative experiences result in solved problems via warranted assertions. These assertions are judgments you make in the process of inquiring. Writes Dewey:

Judgment may be identified as the settled outcome of inquiry. It is concerned with the concluding objects that emerge from inquiry in their status of being *conclusive*. Judgment in this sense is distin-guished from *propositions*. The content of the latter is intermediate and representative and is carried by symbols; while judgment, as finally made, has *direct* existential import. The terms *affirmation* and *assertion* are employed in current speech interchangeably. But there is a difference . . . between the logical status of intermediate subject-matters that are taken for use in connection *with what they lead to as means*, and subject matter which has been prepared to be final. I shall use *assertion* to designate the latter logical status and *affirmation* to name the former . . . However, the important matter is not the words, but the logical properties characteristic of different subject-matters.[15]

---

13   Dewey and Bentley, 81. Emphasis added.

14   Burke, 239.

15   Dewey, *Logic*, 120. Emphasis in original.

Warranted assertions, for Dewey, were part of a project to explain (1) what it means to say that a statement about how things are may or may not correspond to how things actually are, when at the same time, (2) it is not possible to step back and treat this correspondence as if it were a matter of comparing the statement against reality.[16] Burke puts it this way: "It is not as if we have some statement-independent handle on bare reality so that we can hold it up to compare against our statements, since it is the statements themselves and the processes that go into their making which are one's handle on bare reality."[17] What we have to do is make judgments in real time about consequences of actions in solving actual problems. Correspondence, then, becomes a metaphor for Dewey, allowing him to point out that while a spectator version of detachment is not completely wrong, neither does it describe nor explain how people actually use information from their lives to solve problems they face. The relevance of the spectator is in the very detachment Dewey criticizes. Spectators don't assert, they observe—passively. Spectators are outside of experience, at least the kind of experience that is engaging of others.

For classrooms, this means that students-as-spectators merely watch and listen to their teachers tell them facts that correspond to an external world. The teachers may have the correct information and may be telling the students that information in a clear way. But the students are passive. They receive the truth told to them by their (well-meaning) teacher. The students are not active in knowing. They are not inquiring in anything more than an effort to understand why they are told what the teacher is telling them. "In educational terms," writes Stoller, "this represents a danger point because unless students experience inquiry in its full course it is likely that they will apply a solution *meaninglessly*. They will be able to perform an action, but that action is logically ungrounded, because they have not made connections between that action and other parts of experience."[18] Said differently, teaching "is not a kind of *telling* and learning a kind of *hearing*, but pedagogy is an act of shared *making*, resulting in a shared process of creative construction and of praxis in which something new emerges."[19] There

---

16   Burke, 240. See, also, John Dewey, "Propositions, Warranted Assertibility, and Truth," *Journal of Philosophy* 38, 7 (1941): 169-186.

17   Burke, 241.

18   Stoller, 65. Emphasis in original.

19   Ibid., 82. Emphasis in original.

are obvious implications for curriculum here and, in chapter 5, I explain through a case-study of a corporate-supplied ethics curriculum how "telling" is a form of indoctrination. Before then, let's finish the philosophy in this section by summarizing and restating the main points.

For Dewey, traditional knowledge suffered greatly at the hands of correspondence theories because, as he wrote in 1941, "wondering at how something in experience could be asserted to correspond to something by definition outside of experience [STK] . . . is what made me suspicious of the whole epistemological industry."[20] Dewey, therefore, rejected STK and its detachments—the very thing that traditional accounts of correspondence endorse and what teachers tend to practice in traditional classrooms—in order to have individual knowers "concretely and dynamically embedded in the world."[21] As a result, those knowers would have access to mediated and contextual knowledge, where knowledge is not understood in terms separated from experience. "We imaginatively and creatively project certain relationships, or wholes, on to the parts," explains Stoller, "our ability to mold the parts and their response, then, revises the whole. This back and forth between ideas and facts"[22] is the integration and transaction Dewey wants us to do. While it may appear that some of Dewey's views commit him to a form of idealism, the fact that Dewey concentrates so much attention on concrete situations means that his pragmatism mitigates any latent idealism that exists. He is, instead, a functionalist. He values inquiry that demonstrates a connection between expected consequences and actual consequences. Such an integration is linked to schools, as Jim Garrison explains, through what we might call the integration of Dewey's theory of knowing and the teachable moment. The teachable moment is

> perhaps the most sought-after pedagogical prize. All teachers know what it feels like even if they cannot name its characteristics. It is as wonderful as it is elusive. Teachers long for the moment when their

---

20 Dewey, "Propositions, Warranted Assertibility, and Truth," 183. Dewey's rejection of "the whole epistemological industry" may be part of the reason some neopragmatists interpret Dewey as throwing out epistemology altogether. They're still wrong. Dewey is trying to change epistemology just like he's trying to change schooling. Throw out the bath water, not the baby with it.

21 Burke, 243.

22 Stoller, 64.

class has that special quality of intimacy, openness, and creativity that provides the almost ineffable experience of getting through to students, of connecting and of students learning and not just getting ready to take a test.[23]

Garrison's point is one way to merge the theory and the practice Dewey's talking about. Let's consider knowing, knowledge, and intelligence in practical terms to illustrate the link between the theory and practice.

Knowing, Knowledge, and Intelligence: Epistemology Goes to School

Here it may be helpful to distinguish between a few key concepts in order to better understand the importance of warranted assertions and their relationship to classroom interaction. Knowing, knowledge, and intelligence are distinct for Dewey. Knowing is an inquiry. Inquiry involves specific instances of applying oneself to solving problems. Knowing is the stable outcome of inquiry and intelligence is the result of the development and accumulation of inquiring in specific ways. Intelligent action, in other words, is action constructed in the light of properly anticipated consequences. "Knowledge is the result of successful inquiry, whereas knowing consists in using one's intelligence in given inquiries. Intelligence is stabilized knowledge . . . which can be utilized in other inquiries, given the principle of continuity and given the fact that judgments are not merely abstract decisions but constitute a kind of conduct (assertion) . . . Knowing is to intelligence roughly what asserting is to being disposed to assert."[24] Dewey explains further:

> From the standpoint of empirical naturalism, the denotative reference of "mind" and "intelligence" is to funding of meanings and significances, a funding which is both a product of past inquiries or knowings and the means of enriching and controlling the subject-matters of subsequent experiences. The function of enrichment and control is exercised by incorporation of what was gained in past experience in attitudes and habits which, in their interaction

---

23   Jim Garrison, *Dewey and Eros: Wisdom and Desire in the Art of Teaching* (New York: Teachers College Press, 1997), 115.

24   Burke, 256.

with the environment, create the clearer, better ordered, "fuller" or richer materials of later experience—a process capable of indefinite continuance.[25]

Let's break this quote down. What we have in this passage is Dewey's basic argument for classroom interaction. Organic and natural environments for learning impel knowing and the habits of intelligence. Detachment from natural environments for learning foster "spectating" and habits of routine. When one supports a quest for "meanings and significances," one sides with inquiry via warranted assertions. That is, given Dewey's epistemology, classrooms should be places where students make knowledge claims at the very same time they are engaged in knowing (inquiry), since the means and ends are not separable for Dewey, and since the point of inquiry is not to collect detached artifacts or pieces of the dead wood of the past. Active engagement *of the sort Dewey suggests*[26] means students attempt stability rather than certainty. Students should not be in the business of "discovering" the basic beliefs on which traditional epistemology relies. Rather, students should achieve stability in knowing. Stability indicates functionality over universality.

Still, stability is not assured by Dewey either. In fact, much of the point of interacting "with the environment" is "creat[ing] the clearer, better ordered, 'fuller' or richer materials of later experience—a process capable of in indefinite continuance."[27]

[I]ntelligence is more than just a store of habits and context-sensitive dispositions. Intelligence is habitual, but not all habit is intelligent. Experience guided by intelligent habit, rather than merely routine habit, is experience characterized by resourcefulness, inventiveness, ingenuity, tenacity, efficiency, and any such "pragmatic virtue" designed to anticipate not only the regularities and constancies of experience but also the inevitable uncertainties and indeterminacies.[28]

25 John Dewey, "Experience, Knowledge, and Value: A Rejoinder," in *The Philosophy of John Dewey*, ed. Paul A. Schilpp (New York: Tudor, 1939), 520-521.

26 Dewey's organic instrumentalism, not prescription or relativism.

27 Dewey, "Experience, Knowledge, and Value," op. cit.

28 Burke, 256-257.

Remember the differences between educative, miseducative, and noneducative experiences from chapter 1. Educative experiences propel growth and inquiry. Miseducative experiences stunt growth and restrict inquiry. Noneducative experiences are the rare instances when the experience simply is: It doesn't yield understanding or action and it doesn't restrict understanding or action. Also recall the difference in habits discussed in chapter 1. Burke, in the earlier quote, is repeating those distinctions in different words. When he writes that "intelligence is habitual, but not all habit is intelligent," he's distinguishing between habit as unthinking routine and habit as inquiry and solving new problems. All the characteristics he lists (resourcefulness, inventiveness, ingenuity, tenacity, efficiency, etc.) are intended to convey responsible action and the kind of agency he thinks teachers and students should be doing, should be practicing. That we face uncertainty—fallibility—is a basic fact of life Dewey wants us to embrace, not overcome (see chapter 4 for how he makes this case in ecological terms tied to classroom practice). The problem is that US schools seem preoccupied with so much order and control that it suffocates inquiry and limits rather than encourages the habits of mind that yield intelligent knowing.

Students as fallibilist knowers means that knowledge claims can be valid, even if the knowledge claim is not universal. Dewey, as a fallibilist, focuses on stability and the never-ending search for meaning to indicate the limits of traditional epistemology and traditional teaching and learning. He replaces correspondence and foundationalism with warranted assertions and fallibilist knowing. He replaces banking education with active inquiry. Teachers become co-learners, students become engaged thinkers, and knowing more and more is the logical and practical consequence that follows. Let's extend these points in relation to classroom interaction. What would go on in classrooms that would be different from what currently goes on in most schools? What might it look like?

One way to address these questions is to envision new roles for teachers and students. Following the notion of warranted assertions, both teachers and students would become fallible knowers who must defend their claims to knowledge, where knowledge represents a temporal suspension point in the process of making judgments. This is Dewey's theory of inquiry and his theory of logic. In so doing, both teachers and students realize the limitations of universal, foundational, "comfort zones," and demonstrate the kind of continual thinking and rethinking required of those who face change in their lives and who, as a result of that change, must continually defend their claims to knowledge. Knowing the capital of Austria is essentially meaning-less on its own, unless there is a Trivial Pursuit question about it. Whether it's Wien or Vienna, what's the point? This question is *not* a dismissive one like so many "why do we have to learn this stuff?" questions are. "What's the point?" The question intends an answer that comes from inquiry. Why *should* we know Vienna and Austria? This is a productive question that, while open-ended, has a long list of possible answers. Largest emerald? Many composers? Historical links to World War I? Other? The veterans' exhibition, donated books, robin's eggshell, and chair-building examples from earlier chapters have no obvious link—until you start thinking about world wars and veterans, book publishing and music, ecology, and architec-ture and history that are contextualized. My point is that Dewey understood the interrelated nature of knowing. One inquiry *could* lead to inquiries that are life-changing and profound. Not by design, but by the quirks of human curiosity. There is a serendipity about knowing that should be embraced, not organized and arranged. What contexts are required for understanding and what problems are within those contexts that would provide students opportunities for ever-expanding inquiry? This isn't merely an academic problem for Dewey.

Indeed, when characterizing the problem Dewey had with "intellectu-alists" and professional philosophers, David Hildebrand notes the follow-ing: "Sidetracked from the problematic and lived situation that instigated inquiry in the first place, philosophers institutionalize their practice . . . into an ontology with eternal permanence."[29] Teachers are rarely different from this characterization. They, too, institutionalize their practice, even if hege-monically so. That is, teachers are taught that they should rely on profes-sional development sessions that effectively brainwash them into thinking that there are best practices outside of their experience. If only they would apply those best practices, all of the problems of schooling would simply go away. Except, of course, that's a lie. And Dewey knew it when he con-veyed the problem of institutionalizing any field in restrictive, rote ways. This point raises at least two other issues: (1) the superstructure and met-anarrative of schooling; and (2) the specific responsibility of teachers in a given situation.

---

29   David L. Hildebrand, *Beyond Realism & Anti-Realism: John Dewey and the Neo-pragmatists* (Nashville, TN: Vanderbilt University Press, 2003), 64.

For the first point, I'm arguing that schools are structured to support a version of traditional epistemology. If schools aren't truly traditional, insofar as they expect students to amass "pure" knowledge via STK, then they are reliabilist insofar as they require only correct answers without justification. While much more time could be spent on distinguishing the variations of epistemology within schools, one point seems clear: It is rare that teachers recognize emergent contexts for the development of inquiry and knowing in the Deweyan sense. In terms of the superstructure of current, traditional schools, this only makes sense. Order, discipline, and time-on-task expectations do not support inquiry that is varied, serendipitous, and transactional. Except for rare and unique examples within some schools, the reality in most schools is that traditional expectations have been so deeply entrenched prior to teachers and students actually entering the hallways, that the task of changing schools is often seen as impossible. Epistemically, it's as though STK and the correspondence theory of truth is the given and the taken for granted in schools.

For the second point from above, when prospective teachers enter their course work as education majors (or for certification), it's not without ideas and experiences that inform what they want to do and how they want to do it; it's simply with virtually no change whatsoever in the culture from which they came through schooling, themselves. They were reared as spectators (and often spectate in their college classes, too) and even when some students profess to wanting to "engage" their students in "active" learning, it still usually ends up being a souped-up version of traditional schooling—or as Dewey puts it in *Experience and Education*, using "devices of art to cover up obviously brutal features."[30] Fear of losing a job, fear of being reprimanded, and fear of standing out as "different" are common excuses teachers give for not challenging an established school structure they understand to be problematic. It's in this sense that I wish to force the revolutionary point that teachers, *regardless of the superstructure*, have epistemic (and other) responsibilities to their students. At risk of being perceived as another in a long line of people who blame teachers, I nonetheless believe that teachers are in positions of power they may not even understand. What I'm asserting is that teachers already have space and control over what goes on in their

---

30   John Dewey, *Experience and Education* (New York: Collier Books, 1938), 19.

classrooms. Beyond the power that could be actualized from teacher short-ages nationwide, add the possibility that teachers broaden their understand-ing of pedagogy by engaging in discourses of knowing, and change becomes imaginable. There is, of course, no guarantee that teachers who enter such epistemological discourse will value Dewey's idea of knowing over, say, the certainty often attached to state curriculum and content. Still, by champi-oning the intellectual and practical possibilities of the very teachers I risked blaming a moment ago, I'm urging a movement of teachers to claim school spaces for themselves and their students in ways that are grounded in Dew-ey's theory of knowing.

To envision classroom practices that specifically endorse warranted assertions would mean that students *and* teachers would no longer search for or operate under the assumption of "the truth" in Platonic, Kantian, or Common Core terms. Instead, students and teachers would make asser-tions connected to solving their problems (both immediate and connected to as-yet-unknown areas) that are gauged (i.e., judged) in the context of human ecological experience (see chapter 4). This alternative not only rep-resents an epistemological shift, it shifts power away from the traditional quest for certainty and places power with the contexts of student and teacher living—one not divorced from social realities beyond school, and not divorced from parent and social interaction. In short, traditional episte-mology and a power structure that supports it may be largely to blame for the general lack of inquiry found within US classrooms. Students as testable objects themselves, and whose role it is to gather discreet bits of data and information, are repeatedly subjected to classroom spaces where the only evidence of relation is between teacher- and curriculum-imposed artifacts and superimposed goals.

As I've alluded to in previous chapters, even good teachers are bur-dened by the perversion of traditional knowledge acquisition seen in most schools. Never mind that the tests that are claimed to be "objective" and "neutral" are subjectively constructed—all the tests, the standards, the mis-sion statements, the learning objectives. They are controlling features of a power structure frightened to death that teachers and students might learn and think carefully, critically, and productively. It makes little difference. Because the presentation of that reality is repeated as "the real world" or "the way it is," its unassailability is the very feature privileged by STK and traditional understandings of knowledge. It's as though the "view from nowhere" is precisely the view most educators and educational policy makers repeatedly expect. Is it any wonder, then, that most public school classrooms continue to be stultifying spaces for external indoctrination?

Dewey's epistemology, however, is an offering. It is a possible out. It represents one way students and teachers might develop relations in less contrived ways than what currently goes on in most schools. By shifting roles of teachers and students so that both groups are inquirers into problems they face, certitude goes out the window. In place of certainty is stability and it comes about when teachers and students engage in inquiry (knowing) via warranted assertions. As Stoller notes,

> Inquiry is a transactional process of reconstruction of self and world. It opens when there is a disequilibrium between cognitive (thought), emotional (feeling), and habitual (action): when our everyday mode of operating in the world no longer hangs together. The process of inquiry is a process of reconstruction which not only reconstructs the situation such that we can functionally coordinate following the moment of inquiry, but also a reconstruction of self and world, which is the *reason why* we can functionally coordinate following an inquiry.[31]

We must trust ourselves in inquiry. We must understand and appreciate the momentum that comes from learning that leads to more learning in an authentic process of becoming. One way to achieve this fusion of theory and practice is to understand the broader ecological spaces we inhabit and how our interaction with that ecology informs who we are and what we know. The next chapter takes up this point and situates it in a specific historical moment so we can better follow the naturalism and ecological theory that represents, in large measure, Dewey's practical view of the world. Understanding Dewey's view of the world, of reality, also helps in understanding what schools and classrooms should be doing. Make no mistake, Dewey's view of reality has direct consequences for how teaching and learning are done differently from traditional schooling.

---

31 Stoller, 66. Emphasis in original.

References

Burke, Tom. *Dewey's New Logic: A Reply to Russell.* Chicago: The University of Chicago Press, 1994.

Cooper, John M., and D. S. Hutchinson, eds. *Plato: Complete Works.* Indianapolis, IN: Hackett Publishing, 1997.

Dewey, John. *Experience and Education.* New York: Collier Books, 1938a.

Dewey, John. *Logic: The Theory of Inquiry.* New York: Henry Holt and Company, 1938b.

Dewey, John. "Experience, Knowledge, and Value: A Rejoinder." In *The Philosophy of John Dewey,* edited by Paul A. Schilpp, 515-608. New York: Tudor, 1939.

Dewey, John. "Propositions, Warranted Assertibility, and Truth." *Journal of Philosophy* 38 (7) 1941: 169–86.

Dewey, John. *The Quest for Certainty: A Study of the Relation of Knowledge and Action.* New York: Capricorn, 1960.

Dewey, John, and Arthur F. Bentley. *Knowing and the Known.* Boston: Beacon Press, 1949.

Freire, Paulo. *Pedagogy of the Oppressed.* New York: Continuum, 1970.

Freire, Paulo. *Pedagogy of Freedom: Ethics, Democracy, and Civic Education.* Lanham, MD: Rowman & Littlefield, 2001.

Garrison, Jim. *Dewey and Eros: Wisdom and Desire in the Art of Teaching.* New York: Teachers College Press, 1997.

Hildebrand, David L. *Beyond Realism & Anti-Realism: John Dewey and the Neopragmatists.* Nashville, TN: Vanderbilt University Press, 2003.

Mayhew, Katherine Camp, and Anna Camp Edwards. *The Dewey School: The Laboratory School of the University of Chicago, 1896–1903.* New York: J. Appleton-Century Company, 1936.

Stoller, Aaron. *Knowing and Learning as Creative Action: A Reexamination of the Epistemological Foundations of Education.* New York: Palgrave Macmillan, 2014.

CHAPTER FOUR

DEWEY'S NATURALISM AND REALISM:

Ecology and Classroom Practice

L IKE CHAPTER THREE, THIS chapter may take a bit more focus because I'm exploring Dewey's ecological thought and this requires a deep dive into his views on nature, reality, and how humans navigate that reality. To more fully understand Dewey's imaginative vision of teaching, we need to clarify his broader view of the world. What is the world and how do we exist in it? In philosophy, this is the area known as either metaphysics or ontology. Where aesthetics (chapter 2) question what counts as beautiful and epistemology (chapter 3) questions what is known and what constitutes knowing, ontology and metaphysics question what is real. If it's true that each human constructs their own reality and that reality is as legitimate as every other person's reality, even when they are in conflict (and especially when they are in direct opposition to one another), that's a relative world based on very specific, individualized perceptions. If it's true that there's a reality outside of our immediate perception, that's a different view of the world and shifts what counts as true.

In this chapter, I explore Dewey's ecological view of the wider world to better situate his imaginative vision of teaching and the practical implications that follow from his broader philosophical argument. I'm approaching the topic by exploring a specific ecological question that a philosopher of education raised nearly fifty years ago. I then pave two pathways to better understand Dewey's ontology: naturalism and realism. These sometimes-complicated topics, once clarified, yield a more accurate understanding of why Dewey argues for schools and classrooms to be changed from the traditional way they generally operate to the engaging and messy way Dewey wants: classrooms that are more productive of imagination and inquiry. If Dewey's view of the world is accurate, we need to change what it means to teach and to learn. Such a shift would represent a philosophical and ecological transformation of the classroom. I conclude that Dewey does, in fact, offer much to consider in the realm of ecology, especially as it relates to imaginative teaching and learning. To get to that conclusion, let's focus on a specific debate in the history of philosophy of education.

In 1971, Thomas B. Colwell, Jr., published an article in *Educational Theory* in which he argued for an "ecological basis [for] human community."[1] He suggested "naturalistic transactionalism" was being put forward by some ecologists and some philosophers of education at that time, but independently of each other. "I suspect," he wrote, "that some ecologists are working out their own version of a naturalistic transactionalism quite independently of Dewey . . ."[2] Dewey, Colwell argued, was often overlooked

---

1   Thomas B. Colwell, Jr., "The Ecological Basis of Human Community," *Educational Theory* 21, no. 4 (Fall 1971): 418-433, 418.

2   Ibid., 431. Colwell links Dewey to Arthur F. Bentley when he raises the issue of transaction. For the purpose of this chapter, I edit Bentley from the Colwell quotes in order to specifically focus on Dewey. Bentley was important in developing the concept and I do not wish to undervalue or underestimate his contribution, but there is some controversy around Bentley's work with Dewey. See Frank X. Ryan, "The 'Extreme Heresy' of John Dewey and Arthur F. Bentley: A Star Crossed Collaboration?" *Transactions of the Charles S. Peirce Society* 33, no. 3 (Summer, 1997): 774-794. See Sidney Ratner and Jules Altman, eds. (with James E. Wheeler) *John Dewey and Arthur F. Bentley: A Philosophical Correspondence, 1932-1951* (New Brunswick, NJ: Rutgers University Press, 1964); and John Dewey and Arthur F. Bentley, *Knowing and the Known* (Boston: Beacon Press, 1949). See, also, Elizabeth H. Roth, "The Emerging Paradigm of Reader-Text Transaction: Contributions of John Dewey and Louise M. Rosenblatt, with Implications for Educators" (PhD dissertation, Virginia Polytechnic and State University, 1998); Troy Nicholas Deters, "John Dewey's Theory of Inquiry: An Interpretation of a Classical American Approach to Logic" (master's thesis, Texas A&M University, 2006); and Christopher C. Kirby, "Experience and Inquiry in John Dewey's Contextualism" (master's thesis, University of South Florida, 2005).

when it came to his ecological thought.[3] Fourteen years later, in a 1985 article in *Educational Theory*, Colwell argued, again, in favor of understanding
Dewey as an ecological philosopher.[4] Colwell's main claim was that Dewey's theories of knowing, learning, and living are ultimately biocentric and
transactive, not anthropocentric and uni-directional. That is, Colwell inter-
prets Dewey to mean that our lives are not a one-way street where nature
is used by humans solely for their controlling and exploitative interests.
Anthropocentrism (literally, human-centered) situates humans as the ones
who exploit nature for the benefit of humans. Biocentrism (life-centered)
recognizes that humans are not the only living creatures on the planet. Biocentrism also means that humans have an ethical responsibility to care for
the entire world, not just the survival of human beings.[5] Dewey's conception
of science, according to Colwell, "is distinguished not only by its ecological
model of organism-environment interaction, but by the principle of continuity."[6] Colwell complained, however, that much of Dewey's thought had

---

3   Colwell suggests that Baker Brownell, too, was overlooked. "Brownell has suffered
the misunderstanding and neglect of a man ahead of this time. He bears reading again.
And so does John Dewey. Dewey, and Bentley too, had perhaps an even greater ecological sense than Brownell, but never made it explicit. But take another look at Dewey's
account of environment in *Democracy and Education* or his treatment of organism and
environment in the *Logic*—Dewey, who has been rejected because he 'doesn't speak to
our problems,' Dewey who gave ecology a permanent place in the curriculum of his Laboratory School in 1896." Colwell, "The Ecological Basis of Human Community," 432.
See, also, Baker Brownell, *The Human Community* (New York: Harper and Brothers
Publishers, 1950); John Dewey, *Democracy and Education* (New York: The Macmillan
Co., 1916), chapter 2; and John Dewey, *Logic: The Theory of Inquiry* (New York: Henry
Holt and Co., 1938).

4   Tom Colwell, "The Ecological Perspective in John Dewey's Philosophy of Education,"
Educational Theory 35, no. 3 (Summer 1985): 255-266.

5   There are variations on these two concepts and, as will be shown later in the chapter,
Dewey's biocentrism is not meant as restrictively "labeling" or "pigeon-holing" Dewey,
only another means to use language to clarify Dewey's thought. See Larry A. Hickman,
"Nature as Culture: John Dewey's Pragmatic Naturalism," in Andrew Light and Eric Katz,
eds., *Environmental Pragmatism* (New York: Routledge, 1996): 50-72, especially 55.

6   Colwell, "The Ecological Perspective in John Dewey's Philosophy of Education,"
262. See, also, Huey-li-Li, "On the Nature of Environmental Education (Anthropocentrism versus Non-Anthropocentrism: The Irrelevant Debate)," *Philosophy of Education*
(1996): 256-263; Dale Snauwaert, "The Relevance of the Anthropocentric-Ecocentric
Debate," *Philosophy of Education* (1996): 264-267; William Grey, "Anthropocentrism
and Deep Ecology," *Australasian Journal of Philosophy* 74, no. 4 (1993): 463-475; Val
Plumwood, "Androcentrism and Anthrocentrism," *Ethics and the Environment* 1 (1996):
119-152; and William Grey, "Environmental Value and Anthropocentrism," *Ethics and
the Environment* 3, no. 1 (1998): 97-103.

not been interpreted via ecology and that references to Dewey's ecological thought were "few and far between."[7]

Considering Colwell's claims as a continuation of our inquiry into Dewey's thought and its relation to classroom practice means digging into some of the messy debates about the nature of reality. We'll take this part step-by-step so it's not too confusing. Here are the primary questions: (1) Was there and is there a lack of literature regarding Dewey as an ecological philosopher? (2) If a literature exists, what does it say? Should Dewey be seen as biocentric, anthropocentric, or something else entirely? Are the terms helpful or a hindrance? That is, are the terms used to evaluate Dewey better stated as his naturalism, realism, or something else? and (3) Of what importance are the terms and concepts in understanding and, as a result, determining Dewey's ecological thought in relation to imaginative teaching, learning, and classroom practice?

Ignored, Misinterpreted, Revised?

Colwell claimed that Dewey was doing ecology before ecology became popular.[8] "That Dewey was a naturalist is well known," wrote Colwell, "but the interpretation of his work has focused almost exclusively on social experience and has ignored the relationship of education to nature."[9] In interpreting Dewey's thought, particularly in philosophy of education, Colwell believed Dewey to be a "pioneer in ecological thought."[10] His lament, however, was that Dewey may have been overlooked because he "had one foot in the pre-ecological world and one in the ecological."[11] This is a reference

---

7   Colwell, "The Ecological Perspective in John Dewey's Philosophy of Education," 256*n*.

8   Ibid., 265. Ecology, or the study of organisms and their environments, was (and is) a contested domain. Understanding Dewey in terms of ecology allows for a better understanding of his mature form of realism: transactional realism. For more on the history of and distinctions within ecology, see Hickman, "Nature as Culture," 58-72; James L. Wescoat, Jr., "Common Themes in the Work of Gilbert White and John Dewey: A Pragmatic Appraisal," *Annals of the Association of American Geographers* 82, no. 4 (December 1992): 587-607; and an interesting link made between Dewey and Darwin in William S. Knickerbocker, "John Dewey," *The Sewanee Review* 48, no. 1 (January-March 1940). Knickerbocker attacked Dewey's use of language, but otherwise provides a short but insightful look into "ecology" via Darwin and Dewey, 9*ff.*

9   Colwell, "The Ecological Perspective in John Dewey's Philosophy of Education," 255.

10   Ibid., 265.

11   Ibid.

to Dewey's long life and that he was born in the middle of the nineteenth
century. Taken as a whole, Colwell thought that Dewey's ecological thinking, that is, his naturalistic philosophy, was forward-looking and focused on
practical action and organic change. In support of this view, Colwell noted
a number of philosophical works dealing with ecology.[12] His concern was
that Dewey was only rarely mentioned and when Dewey was mentioned it
was disparagingly so.[13] Those who utilized Dewey were criticized by Colwell as misinterpreting or limiting their analyses.[14] For example, Colwell
criticized Roderick French and D.C. Phillips: French considered Dewey too
briefly and Phillips did not make explicit the "connection between organ-
icism and ecology."[15] Colwell suggested that James Bowen was a rarity in
seeing Dewey's ecological merits, though Colwell claimed that "it is curious
that in his otherwise accurate and sympathetic account of Dewey, [Bowen]
finds that Dewey excluded humanity from nature, even though he quotes

---

12   Among his references are John Passmore, *Man's Responsibility for Nature* (New
York: Scribner's, 1974); K.E. Goodpastor and K.M. Sayre, eds., *Ethics and the Problems
of the 21st Century* (Notre Dame, IN: University of Notre Dame Press, 1979); Stephen
Toulmin, *The Return to Cosmology* (Berkeley: University of California Press, 1982); and
R.G. Collingwood, *The Idea of Nature* (New York: Oxford University Press, 1960). In
an earlier article, Colwell also cited William Leiss, *The Limits to Satisfaction* (Toronto:
The University of Toronto Press, 1976); and David Ehrenfeld, *The Arrogance of Human-
ism* (New York: Oxford University Press, 1981). See Tom Colwell, "The Significance
of Ecology for Philosophy of Education," *Philosophy of Education, 1982* (Normal, IL:
Illinois State University, 1983): 177-185. In his 1971 article, Colwell also indicates the
importance of Paul Shepard and Daniel McKinley, eds., *The Subversive Science: Essays
Toward and Ecology of Man* (Boston: Houghton Mifflin Co., 1969); Marston Bates, *The
Forest and the Sea* (New York: New American Library, 1960); and Baker Brownell, *The
Human Community* (New York: Harper and Brothers Publishers, 1950). See Colwell,
"The Ecological Basis of Human Community." See also, Thomas B. Colwell, Jr., "The
Balance of Nature: A Ground for Human Values," *Main Currents in Modern Thought* 26
(1969): 46-52.

13   See Michael Zimmerman, "Dewey, Heidegger and the Quest for Certainty," *Southwest Journal of Philosophy* 9, no. 1 (1978): 87-95.

14   See Roderick French, "Is Ecological Humanism a Contradiction in Terms? The
Philosophical Foundations of the Humanities under Attack," in Robert C. Shultz and J.
Donald Hughes, eds., *Ecological Consciousness* (Washington, D.C.: University Press of
America, 1981): 59-61; and D.C. Phillips, "John Dewey and the Organismic Archetype,"
in R.J.W. Selleck, ed., *Melbourne Studies in Education* (Melbourne: Melbourne Univer-
sity Press, 1971): 232-71. Richard Rorty is also mentioned but dismissed as "thoroughly
unecological." See Colwell, "The Ecological Perspective in John Dewey's Philosophy of
Education," 256n. See, also, James Bowen, *A History of Western Education* (New York:
St. Martin's Press, 1981), chapters 12 and 15.

15   Colwell, "The Ecological Perspective in John Dewey's Philosophy of Education,"
256n.

Dewey to the contrary."[16] The degree to which Colwell may have been correct will be explored later in the chapter—in the sections dealing with naturalism and realism. For now, I want to highlight a consequence of Colwell's article, explore some follow-up issues that resulted from it, and identify literature Colwell doesn't cite but might be helpful in examining Colwell's (and others') interest in Dewey's ecological thought. The debate is juicy and the ideas are a bit complicated, but the literature helps explain the practical links to classrooms. Perhaps more coffee and a deep breath? Here we go.

One result of Colwell's article was a 1995 essay by Paul Morgan in which he reflected on Colwell's work and claimed that Colwell's interpretation of Dewey had merit, but only if Dewey was read selectively.[17] Morgan began with Colwell's work but turned to C.A. Bowers and George Sessions for criticism of Colwell and Dewey. In citing Bowers, Morgan was persuaded that Dewey had, as Bowers articulated it, a disguised cultural agenda that disqualified Dewey from being an ecological leader.[18] Morgan determined that Dewey's naturalism was his weak spot, his Achilles' heel. He wrote that the "potential problem for Dewey is that those who proclaim a naturalistic philosophy and see nature as a unitary, dynamic whole, still have questions to answer *if they see that same nature as primarily a source of problems to be overcome or an unruly force to be subdued.*"[19] Morgan's emphasis within the claim (noted in italics) led him immediately to George Sessions' criticism of Dewey. Morgan cited Sessions as follows: "Many naturalistic philosophies, from the Enlightenment to Marx and Dewey, claimed that humans were a part of Nature. But they seem to have meant this in a somewhat superficial sense for they still pictured humans as dominating the rest of Nature, as manipulating, controlling, or managing the

---

16   Ibid.

17   Paul Morgan, "Reconceiving the Foundations of Education: An Ecological Model," *Philosophy of Education, 1996* (Urbana: University of Illinois, 1997): 294-302, especially 295-297.

18   Ibid., 298. See also, C.A. Bowers, *Education, Cultural Myths, and the Ecological Crisis* (Albany: SUNY Press, 1993); C.A. Bowers, "Toward an Ecological Perspective," in Wendy Kohli, ed., *Critical Conversations in Philosophy of Education* (New York: Routledge, 1995): 310-323; and C.A. Bowers, "The Case Against John Dewey as an Environmental and Eco-Justice Philosopher," (2002): http://www.cabowers.net/pdf/DeweysRelevance2003.pdf.

19   Morgan, 297. Emphasis added.

biosphere."[20] What's interesting about the progression of Morgan's essay is that he acknowledges Colwell's line of reasoning in support of Dewey's naturalism, but then questions whether Dewey saw *"nature as primarily a source of problems to be overcome or an unruly force to be subdued."*[21] If put this way, Dewey's naturalism means that nature provides two, *and only two*, possible consequences and both of these consequences are negative: Nature's either a source of problems to be overcome or an unruly force to be subdued. In this view, to "overcome" and "subdue" nature separates nature from those who would "overcome" and "subdue" it. Putting Dewey's ideas in those terms appears to set up a dualism that is inconsistent with Dewey's anti-dualist stance, as noted in the previous chapters.[22]

Morgan is persuaded by Sessions' conclusion that Dewey "wanted to overcome nature and not cooperate with it."[23] Morgan writes the following:

> What is needed is a commitment to ensuring that human creations and practices complement and conserve the rest of nature and pro- mote the long-term existence of communities, human and other, including all the qualitative aspects of life that make for thriving. This is where Dewey begins rating poorly as an ecological pioneer, and where Colwell, given his opposition to viewing nature as "an object of control, alteration, and exploitation," should have been more cautious about painting Dewey as a visionary ecologist.[24]

---

20 George Sessions, "Ecophilosophy, Utopias, and Education," *The Journal of Environmental Education* 15, no. 1 (1983): 27-42, cited in Morgan, 297. Jonathan D. Moreno and R. Scott Frey offer a different take on the naturalism of Dewey and Marx. In an article primarily dealing with politics and justice, they nonetheless determine that "Marx's naturalism leads to the elimination of value and Dewey's naturalism finds value as an inescapable component of social life." See Jonathan D. Moreno and R. Scott Frey, "Dewey's Critique of Marxism," *The Sociological Quarterly* 26, no. 1 (Spring, 1985): 21-34, 27.

21 Morgan, 297. Emphasis added.

22 For more on Dewey's anti-dualist stance, see Dewey's *Experience and Education* (New York: Collier, 1938). Dewey employs a form of dualistic representation in *Experience and Education* to get rid of dualisms themselves. That is, he lays out traditional and child-centered approaches to understanding schooling and argues that both are wrong in their extremes. Instead, he offers a more moderate "third way." Dewey's version of progressivism doesn't indulge in student whim, but it doesn't solely rely on imposed curriculum, either.

23 Morgan, 297.

24 Ibid.

As part of this conclusion, Morgan takes a quote from Colwell as a criticism of Dewey. He presumes, in other words, that "viewing nature as 'an object of control, alteration, and exploitation,'"[25] is Dewey's view and one that Colwell already rejects. Therefore, viewing nature this way should be a good reason for criticizing Dewey rather than advancing him as ecological. The question is still the same: What is naturalism? Did Dewey regard nature in the way that Sessions and Morgan claim? I suggest the answer is "no" and that support for this conclusion is best found in Dewey's integration of naturalism and realism, particularly in his mature thought.[26] Bear with me as I go through this next section. It has a direct link to classrooms because what we take to be *real* influences the way we view children, students, schools and teaching in the context of nature. Stay with me as I explain the meaning of naturalism and realism in order to link them to Dewey's view of the world and the implications that follow for imaginative teaching and learning.

Naturalism

Michael Eldridge's analysis of the development and varieties of naturalism in the nineteenth and twentieth centuries in the US provides context for understanding Dewey's naturalism.[27] In short, Eldridge points out that naturalism in nineteenth century America meant materialism and empiricism in opposition to idealism. Stick with me. Theorists like George Santayana, William James, F.J.E. Woodbridge, and John Dewey debated the meaning of "naturalism." While each theorist can be broadly defined as a naturalist,

---

25   Ibid. The Colwell quote is from "The Ecological Basis of Community," 427.

26   Before focusing on those aspects of Dewey's philosophy, I want to point out that Colwell was likely correct that there was a lack of literature relating to Dewey and ecological thought, at least in the specific terms of ecology and in the timeframe to which Colwell refers. What I mean is related to the next sections on naturalism and realism: while there may be a lack of literature relating to Dewey and ecological thought prior to Colwell's 1985 article (and even granting Colwell's 1971 essay), there's a substantial literature debating Dewey's version of naturalism and realism and I turn to some of that literature next. Dewey is cited and philosophy and ecology are not wholly excluded, to be sure. My point is that there's more literature on naturalism and realism relating to Dewey than ecology. For an example of Dewey linked to ecology, see Eduard C. Lindeman, "Ecology: An Instrument for the Integration of Sciences and Philosophy," *Ecological Monographs* 10, no. 3 (July 1940): 367-372. See, also, Amos H. Hawley, "Ecology and Human Ecology," *Social Forces* 22, no. 4 (May 1944): 398-405.

27   Michael Eldridge, "Naturalism," in Armen T. Marsoobian and John Ryder, eds., *The Blackwell Guide to American Philosophy* (Malden, MA: Blackwell Publishing, 2004): 52-71.

distinctions nonetheless developed over time. "[These distinctions] are the Aristotelian orientation of F.J.E. Woodbridge, and his prominent student, John Herman Randall, Jr., the pragmatic naturalism of John Dewey, and the non-pragmatic (or refusal to privilege the human) approaches of George Santayana and Morris Raphael Cohen."[28] There was a notable exchange between Santayana and Dewey that helps us understand Dewey's position.

In the exchange, Santayana accused Dewey of not being a naturalist at all. He charged that Dewey's views in *Experience and Nature* could be summed up in the phrase "the dominance of the foreground." Wrote Santayana,

> In nature there is no foreground or background, no here, no now, no moral cathedra, no centre so really central as to reduce all other things to mere margins and mere perspectives. A foreground is by definition relative to some chosen point of view, to the station assumed in the midst of nature by some creature tethered by fortune to a particular time and place. If such a foreground becomes dominant in a philosophy naturalism is abandoned.[29]

Dewey replied to Santayana's critique by claiming that Santayana had separated humans from nature. "In short, [Santayana's] presupposition is a break between nature and man . . . The former is real, substantial; the latter specious, deceptive, since it has centers and perspectives."[30] This is like

---

28   Ibid., 55. For more on the disagreements, see George Santayana, "Dewey's Naturalistic Metaphysics," *The Journal of Philosophy* 22, no. 25 (December 3, 1925): 673-88; John Dewey, "Half-Hearted Naturalism," *The Journal of Philosophy* 24, no. 3 (February 3, 1927): 57-64; Morris R. Cohen, "Some Difficulties in Dewey's Anthropocentric Naturalism," *The Philosophical Review* 49, no. 2 (March 1940): 196-228; Roy Wood Sellars, "Dewey on Materialism," *Philosophy and Phenomenological Research* 3, no. 4 (June 1943): 381-392; John Dewey, *Reconstruction in Philosophy* (New York: Henry Holt, 1920), 103-131; and John Dewey, *Experience and Nature*, in Jo Ann Boydston, ed., *John Dewey: The Later Works, 1925-1953, Volume 1* (Carbondale: Southern Illinois University Press, 1981). For a review of the debate long after it took place, see Bernard Suits, "Naturalism: Half-Hearted or Broken-Backed?" *The Journal of Philosophy* 58, no. 7 (March 30, 1961): 169-179. The listing of sources in this footnote should also help justify the earlier claim in the chapter that while "ecology" may not have been a term directly associated with Dewey, "naturalism" and "realism" were. See, also, Sholom J. Kahn, "Experience and Existence in Dewey's Naturalistic Metaphysics," *Philosophy and Phenomenological Research* 9, no. 2 (December 1948): 316-321.

29   Santayana, "Dewey's Naturalistic Metaphysics," 679. See, also, Eldridge, 56-57.

30   Dewey, "Half-Hearted Naturalism," 58.

86 John Dewey's Imaginative Vision of Teaching

separating students' lives outside of school from classroom interaction. It's a false split.

Dewey claimed that the "broken-backed" naturalism of Santayana divided humans from nature, was actually unnatural, and reminded Dewey of transcendental, "supernatural beliefs."[31] Dewey's naturalism spanned the gulf by imploding the dualism between humans and nature. "In other words," wrote Dewey, "I have tried to bring together on a naturalistic basis the mind and matter that Santayana keeps worlds apart."[32] What is important to underscore about this quote, and part of the focus of this part of the chapter is that Dewey is bringing together "mind and matter."[33] Think about joining inquiry with course content. Mind is inquiry. Matter is content. There must be a connection, a transaction, between them to be meaningful, otherwise they are artificial and separate. Aaron Stoller puts it this way:

> In educational terms . . . unless students experience inquiry in its full course it is likely that they will apply a solution *meaninglessly*. They will be able to perform an action, but that action is logically ungrounded, because they have not made connections between that action and other parts of experience.[34]

Significantly, Dewey also responds to claims that his view is anthropocentric. "In order to be understood," Dewey wrote, "what I have said about genesis and function, about antecedents and consequences, has to be placed in the perspective suggested by this emphasis upon the need of formulating a theory of nature and of the connections of man *in* (not *to*) nature on the basis of a temporal continuum."[35] Dewey is drawing a distinction between human application and human embedding. Humans are part of nature, not

---

31   Ibid.

32   Ibid., 62.

33   John Dewey, "Nature in Experience," *The Philosophical Review* 49, no. 2 (March 1940): 244-258. Dewey's paper is in reply to Morris R. Cohen, op. cit., and William Ernest Hocking, "Dewey's Concepts of Experience and Nature," *The Philosophical Review* 49, no. 2 (March 1940): 228-244.

34   Aaron Stoller, *Knowing and Learning as Creative Action: A Reexamination of the Epistemological Foundations of Education* (New York: Palgrave Macmillan, 2014), 65.

35   Dewey, "Nature in Experience," 249. Emphasis in original.

set apart from it. Nature is not a fully formed entity set apart from humans, either. "Nature," as Larry Hickman puts it, "as a complex of objects of knowledge, is neither complete in itself apart from human interaction, nor the locus of extra-human deliberation."[36]

Dewey's theory of nature is like his theory of knowledge. Reconsider the role of the spectator theory of knowledge that separates the object of knowledge and the subject who knows. Remember chapter 3, when Dewey is talking about either being a spectator or a participant? We shouldn't just watch a ball game; we should play it. In doing, we know. In being, we exist. We aren't set apart from nature, we are surrounded by, infused with, and part of nature, too. By emphasizing "in nature," Dewey echoes Eduard Lindeman's definition of ecology as "a relational discipline," one that integrates science and philosophy.[37] Dewey's naturalism merges rather than separates; joins rather than separates. Relating Dewey's naturalism to the question of human-centered selfishness, Hickman writes the following:

> To speak of non-human species or non-human individuals as the possessors of intrinsic rights would in Dewey's view amount either to anthropomorphizing non-human nature or to opening up a chasm between human and non-human nature by positing a domain of moral rights that does not involve moral agency and is therefore entirely separate from what human beings understand by the term. Does this mean that Dewey's naturalism regresses to a modernist anthropocentrism? Does his naturalism open the door to treating non-human species in any way we choose? It does neither.[38]

Hickman provides a bridge between Dewey's view of realism and how it informs his broader theory of naturalism. To connect this point with the

36 Larry A. Hickman, "Nature as Culture: John Dewey's Pragmatic Naturalism," in *Environmental Pragmatism*, ed. Andrew Light and Eric Katz (New York: Routledge, 1996), 50–72, 53.

37 Lindeman, 369.

38 Hickman, "Nature as Culture," 64-65. Hickman also adds that "Dewey's naturalism is capable of promoting a piety with respect to non-human nature that is not encumbered by the epistemological problems of transcendent views of nature." (65)

larger purpose of this chapter, I now turn to a brief exploration of real-ism (or better, realisms).[39] In doing so, it might be helpful to remember the Johnny and Susie illustration from chapter 1. Johnny and Susie found a robin's eggshell and took parts of the shell to their teachers. Dewey wants us to consider whether our actions in the world (in nature) negatively influ-ence the world. Without turning Johnny and Susie into poachers, there is still an important question about their (and our) actions. Consider habitat, extinction, climate change, and whether we contribute to global warming. Johnny and Susie are just kids on their way to school, but their basic (onto-logical) question ("What is this?") is answered in ways that go beyond blue eggshells and birds. It is, said differently, larger than the eggshells alone. Their question is ecological, and Dewey thinks a broader and more careful consideration of our interactions in the world are important to understand. To comprehend this point more fully means we need to explore what Dewey meant by realism and transaction.

Realism(s) and Transaction

As a general definition, realism claims that objects exist outside of our per-ceptions. Simple enough, on first blush, there are a series of distinctions that help clarify which version of realism Dewey holds, how it informs his natu-ralism, and how to evaluate his ecological thought and standing. Realism is distinct from idealism in that idealism claims that no external reality exists apart from our knowledge or consciousness of material objects. Mind, for idealists, is central. Realism is also distinct from phenomenalism in that phenomenalism regards groups or sequences of actual and possible sensa.[40] Sensa, including things like sound, shape, color, smell, and tactile feelings, are taken by phenomenalists to be private and known directly. Varieties of realism include, but are not limited to, naïve realism, common-sense real-ism, critical realism, new realism, scholastic realism, and subjectivist real-ism. Dewey's realism is distinct from each of these versions and is central to

---

39   Just as I argue that there are a variety of "realisms," so, too, are there different ver-sions of idealism, hence, "idealisms." My point is not to reduce either view, but to point out the complexities within and surrounding various versions of realism in order to better situate and clarify Dewey's ideas and their link to classroom practice.

40   See, for example, Nicholas Bunnin and Jiyuan Yu, eds., *The Blackwell Dictionary of Western Philosophy* (London: Blackwell, 2004), 634.

understanding his ecological view.[41] Here's why.

Naïve realism is the position that sensations yield accurate descriptions of the world. Common-sense realism ranges from G.E. Moore's defense of the certainty of the claim "this is a hand," to J.L. Austin's and Anthony Quinton's arguments that perception (even illusions) means actually seeing physical objects.[42] Naïve realism and common-sense realism fall under the broader category of direct realism because they hold that perception is the "direct" awareness of an external, fixed object. Dewey's ultimate criticism of such forms of realism is that they represent "a last desperate stand and fortress of the classic doctrine that knowledge is immediate grasp, intuition, envisagement, possession" and that "until the assumption of immediate intrinsic differences in the meaning-objects of sensory perceptions, reveries, dreams, desires, emotions, has been expelled, the actual relation of ideas to existences must remain an obscure and confused matter."[43] For classrooms, Dewey's point is that "direct awareness" should result in students knowing chemistry by looking at the periodic table or understanding Shakespeare when they first read his sonnets. This isn't the way students learn. They may perceive charts and texts, but perceiving is not the same thing as knowing.

---

41   For a further, if different, analysis of Dewey's realism, see David L. Hildebrand, *Beyond Realism & Anti-Realism: John Dewey and the Neopragmatists* (Nashville, TN: Vanderbilt University Press, 2003); John R. Shook, Dewey's *Empirical Theory of Knowledge and Reality* (Nashville: Vanderbilt University Press, 2000): 217*ff*; Peter Godfrey-Smith, "Dewey on Naturalism, Realism, and Science," *Philosophy of Science* 69, no. 3 (September 2002): S25-S35; and Frank X. Ryan, "Skepticism, Realism, and Transactional Pragmatism," paper presented at the 10th Annual Summer Institute in American Philosophy, University of Colorado, Boulder, July 9-14, 2007. Tom Burke calls Dewey's view "ecological psychology." See Tom Burke, *Dewey's New Logic: A Reply to Russell* (Chicago: The University of Chicago Press, 1994): 83-96.

42   See G.E. Moore, *Philosophical Papers* (London: George, Allen, and Unwin, 1959); J.L. Austin, *Sense and Sensibilia* (Oxford: Oxford University Press, 1962); and Anthony M. Quinton, "The Problem of Perception," *Mind* 64, no. 253 (1955): 28-51. For Dewey's interpretation, see John Dewey, "Common Sense and Science: Their Respective Frames of Reference," *The Journal of Philosophy* 45, no. 8 (April 8, 1948): 197-208.

43   Dewey, *Experience and Nature*, in Boydston, 256. See, too, Ernest Nagel, "Dewey's Theory of Natural Science," in Sidney Hook, ed., *John Dewey: Philosopher of Science and Freedom* (New York: The Dial Press, 1950): 231-248, especially 237-238 relating to naïve realism. Christine McCarthy and Evelyn Sears argue differently. They explicitly claim that Dewey "specifically endorses naïve realism." See McCarthy and Sears, "Deweyan Pragmatism and the Quest for True Belief," *Educational Theory* 50, no. 2 (Spring 2000): 213-227, 217.

Again, recall chapter 3. If all students have to do is look at x to know x, they'd confirm the long-standing, but misleading, metaphor that students are merely sponges. Students *are* influenced by their surroundings. Kids see a lot and imitate and copy or mimic behaviors. But Dewey claims that "the first stage of contact with any new material, at whatever stage of maturity, must inevitably be of the trial and error sort."[44] Blank stares don't count. Skimming words on pages aren't enough. Instead, we "must actually try, in play or work, to do something with the material in carrying out . . . impulsive activity, and then note the interaction of . . . energy and that of the material employed."[45] Stoller explains the point this way:

> In educational terms, students are cheated of their own learning when they are not allowed the experience of turning an indeterminate situation into a problematic one. Students must encounter the very existential process of an *emerging problematic* if they are to learn how to creatively solve problems and reconstruct their environment.[46]

Students must do something with chemistry to solve a problem or use Shakespeare to understand a concept, phrase, or idea. The realism of the classroom is interpretive. When Stoller talks about student learning in terms of creativity to solve problems and reconstruct their environment, he means making learning personal. The realism of classroom interaction or transaction is found in student experience: doing is knowing (chapter 3).

But note that Dewey's realism is also distinct from C. S. Peirce's "scholastic realism," otherwise understood as closer to an objectivist end of a pragmatist spectrum. For Peirce, there are "real" and fixed essences that exist before reflective inquiry.[47] As Jim Garrison puts it, "Peirce believed in the reality of universals [like] fixed laws of science. The predetermined end of scientific inquiry for Peirce was correspondence to the fixed and final structures

---

44   John Dewey, *Democracy and Education* (New York: The Free Press, 1916), 160.

45   Ibid.

46   Stoller, 62.

47   See, for example, Christopher Hookway, *Peirce* (New York: Routledge, 1985/ 1992), 37-40; 51-58. See, also, Justus Buchler, *Philosophical Writings of Peirce* (New York: Dover Publications, Inc., 1950), 274-301.

of external reality."[48] Dewey's realism is unlike William James' "subjectivist realism," too, otherwise understood as a reality having no pre-ordained essence or final end to inquiry. "All reality," wrote James, "whether from the absolute or the practical point of view, is thus subjective . . ."[49] Dewey's realism differed from both Peirce and James insofar as Dewey rejected Peirce's notion of fixed essences and refused to slide down James' slippery slope of potential relativism. While these characterizations tell us what Dewey's view was *not*, what was it?

Dewey's realism is what Garrison calls a "reconstructed combination" of both Peirce's and James' philosophies.[50] Dewey took Peirce's pragmatic maxim (all things are fixed by their consequences) and James' view of constructed essences as part of ongoing human inquiry.[51] Dewey's realism is, therefore, transactional realism. In 1986, R. W. Sleeper describes Dewey's transactional realism as follows:

> Dewey's pragmatism is . . . a radical form of realism—transactional realism in which instrumentalism plays a subordinate role . . . and thinking entails active involvement with independent reality, an involvement that is causally efficacious. Even reflection is a means of conducting transformational transactions with the world, a means of changing or reconstructing the world.[52]

---

48 Jim Garrison, "Realism, Deweyan Pragmatism, and Educational Research," *Educational Researcher* (January-February 1994): 5-14, 6.

49 William James, *The Principles of Psychology, Volume 2* (New York: Dover, 1890/1950), 296-97.

50 Garrison, "Realism, Deweyan Pragmatism, and Educational Research," 7.

51 Thomas Alexander notes that "Rather than fighting the ghosts of idealism in Dewey's thought, we would do far better to see his work presenting the rudiments of an evolutionary metaphysics that replaces the Greek ideal-knower with that of a creative ecosystem in which change, plurality, possibility, and mutual interdependence replace the canonical concepts of substance, timelessness, logical identity, self-sufficiency, and completion. Such a position might be called 'ecological emergentism' and its metaphysics in particular, 'eco-ontology.'" See Thomas Alexander, "The Aesthetics of Reality: The Development of Dewey's Ecological Theory of Experience," in F. Thomas Burke, D. Micah Hester, and Robert B. Talisse, eds., *Dewey's Logical Theory: New Studies and Interpretations* (Nashville, TN: Vanderbilt University Press, 2002), 21.

52 R.W. Sleeper, *The Necessity of Pragmatism* (New Haven, CT: Yale University Press, 1986), 3.

Transactional realism appears to support the view that Dewey was not anthropocentric in his ecological outlook because the change and reconstruction to which Sleeper refers are not done "to" the world, but "with" and "in" the world. Human understanding and knowing come about from more than mere *inter*action between humans and artifacts or objects. When students at Chrysalis developed a veteran's museum and figured out the meaning of donated books, they did more than gather artifacts of war and pages in texts. The students were *transactional* with veterans, their experiences, their lives after service, the materials associated with military engagement, and more. This was done through initial contact and naïve conversations that developed and deepened and clarified because of the transactional nature (reality/realism) of human being.

Wrote Dewey, "nature's place in man [*sic*] is no less significant than man's place in nature. Man in nature is man subjected; nature in man, recognized and used, is intelligence and art."[53] Dewey also wrote that thought "is thus conceived of as a control-phenomenon biological in origin, humane, practical, or moral in import, involving in its tissue real transformation in real reality."[54] Remember that society and nature are connected, for Dewey. "Real reality" is learning through transactions with other humans, artifacts (like donated books), and all that develops from that ongoing series of inquisitive processes. Malcolm P. Cutchin argues that while some have indicted Dewey for being anthropocentric, Dewey ultimately "never proposed the necessity of human perception or being; indeed he emphasized the primordial character and role of nature in experience."[55] Reconstruction occurs when individuals make meaning from "ordinary experiences." Donated books. War bond posters. Eggshells. Students make intellectual meaning from their lives. As Ernest Nagel notes, "Dewey does not achieve his aim [of transactional realism] by viewing the whole of nature in terms of distinctions that are known to be relevant only for the human scene. He does not offer a resolution of the standing problems of modern philosophy

53   John Dewey, *Experience and Nature* in *The Collected Works of John Dewey*, 1882-1953, ed. Jo Ann Boydston (Carbondale and Edwardsville: Southern Illinois University Press, 1967-1991), LW 4: 384.

54   *The Collected Works of John Dewey*, 1882-1953, ed. Jo Ann Boydston (Carbondale and Edwardsville: Southern Illinois University Press, 1967-1991), MW 4: 123.

55   Malcolm P. Cutchin, "John Dewey's Metaphysical Ground-Map and its Implications for Geographical Inquiry," *Geoforum* 39 (2008): 1555-1569, 1559.

by clothing all of nature with anthropomorphic traits, or interpreting the course of cosmic events in terms of values that are of paramount concern only to [humans]."[56] Recall the distinction between anthropocentrism and biocentrism: Anthropocentrism situates humans as the intermediaries of utility and exploitation *over* nature whereas biocentrism situates humans within a world that is reciprocal. Some may be concerned that Dewey is being "pigeon-holed" by this dualism, but the purpose, in part, for making the distinction is to underscore how Dewey's realism follows from a bio-centrism that yields—and necessarily requires—transaction. Hickman concludes that Dewey *was* biocentric, given the following stipulation:

> If "biocentrism" means taking a perspective that is other than human, then Dewey was no biocentrist. If it means, on the other hand, that it is characteristic of human intelligence that it continually broadens its purview, and that its best and most productive perspective is holistic, then Dewey's work from the 1890s onward *was* "biocentric."[57]

So, while Dewey may make claims regarding the use of tools, technology, etc., in relation to the world and environment in otherwise anthropocentric terms (i.e., humans sometimes exploit the environment for their ends), the "thrust" of Dewey's mature thought is far more consistent with biocentrism. Indeed, Dewey's goal is to minimize exploitation and emphasize interdependence. Our dispositions toward investigation are merged with our surroundings in such a way that consequences, meaning-making, and problem-solving organically intertwine and influence each other. This is Dewey's view of classrooms, too.

Transaction v. Interaction and Imaginative Teaching

Before moving on to implications that might follow from Dewey's transactional realist view of ecology for education and classroom practice, I argue that *interaction* and *transaction* should be reconsidered in terms of their interchangeability. My point is that conflating the two concepts may lead

---

56 Nagel, "Dewey's Theory of Natural Science," 246.

57 Hickman, "Nature as Culture," 55. Emphasis added.

to unnecessary confusion regarding Dewey's naturalism, realism, and, by extension, ecological and educational views. Interaction signifies part of educational experience (along with the principle of continuity), but Dewey clarifies what he means when he writes about people living "in" the world and "interacting" in various "situations."

> The statement that individuals live in a world means, in the concrete, that they live in a series of situations. And when it is said that they live *in* these situations, the meaning of the word "in" is different from its meaning when it is said that pennies are "in" a pocket or paint is "in" a can. It means, once more, that interaction is going on between an individual and objects and other persons. The conceptions of *situation* and *interaction* are inseparable from each other. An experience is always what it is because of a <u>transaction</u> taking place between an individual and what, at the time, constitutes his [*sic*] environment . . .[58]

Dewey might have been better off using the principle of "transaction" rather than "interaction" because he means, in addition to continuity, that the back and forth between individual and environment is neither passive nor trite. We might interact with other drivers on the highway, but the qualitative difference of the experience (as between educative, miseducative, or noneducative experiences) depends on the depth or degree of exchange, growth, and meaning-making that takes place. You can interact without considering the consequences of the interaction. Your chatting at a party might require polite banter about popular topics by those in attendance. You interact. You may even contextually solve the social problem of navigating niceties. But transaction occurs at the party when the polite banter is regarded substantively or meaningfully: when the objects of inquiry organically develop and are not regarded as extant, already formed as the topic, or given. In short, when it becomes *meaningful*.

For Dewey, this back-and-forth transaction illustrates the difference between a spectator theory of knowledge where the knower is merely an observer within the *inter*action, not one who inquires into the meanings,

---

58 John Dewey, *Experience and Education* (New York: Collier Books, 1938), 43. Italics in original, underline added.

possibilities, or ends-in-view of knowing (chapter 3). *Trans*action, differently, requires making meaning of the world relationally and contextually. As Garrison notes, "interaction, or more exactly *trans*action, is meaningless in itself . . . Unless thought connects the doing and the being done to, unless the activity is continued into the consequences and reflected back into a change . . . no learning takes place [no transaction occurs]."[59] In close succession, think about the following five points regarding transaction.

Dewey, with Arthur Bentley, distinguishes between interaction and transaction as follows:

> If interaction is inquiry of a type in which events enter under the presumption that they have been adequately described prior to the formulation of inquiry into their connection, then—

> Transaction is inquiry of a type in which existing descriptions of events are accepted only as tentative and preliminary, so that new descriptions of the aspects and phases of events, whether in widened or narrowed form, may freely be made at any and all stages of the inquiry.[60]

In *Reconstruction in Philosophy* Dewey also clarifies transactional realism when he writes about those who regard what appears to them "only as

---

59   James W. Garrison, "John Dewey's Philosophy as Education," in Larry Hickman, ed., *Reading Dewey: Interpretations for a Postmodern Generation* (Bloomington, IN: Indiana University Press, 1998): 63-81, 66-67.

60   John Dewey and Arthur F. Bentley, "Transactions as Known and Named," *The Journal of Philosophy* 43, no. 20 (September 26, 1946): 533-551, 535. Some may object to this interpretation on the grounds that Dewey, at times, makes clear reference to the use of tools and the role of technology. Hickman is helpful here insofar as he characterizes Dewey and Bentley's *Knowing and the Known* as "an attempt to move beyond models of 'self-action' utilized in classical philosophy and the 'interactional' models of modern mechanistic physics in order to develop a 'transactional' way of thinking that honors the dynamic features of human behavior." Larry Hickman, "Introduction," in Larry Hickman, ed., *Reading Dewey: Interpretations for a Postmodern Generation* (Bloomington, IN: Indiana University Press, 1998): ix-xxi, xi. Burke, Hester, and Talisse note that "Experience...is not a matter of a mind being passively affected by objects, nor a matter of a mind receiving and filtering sensory data from an external world. It is rather an *exchange*, a *transaction*, between an organism and the physical and social factors within its environment...." F. Thomas Burke, D. Micah Hester, and Robert B. Talisse, eds., *Dewey's Logical Theory: New Studies and Interpretations* (Nashville: Vanderbilt University Press, 2002), xiv. Emphasis in original.

material for change."[61] Recall the story of the student in Dewey's lab school who wanted to build a chair. Think of that student as the carpenter in the following quote:

> It is accepted precisely as the carpenter, say, accepts things as he finds them. If he took them as things to be observed and noted for their own sake, he never would be a carpenter. He would observe, describe, record the structures, forms and changes which things exhibit to him, and leave the matter there. If perchance some of the changes going on should present him with a shelter, so much the better. But what makes the carpenter a *builder* is the fact that he notes things not just as objects in themselves, but with reference to what he wants to do to them and with them; to the end he has in mind . . . It is only by these processes of active manipulation of things in order to realize his purpose that he discovers what the properties of things are.[62]

Transactional realism, akin to what Gert Biesta refers to as Dewey's "transactional theory of knowledge," is a particular kind of connection between thinking and action.[63] Writes Biesta,

> To understand Dewey's ideas about the role of thinking in action, it is important to see that we only learn, or acquire new habits, in those situations in which the organism-environment transaction is interrupted. After all, as long as the transaction goes "smoothly"— that is, when there is coordination between our doings and undergoings—we apparently have all the habits we need. The situation is different when we are *not* able to maintain coordinated transaction, when we do not "know," in other words, how to respond.[64]

---

61   John Dewey, *Reconstruction in Philosophy* (Boston: Beacon Press, 1920/1957), 114.

62   Ibid., 114-115. Emphasis in original.

63   Gert Biesta, "Why 'What Works' Won't Work: Evidence-Based Practice and the Democratic Deficit in Educational Research," *Educational Theory* 57, no. 1 (2007): 1-22, 13.

64   Ibid., 14. Emphasis in original. See, also, Gert J.J. Biesta, "Education as Practical Intersubjectivity: Towards a Critical-Pragmatic Understanding of Education," *Educational Theory* 44, no. 3 (Summer 1994): 299-317.

Connecting transaction in terms of human-ecological processes, consider Dewey's basic illustration of breathing, walking, and speaking from *Human Nature and Conduct*:

> Breathing is an affair of the air as truly as of the lungs; digesting an affair of food as truly as of the tissues of the stomach. Seeing involves light just as certainly as it does the eye and optic nerve. Walking implicates the ground as well as the legs; speech demands physical air and human companionship and audience as well as vocal cords. We may shift from the biological to the mathematical use of the word function and say that natural operations like breathing and digesting, acquired ones like speech and honesty, are functions of the surroundings as truly as of a person. They are things done *by* the environment by means of organic structures or acquired dispositions.[65]

Dewey directly extends this point, in similar terms, in his *Logic*:

> Whatever else organic life is or is not, it is a process of activity that involves an environment. It is a <u>transaction</u> extending beyond the spatial limits of the organism. An organism does not live *in* an environment; it lives by means of an environment. Breathing, the ingesting of food, the ejection of waste products, are cases of *direct* intergration; the circulation of the blood and the energizing of the nervous system are relatively *indirect*. But every organic function is an interaction of intra-organic and extra-organic energies, either directly or indirectly . . . The processes of living are enacted by the environment as truly as by the organism; for they *are* an integration.[66]

Taken together, these long quotes, analyses, and interpretations offer a clearer sense of the qualified importance of transaction—not in place of interaction, but in addition to it.

---

65 Dewey, *Human Nature and Conduct*, 15. See, also, Tanya Jeffcoat, "The Ecological Individual, Pragmatist Ecology, and Patch Dynamics: Putting the Ecological Individual to Work for the Environment," paper presented at the Mid-South Philosophy Conference, Memphis, Tennessee, March 5-6, 2010.

66 Dewey, *Logic*, 25. Italics in original, underline added.

There is, as Robin Zebrowski puts it, a key qualifier for transaction: agency. Human transaction with others and the environment requires "a constant remaking of both the world and the individual."[67] For Dewey, individuals are innately curious, inquiring beings who transact the world as both the means and ends of understanding self and environment. Dewey's view necessarily integrates individuals with nature. Environment may begin as a crib, a room, or a classroom, but it's by extension that a better understanding of an ecological environment follows from inquiry and meaning making. Inquiry, after all, does not stop at the bedroom door or at the end of a driveway or at the schoolhouse doors. Inquiry, as transactional realism, merges physicality with meaningfulness. It is another way of talking about Dewey's epistemology and it cannot be divorced or severed from his classroom practice.

Links to Classroom Practice

To relate back to the beginning of this chapter, I noted Tom Colwell's scholarship on Dewey and ecology—as well as his concern. He was disturbed that little work had been done in the 1960s, 1970s, and up to his essay in 1985, to link Dewey's philosophy to the broader movement of ecology. A review of the literature bears out Colwell's worry, but he might be reassured by work that followed his 1985 essay. From Ralph Sleeper's 1986 work, *The Necessity of Pragmatism*, to Peter Manicas' 1992 Romanell Lecture to the American Philosophical Association, to Andrew Light and Eric Katz's 1996 work in "environmental pragmatism," some discussion of Dewey's ecology did follow.[68] Even those who argue against Dewey as an ecologist, including C. A. Bowers, George Sessions, and Paul Morgan, at least picked up on Colwell's theme. Still, Colwell might be happy to see even more recent scholarship that takes up Dewey's ideas and relates them to more current ecological thought. From what I think is an underused work by Paul Thompson and Thomas Hilde to the more recent work by Neil W. Browne, Lorraine Code, Ben Minteer, Bradley Rowe, Tanya Jeffcoat, and Deborah Seltzer-Kelly, it appears

---

67   Robin L. Zebrowski, "Mind is Primarily a Verb: An Examination of Mistaken Similarities Between John Dewey and Herbert Spencer," *Educational Theory* 58, no. 3 (2008): 305-320, 316.

68   Sleeper, *The Necessity of Pragmatism*; Peter Manicas, "Nature and Culture," *Proceedings and Addresses of the American Philosophical Association* 66, no. 3 (November 1992): 59-76; and Andrew Light and Eric Katz, *Environmental Pragmatism* (New York: Routledge, 1996).

that Dewey is, indeed, being linked to questions of ecology.[69] I use Browne's and Seltzer-Kelly's work to illustrate how Dewey is currently being discussed in the field of ecology and suggest that Dewey be re-visited and re-read in an effort to change current education practice in the US. The change should be from a detached, objectified, narrow, and dualist one to one that is ecologically organic, engaging, expanding, and meaningful.

Neil Browne's *The World in Which We Occur: John Dewey, Pragmatist Ecology, and American Ecological Writing in the Twentieth Century* is an examination of non-fiction ecological writing by the likes of John Muir, John Steinbeck, and Rachel Carson. Browne uses Dewey to extend, compare, and critique questions of environmentalism and ecology by reminding readers that Dewey's notion of inquiry was directed at joining art and science, nature and culture, philosophy and social problems, etc. As Browne notes, "Dewey's inclusive interpretation of experience underwrites [the] contention that in ecological writing we witness the attempt to articulate the complex interaction and interpenetration of human culture and the physical world."[70] Browne uses the term "ecotone" as a link between Dewey's philosophy and the ecological writing of Muir, Steinbeck, Carson, etc. An ecotone is a

> transitional zone between two or more ecosystems where evolutionary potential becomes most possible. It is a place of growth and contingency, and mediated space where change can happen.

---

69   Paul B. Thompson and Thomas C. Hilde, eds., *The Agrarian Roots of Pragmatism* (Nashville: Vanderbilt University Press, 2000); Neil W. Browne, *The World in Which We Occur: John Dewey, Pragmatist Ecology, and American Ecological Writing in the Twentieth Century* (Tuscaloosa: The University of Alabama Press, 2007); Lorraine Code, *Ecological Thinking: The Politics of Epistemic Location* (Oxford: Oxford University Press, 2006); Ben A. Minteer, *The Landscape of Reform: Civic Pragmatism and Environmental Thought in America* (Cambridge: MIT Press, 2006); Bradley Rowe, "Deep Ecology and Disruptive Environmental Education," *Philosophy of Education 2017*, Ann Chinnery, editor (Urbana: University of Illinois Press, 2017): 521-525; and Deborah Seltzer-Kelly, "Deweyan Darwinism for the Twenty-First Century: Toward an Educational Method for Critical Democratic Engagement in the Era of the Institute of Education Sciences," *Educational Theory* 58, no. 3 (2008): 289-304. See, also, Burke, Hester, and Talisse, *Dewey's Logical Theory*; Stephanie Raill Jayanandhan, "John Dewey and a Pedagogy of Place," *Philosophical Studies in Education* 40 (2009): 104-112; and Jerome A. Popp, *Evolution's First Philosopher: John Dewey and the Continuity of Nature* (Albany, NY: SUNY Press, 2007).

70   Browne, 13.

An ecotone exists between ecology and democracy . . . Some of the nodes where the two ideas rub up against one another are the concept of interdependence; the notion of borders and barriers as permeable and transitional; and the need for public access to knowledge; further, acts of intelligence participate in nature and culture; experience is a cumulative process, with an emphasis on the input of everyday life; human culture is embedded in physical nature, and physical nature is embedded in human culture. There is an ongoing exchange of creative energy among these ideas that powers pragmatist ecology.[71]

Browne uses ecotones to underscore the potential for relationships, border-crossing, and, yes, imaginative teaching. The transitional zones ecotones represent are pregnant with possibility, in other words. They indicate spaces where the push-and-pull of evolutionary meaning-making emerges—where social intelligences are developed and refined over time. Think of ecotones as classrooms. As transitional spaces, ecotones are places where continuity and change supportively struggle in order to yield intelligence. Understanding ecotones as transitional spaces infused with activity underscores the Deweyan view that directing relations is actually *re*directing relations in an on-going process of meaning-making and understanding (i.e., knowing). The purpose of inquiry in ecotones is less about the object of inquiry and more about the action of inquiry. As Hugh McDonald puts it, "Value is primarily connected with activity . . . rather than the object."[72] This shouldn't be taken to mean than process is more important than product, remember, since Dewey intricately joins the two concepts when he points out that means and ends are really the same thing. Instead, the point behind championing activity over objects is to position inquiry over goals or outcomes. Otherwise, static and imposed goals and outcomes devolve into restrictions on inquiry. Such required objectives limit the possibilities for understanding alternatives (or even that there *are* alternatives) to the objects of inquiry

---

71 Ibid., 18.

72 Hugh P. McDonald, *John Dewey and Environmental Philosophy* (Albany, NY: SUNY Press, 2004), 108. Barry Duff argues that in order to understand Dewey's ideas regarding experience and nature, we should focus our attention on the idea of "events." See Barry E. Duff, "'Event' in Dewey's Philosophy," *Educational Theory* 40, no. 4 (Fall, 1990): 463-470.

because imagination is marginalized, and thinking is already done for teachers and students. The ecotone—the classroom—becomes a manufactured and fake place unlike living, natural ecosystems.

Seltzer-Kelly similarly notes that ends-in-view are part of Dewey's scientific method, where that method is neither restrictive nor habitual. "However much Dewey advocated scientific rigor," she notes, "it was not directive; the insights to be developed through pragmatism were anything but predictable . . ."[73] Emphasizing this point, Dewey argued that inquiry functions "to project new and more complex ends—to free experience from routine and from caprice."[74] The importance of this sort of inquiry for Seltzer-Kelly is to highlight the role that Charles Darwin played in influencing what she calls Dewey's "evolutionary epistemology." For the purpose of this chapter, her investigation also leads to an understanding of ecology and classroom practice. This is so not only because of Darwin's theory but also because transactional realism requires the sort of inquiry she identifies as central to Dewey's project. Her work is also instructive because she links her arguments to the issue of educational method as inquiry. In linking Dewey to ecology and education in this way, Seltzer-Kelly notes that "each of the individual beings in every classroom ecosystem comes with prior adaptations and interests of its own, arrived at as a result of other pressures and experiences, and all of these individual differences interact with each other and with the broader system of education."[75] Classrooms as ecosystems, akin to Browne's ecotones, means that teacher and student inquiry are not "ready-made" with pre-ordained activities. To do so would be to anthropomorphize nature: to have humans structure the world artificially and exploitatively—to view schooling "as primarily a source of problems to be overcome or an unruly force to be subdued."[76] Such reductionism isn't what Dewey wanted.

To use some of the big words from earlier in this chapter, anthropomorphism opposes naturalistic transactions because transaction requires movement and change from contextual situations upward and outward.

---

73 Seltzer-Kelly, 294.

74 John Dewey, "The Need for a Recovery of Philosophy," in *John Dewey: The Middle Works, 1899–1924*, vol. 3, ed. Jo Ann Boydston (Carbondale, IL: Southern Illinois University Press, 1917/1981), 257.

75 Seltzer-Kelly, 299.

76 Morgan, 297.

Remember the upward spiral from chapter 1. For schooling situations, meaning emerges from student and teacher experiences and is not confined to an imposed view of only what others think students should learn and teachers should teach. This point is significant because it underscores the dramatic difference between imposition and transaction. As noted earlier in this book, most schools, most of the time, in most of the US, are bounded by external learning objectives that have to be confined to lesson planning and, thus, conforming to the assumption that, for example, "best practices" already exist and need only be adopted in order for good teaching and learning to take place. Recall that in the typical classroom, teachers talk and students listen, rules of order are followed, quizzes are taken, grades are noted, and students (and teachers) become habituated to routines that, in circular fashion, reinforce more routines. This is the opposite of Dewey's educational point—and his ecological concern, too. Classrooms as environments (or ecotones) are, merging Browne with Dewey, supposed to be places where transacting existing capacities of children with the social set-up of situations, including others (e.g., teachers, too), leads to worthwhile experiences. Traditional schools, Dewey complained in 1938 (and I think he would still complain today), provided an environment, but one that was so stacked with inauthentic and contrived "exercises" that ecological engagement is petrified by the very routines and unthinking habits outlined in chapter 1 and noted throughout this book. Any learning that results from manufacturing nature is, according to Dewey, merely "accidental."[77] Teachers and students benefit from inspired learning—a result of freeing teachers and students from routine and over-bearing structure—but this is different from an accidental learning or learning *in spite of* the structure of schools.

Instead of accidental learning, classrooms should be environments understood as extensions of nature. Classrooms should be ecological spaces for conjoint inquiry where that inquiry is neither canned nor prepackaged, like much curricula today. Just as Dewey denied that schools are separate from society, classrooms are not separate from the broader notion of the environment either. This includes, but is much broader than, global warming or plastic islands in oceans. The relevant consequences of this point are relatively straightforward: We should see classrooms as reconstructed,

---

77   Dewey, *Experience and Education*, 45.

organic spaces safe for and productive of imaginative transactions between and among students, teachers, and emergent content. The problem, of course, is that Dewey's ecological argument regarding classrooms means that the comfortable routines, traditional attitudes, and entrenched expectations for "preparation for the future" that characterize most US schools will reinforce an anthropocentric understanding of the nature of teaching and learning. As Stoller sees it, teaching "is not a kind of *telling* and learning a kind of *hearing*, but pedagogy is an act of shared *making*, resulting in a shared process of creative construction and praxis in which something new emerges."[78] And Stoller also understands how his point may be lost of those who have already navigated schools that do not operate in a Deweyan way. He writes that his views,

> will likely seem foreign in the context of an educational system which has so deeply maintained that methodological certainty (e.g. uniform teaching strategies) or epistemological certainty (e.g. quantifiable testing measures) is the only ground on which education might possibly stand. Asking teachers to conform to a narrow set of predetermined lesson plans or to submit their students to a test developed by external authority is equivalent to asking a poet to begin her writing practice by adhering to pre-determined conditions for the beautiful. A poem, like a pedagogical moment, cannot begin within and should not be judged in terms of an *a priori* metric, but only in terms of its transactional, reconstructive, and context-laden being in the world. This is why central educational concepts like cognitive certainty, rational criteria, and objective truth—rather than remedying—actually become the very barrier which prohibits creative action and growth in educational practice.[79]

Stoller's right. The challenge is to change the practices in schools that inhibit genuine inquiry. That it's a challenge does not change the fact that Dewey's ecological view should be best understood as a bridge between ecological and educational worlds.

---

78 Stoller, 82. Emphasis in original.

79 Ibid., 82-83.

At Dewey's lab school, students built on previous educative experiences by focusing on earth science (or what we now call ecology, generally, and geology specifically). As Mayhew and Edwards report, "the child at ten years was ready to take up the growth of the continent as a convenient basis, on the geographic side, for gathering together all his [sic] previous experience."[80] The bridge here is between previous experience and new study, in this case nature in the form of geology and earth science. They also make note of imagination and I'm going to cite a few passages from their experiences teaching in the lab school to emphasize the point. Regarding the purpose of such ecological study, Mayhew and Edwards report that it was "to help the child form a notion of the dynamic character of the changes in the earth's surface, to see that its present condition is but one stage in a long series, and that the same forces which acted in the past still act."[81] Again, the metaphor of bridge comes in handy. It's the continuity of inquiry and experience that builds upon itself to develop knowing (chapter 3). It's also directly linked to imagination: the students were "led to construct *imaginatively* the conditions which must have obtained in very early stages of geological history."[82] And they also write that "experimentation accompanied this *imaginative* remaking of the continent, in order to secure typical concrete illustrations of such things as the action of a gas on a solid, the solution in water of the solids changed by such action and the subsequent crystallization of the solid from that solution, the solution of a gas in a liquid, and of the conditions that determine, roughly speaking, that solution."[83] You don't need to follow all of the illustrations they note in order to get the point: Learning as inquiry and learning as knowing are active and engaged processes that build on educative experiences that require imagination. There are realities (see the section on realism above), of course, but they are not understood if they are merely told to students. There is no activity—no agency—demonstrated in canned approaches to covering content.

---

80   Katherine Camp Mayhew and Anna Camp Edwards, *The Dewey School: The Laboratory School of the University of Chicago, 1896-1903* (New York: J. Appleton-Century Company, Inc., 1936), 291.

81   Ibid., 292.

82   Ibid. Emphasis added.

83   Ibid. Emphasis added.

At Chrysalis, Dewey's ecological view was illustrated in recycling programs and the fun competitions held between groups of students to see who
could recycle more plastic, tin cans, and glass bottles. But these obvious
actions are not quite the point. Let's link back to Dewey's lab school and
consider a long quote from Mayhew and Edwards. They explain the connection, the relation, the transaction that we're considering in terms of the
purpose of education in Dewey's school:

> The pedagogical problem was to direct the child's power of ob-
> servation, to nurture his [sic] sympathetic interest in characteristic
> traits of the world in which he lives, to afford interpreting material
> for later, more special studies, and yet to supply a carrying medium
> for the variety of facts and ideas through dominant, spontaneous
> emotions and thoughts of the child. No separation was made be-
> tween the social side of the work, its concern with people's activities
> and their mutual dependencies, and the scientific side, its regard
> for physical facts and forces . . . To make the child study earth, air,
> or water, bird, beast, or flower apart from environment and out
> of relation to their use by other factors in the environment, their
> function in the total life-process, cuts the tie that relates and binds
> natural facts and forces to people and their activities. The child's
> interest fades for he misses the way. His imagination finds no av-
> enue of connection that makes object, fact, or process concrete to
> him. He loses his original open, free attitude to natural facts. Na-
> ture herself is reduced to a mass of meaningless details. In contrast,
> however, when a natural object is clothed with human significance
> and human association, a road lies open from the child's mind to
> the object through the connection of the latter with life itself.[84]

In this extended passage, Mayhew and Edwards link many of the central
claims I'm making in this chapter. Their language may be dated, but the
ideas should be clear. Classrooms are not supposed to be places where artificial imposition of standardized material is the goal. Students learn via
active means and imaginative processes that are linked to emergent content.

---

84   Ibid., 78.

Another important point they raise is the degree to which learning is not separated from social relations.

In an updated interpretation of Mayhew and Edwards, consider that the students at Chrysalis prided themselves on amassing thousands upon thousands of volunteer hours. Some of those hours were spent in bilingual after school programs with a local elementary school. Reading and translating were made humane by one-to-one mentoring that was not one-way. That is, the Spanish-speaking elementary students learned from their Chrysalis mentors, but the volunteer mentors also learned from the elementary students. What they learned wasn't canned. It wasn't predetermined. It grew, authentically, out of both human interaction and problem solving—in this case two young people and two languages.

Some of those volunteer hours were spent in retirement homes where students would perform on musical instruments or act out parts of plays. But beyond performances, there was interaction that wasn't scripted. Questions and answers were tossed around and conversations were had that at least sometimes were profound and often very meaningful. Reflection took place. Follow-up actions came about that nobody knew would happen. The ecological environment, for Dewey, is not only clean water and fresh air. It includes these things, to be sure, but Dewey's notion of community—ecological community—was a more robust one. Students learn that volunteering isn't done because it's part of a service-learning program. It's done because that's what healthy social ecologies do.[85] And we learn a lot from the kind of interaction or transaction that takes place in these out-of-school teaching and learning spaces. The students rarely had a theoretical understanding of the undertaking of volunteering. But through the educative experiences they *had*, they linked community with learning in ways that went far beyond the school walls. So, Dewey's imaginative vision of teaching and learning reinforces his point that school and society are the same thing. There may be school buildings but teaching and learning go on in many other arenas, too. In fact, if Dewey is correct, much of what goes on in schools today rarely rises to what he considers imaginative teaching and learning to be. And this point raises ethical questions, the focus of chapter 5.

---

85 See, also, Jeff Frank, *Teaching in the Now: John Dewey on the Educational Present* (West Lafayette, IN: Purdue University Press, 2019).

References

Alexander, Thomas. "The Aesthetics of Reality: The Development of Dewey's Ecological Theory of Experience." In *Dewey's Logical Theory: New Studies
and Interpretations*, 3-26, edited by F. Thomas Burke, D. Micah Hester, and
Robert B. Talisse. Nashville, TN: Vanderbilt University Press, 2002.

Austin, J. L. *Sense and Sensibilia*. Oxford: Oxford University Press, 1962.

Bates, Marston. *Forest and the Sea*. New York: New American Library, 1960.

Biesta, Gert. "Why 'What Works' Won't Work: Evidence-Based Practice and the
Democratic Deficit in Educational Research." *Educational Theory* 57 (1)
2007: 1–22.

Biesta, Gert J. J. "Education as Practical Intersubjectivity: Towards a Critical-
Pragmatic Understanding of Education." *Educational Theory* 44 (3) 1994:
299–317.

Bowen, James. *A History of Western Education*. New York: St. Martin's Press,
1981.

Bowers, C. A. *Education, Cultural Myths, and the Ecological Crisis*. Albany, NY:
SUNY Press, 1993.

Bowers, C. A. "The Case against John Dewey as an Environmental and Eco-Justice
Philosopher." 2002. http://www.cabowers.net/pdf/DeweysRelevance2003.
pdf.

Browne, Neil W. *The World in which We Occur: John Dewey, Pragmatist Ecology,
and American Ecological Writing in the Twentieth Century*. Tuscaloosa: The
University of Alabama Press, 2007.

Brownell, Baker. *The Human Community*. New York: Harper and Brothers, 1950.

Buchler, Justus. *Philosophical Writings of Peirce*. New York: Dover Publications,
1950.

Bunnin, Nicholas and Jiyuan Yu, eds. *The Blackwell Dictionary of Western Philosophy*. London: Blackwell, 2004.

Burke, Tom. *Dewey's New Logic: A Reply to Russell*. Chicago: The University of
Chicago Press, 1994.

Code, Lorraine. *Ecological Thinking: The Politics of Epistemic Location*. Oxford:
Oxford University Press, 2006.

Cohen, Morris R. "Some Difficulties in Dewey's Anthropocentric Naturalism." *The
Philosophical Review* 49 (2) 1940: 196–228.

Collingwood, R. G. *The Idea of Nature*. New York: Oxford University Press, 1960.

Colwell, Thomas. "The Significance of Ecology for Philosophy of Education." In
Philosophy of Education, 1982, 177–85. Normal: Illinois State University
Press, 1983.

Colwell, Thomas. "The Ecological Perspective in John Dewey's Philosophy of Education." *Educational Theory* 35 (3) 1985: 255–66.

Colwell, Thomas B., Jr. "The Balance of Nature: A Ground for Human Values."
Main Currents in Modern Thought 26 (1) 1969: 46–52.

Colwell, Thomas B., Jr. "The Ecological Basis of Human Community." *Educational
Theory* 21 (4) 1971: 418–33.

Cutchin, Malcolm P. "John Dewey's Metaphysical Ground-Map and its Implications for Geographical Inquiry." *Geoforum* 39 (4) 2008: 1555–69.

Deters, Troy Nicholas. "John Dewey's Theory of Inquiry: An Interpretation of a Classical American Approach to Logic." Master's thesis, Texas A&M University, 2006.

Dewey, John. *Democracy and Education.* New York: The Free Press, 1916.

Dewey, John. *Reconstruction in Philosophy.* New York: Henry Holt, 1920.

Dewey, John. "Half-hearted Naturalism." *The Journal of Philosophy* 24 (3) 1927: 57–64.

Dewey, John. *Experience and Education.* New York: Collier Books, 1938.

Dewey, John. *Logic: The Theory of Inquiry.* New York: Henry Holt and Company, 1938.

Dewey, John. "Nature in Experience." *The Philosophical Review* 49 (2) 1940: 244–58.

Dewey, John. "Common Sense and Science: Their Respective Frames of Reference." *The Journal of Philosophy* 45 (8) 1948: 197–208.

Dewey, John. *Experience and Nature.* In *The Collected Works of John Dewey,* 1882-1953, ed. by Jo Ann Boydston (Carbondale and Edwardsville: Southern Illinois University Press, 1967-1991), LW 1981: 14.

Dewey, John. "The Need for a Recovery of Philosophy." In *The Collected Works of John Dewey,* 1882-1953, ed. by Jo Ann Boydston (Carbondale and Edwardsville: Southern Illinois University Press, 1967-1991), MW 1981: 3.

Dewey, John. *Human Nature and Conduct.* In *The Collected Works of John Dewey,* 1882-1953, ed. by Jo Ann Boydston (Carbondale and Edwardsville: Southern Illinois University Press, 1967-1991), MW 1983: 14.

Dewey, John, and Arthur F. Bentley. "Transactions as Known and Named." *The Journal of Philosophy* 43 (20) 1946.: 533–51.

Dewey, John, and Arthur F. Bentley. *Knowing and the Known.* Boston: Beacon Press, 1949.

Duff, Barry E. "'Event' in Dewey's Philosophy." *Educational Theory* 40 (4) 1990.: 463–70.

Ehrenfeld, David. *The Arrogance of Humanism.* New York: Oxford University Press, 1981.

Eldridge, Michael. "Naturalism." In *The Blackwell Guide to American Philosophy,* edited by Armen T. Marsoobian and John Ryder, 52–71. Malden, MA: Blackwell Publishing, 2019.

Frank, Jeff. *Teaching in the Now: John Dewey on the Educational Present.* West Lafayette, IN: Purdue University Press, 2019.

French, Roderick. "Is Ecological Humanism a Contradiction in Terms? The Philosophical Foundations of the Humanities under Attack." In *Ecological Consciousness,* edited by Robert C. Shultz and J. Donald Hughes, 43-66. Washington, DC: University Press of America, 1981.

Garrison, James. "Realism, Deweyan Pragmatism, and Educational Research." *Educational Researcher* 23 (1) 1994: 5–14.

Garrison, James W. "John Dewey's Philosophy as Education." In *Reading Dewey: Interpretations for a Postmodern Generation,* edited by Larry Hickman, 63–81. Bloomington: Indiana University Press, 1998.

Godfrey-Smith, Peter. "Dewey on Naturalism, Realism, and Science." *Philosophy of Science* 69(3) 2002: S25–S35.

Goodpastor, K. E., and K. M. Sayre, eds. *Ethics and the Problems of the 21st Century*. Notre Dame, IN: University of Notre Dame Press, 1979.

Grey, William. "Anthropocentrism and Deep Ecology." *Australasian Journal of Philosophy* 74 (4) 1993: 463–75.

Grey, William. "Environmental Value and Anthropocentrism." *Ethics and the Environment* 3 (1) 1998: 97–103.

Hawley, Amos H. "Ecology and Human Ecology." *Social Forces* 22 (4) 1944: 398–405.

Hickman, Larry. "Introduction." In *Reading Dewey: Interpretations for a Postmodern Generation*, edited by Larry Hickman, ix-xxi. Bloomington: Indiana University Press, 1998.

Hickman, Larry A. "Nature as Culture: John Dewey's Pragmatic Naturalism." In *Environmental Pragmatism*, edited by Andrew Light and Eric Katz, 58–72. New York: Routledge, 1996.

Hildebrand, David L. *Beyond Realism & Anti-Realism: John Dewey and the Neopragmatists*. Nashville, TN: Vanderbilt University Press, 2003.

Hocking, William Ernest. "Dewey's Concepts of Experience and Nature." *The Philosophical Review* 49 (2) 1940: 228–44.

Hookway, C. (1992). *Peirce*. New York: Routledge.

James, William. (1890) *The Principles of Psychology, Volume 2*. New York: Dover., 1950.

Jayanandhan, Stephanie Raill. "John Dewey and a Pedagogy of Place." *Philosophical Studies in Education* 40 (1) 2009: 104–12.

Jeffcoat, Tanya. "The Ecological Individual, Pragmatist Ecology, and Patch Dynamics: Putting the Ecological Individual to Work for the Environment." Paper presented at the Mid-South Philosophy Conference, Memphis, Tennessee, March 5–6, 2010.

Kahn, Sholom J. "Experience and Existence in Dewey's Naturalistic Metaphysics." *Philosophy and Phenomenological Research* 9 (2) 1948: 316–21.

Kirby, Christopher C. "Experience and Inquiry in John Dewey's Contextualism." Master's thesis, University of South Florida, 2005.

Knickerbocker, William S. "John Dewey." *The Sewanee Review* 48 (1) 1940: 119-137.

Leiss, William. *The Limits to Satisfaction*. Toronto: The University of Toronto Press, 1976.

Li, Huey-li. "On the Nature of Environmental Education (Anthropocentrism versus Non-Anthropocentrism: The Irrelevant Debate)." *Philosophy of Education* (1996): 256–63.

Light, Andrew, and Eric Katz. *Environmental Pragmatism*. New York: Routledge, 1996.

Lindeman, Eduard C. "Ecology: An Instrument for the Integration of Sciences and Philosophy." *Ecological Monographs* 10 (3) 1940: 367–72.

Manicas, Peter. "Nature and Culture." *Proceedings and Addresses of the American Philosophical Association* 66 (3) 1992: 59–76.

Mayhew, Catherine Camp, and Anna Camp Edwards. *The Dewey School: The Laboratory School of the University of Chicago, 1896-1903*. New York: D. Appleton-Century Company, Inc., 1936.

McCarthy, Christine, and Evelyn Sears. "Deweyan Pragmatism and the Quest for True Belief." *Educational Theory* 50 (2) 2000: 213–27.

McDonald, Hugh P. *John Dewey and Environmental Philosophy.* Albany, NY: SUNY Press, 2004.

Minteer, Ben A. *The Landscape of Reform: Civic Pragmatism and Environmental Thought in America.* Cambridge, MA: MIT Press, 2006.

Moore, G. E. *Philosophical Papers.* London: Allen & Unwin, 1959.

Moreno, Jonathan D., and R. Scott Frey. "Dewey's Critique of Marxism." *The Sociological Quarterly* 26 (1) 1985: 21–34.

Morgan, Paul. "Reconceiving the Foundations of Education: An Ecological Model." In *Philosophy of Education, 1996,* 294–302. Urbana: University of Illinois Press, 1997.

Nagel, Ernest. "Dewey's Theory of Natural Science." In *John Dewey: Philosopher of Science and Freedom,* edited by Sidney Hook, 231–48. New York: The Dial Press, 1950.

Passmore, John. *Man's Responsibility for Nature.* New York: Scribner's, 1974.

Phillips, D. C. "John Dewey and the Organismic Archetype." In *Melbourne Studies in Education,* edited by R. J. W. Selleck, 232-271. Melbourne: Melbourne University Press, 1971.

Plumwood, Val. "Androcentrism and Anthrocentrism." *Ethics and the Environment* 1 (2) 1996: 119–52.

Popp, Jerome A. *Evolution's First Philosopher: John Dewey and the Continuity of Nature.* Albany, NY: SUNY Press, 2007.

Quinton, Anthony M. "The Problem of Perception." *Mind* 64 (253) 1955: 28–51.

Ratner, Sidney, and Jules Altman, eds., with James E. Wheeler. *John Dewey and Arthur F. Bentley: A Philosophical Correspondence, 1932–1951.* New Brunswick, NJ: Rutgers University Press, 1964.

Roth, Elizabeth H. "The Emerging Paradigm of Reader-Text Transaction: Contributions of John Dewey and Louise M. Rosenblatt, with Implications for Educators." Ph.D. dissertation, Virginia Polytechnic and State University, 1998.

Rowe, Bradley. "Deep Ecology and Disruptive Environmental Education." In *Philosophy of Education 2017,* edited by Ann Chinnery, 531–25. Urbana: University of Illinois Press, 2017.

Ryan, Frank X. "The 'Extreme Heresy' of John Dewey and Arthur F. Bentley: A Star Crossed Collaboration?" *Transactions of the Charles S. Peirce Society* 33 (3) 1997: 774–94.

Ryan, Frank X. "Skepticism, Realism, and Transactional Pragmatism." Paper presented at the 10th Annual Summer Institute in American Philosophy, University of Colorado, Boulder, July 9–14, 2007.

Santayana, George. "Dewey's Naturalistic Metaphysics." *The Journal of Philosophy* 22 (25) 1925: 673–88.

Sellars, Roy Wood. "Dewey on Materialism." *Philosophy and Phenomenological Research* 3 (4) 1943: 381–92.

Seltzer-Kelly, Deborah. "Deweyan Darwinism for the Twenty-First Century: Toward an Educational Method for Critical Democratic Engagement in the Era of the Institute of Education Sciences." *Educational Theory* 58 (3) 2008: 289–304.

Sessions, George. "Ecophilosophy, Utopias, and Education," *The Journal of Environmental Education* 15 (1) 1983: 27–42.

Shepard, Paul, and Daniel McKinley, eds. *The Subversive Science: Essays toward and Ecology of Man*. Boston: Houghton Mifflin Co., 1969.

Sleeper, R. W. *The Necessity of Pragmatism*. New Haven, CT: Yale University Press, 1987.

Snauwaert, Dale. "The Relevance of the Anthropocentric-Ecocentric Debate." *Philosophy of Education* (1996): 264–67.

Stoller, Aaron. *Knowing and Learning as Creative Action: A Reexamination of the Epistemological Foundations of Education*. New York: Palgrave Macmillan, 2014.

Suits, Bernard. "Naturalism: Half-Hearted or Broken-Backed?" *The Journal of Philosophy* 58 (7) 1961: 169–79.

Thompson, Paul B., and Thomas C. Hilde, eds. *The Agrarian Roots of Pragmatism*. Nashville, TN: Vanderbilt University Press, 2000.

Toulmin, Stephen. *The Return to Cosmology*. Berkeley: University of California Press, 1982.

Wescoat, James L., Jr. "Common Themes in the Work of Gilbert White and John Dewey: A Pragmatic Appraisal." *Annals of the Association of American Geographers* 82 (4) 1992: 587–607.

Zebrowski, Robin L. "Mind Is Primarily a Verb: An Examination of Mistaken Similarities between John Dewey and Herbert Spencer." *Educational Theory* 58 (3) 2008: 305–20.

Zimmerman, Michael. "Dewey, Heidegger and the Quest for Certainty." *Southwest Journal of Philosophy* 9 (1) 1978: 87–95.

CHAPTER FIVE

DEWEY'S ETHICS APPLIED TO SCHOOLS:

Against School-Business Partnerships and Corporate Exploitation

U NDERSTANDING DEWEY'S VIEW OF imaginative teaching is almost impossible without understanding his ethics. Ethics is the field of philosophy that deals with what's fair and what's proper. Ethics asks, "What are the moral principles that govern our behavior and our actions?" Typical for Dewey, as illustrated in the previous chapters, ethics is not a separate domain or sphere somehow walled-off from discussions about school and society. More importantly, Dewey's ethics begins with everyday experience. Ethics may sound abstract, but Dewey argues that we make meaning of our lives from our beginning, our growth, our lives. This means that Dewey recognizes the importance of context. He's an empiricist. Our senses inform our understanding. When we use our life experiences as the starting point for understanding purpose and meaning, we don't begin with a theory that is imposed. "To be empirical in Dewey's sense is to be a contextualist," writes Gregory Pappas, "but the ultimate context is the stream of unique

and qualitative situations that make up our lives."[1] Those lives face ethical
challenges every day. In what follows, I explore Dewey's ethics from the
standpoint of his critique of business. I do so, part, because I think our lives
as Americans and our lives as teachers and students are constantly bombarded by corporate and commercial messages. If we can understand how
those challenges are ethical ones, we might be better at imagining what good
teaching and living well mean.

This chapter outlines Dewey's business ethics. I then provide a series of
examples of how corporations exploit public schools. Part of the point is to
show what teachers face when they are bombarded with advertising and other
initiatives to promote business interests in schools. The way I explore ethical
considerations should be useful in any situation teachers face in schools. So,
what this chapter does is approach the broad field of ethics through Dewey's
business ethics. Those ethics are then used to explore a series of instances—
lots of mini-illustrations—of ethical problems students and teachers face in
actual classroom contexts. Instead of seeing school-business partnerships as
a good thing, I'm arguing that they exploit teachers, students, and schools.
I ultimately propose that we use the illustrations of exploitation as object
lessons to help bring about Dewey's imaginative vision of teaching. We are,
in other words, still combining theory and practice.

I think you could easily argue that Dewey's ethics is seen in all his
writing and all his thought. He is, recall, against dualisms and binaries:
the choice that you are either a democrat or a republican, right or wrong,
succeeding or failing, selfish or generous, educated or ignorant, etc. Each
of these opposing forces represent values, but, like the difference between
knowledge and knowing (see chapter 3), Dewey activates value to become
valuing. Because of our contextual living, our valuing may change and alter
over time. This is part of Dewey's ethics because his ideas about valuing
are related to actions like self-realization, growth, and human fulfillment.
Dewey specifically takes up the topic of ethics in a textbook he wrote with

1   Gregory Pappas, *John Dewey's Ethics: Democracy as Experience* (Bloomington, IN:
Indiana University Press, 2008), 11. There are lots of sources to support this point. See,
for example, Jennifer Welchman, *Dewey's Ethical Thought* (Ithaca, NY: Cornell University
Press, 1995); J.E Tiles, *Dewey* (New York: Routledge, 1988); Andrew Altman, "John Dew-
ey and Contemporary Normative Ethics," *Metaphilosophy* 13, no. 2 (1982): 149-160; Axel
Honneth, "Between Proceduralism and Teleology: An Unresolved Conflict in Dewey's Mor-
al Theory," *Transactions of the Charles S. Peirce Society* 34, no. 3 (1998): 689-711; Hilary
Putnam, *Renewing Philosophy* (Cambridge, MA: Harvard University Press, 1992); and
James Campbell, *Understanding John Dewey* (Chicago: Open Court Publishing, 1995).

James Hayden Tufts in 1908. They revised the book to be a bit broader in scope in 1932. To clarify Dewey's ethics, I'm using five chapters from his *Ethics* to show how school and society are not separate, how businesses exploit social and educational spaces, and what at least some of the implications are for imaginative teaching and learning. Considering ethics and ethical education is another way to understand Dewey and the kind of imaginative teaching he advocates.

Toward the end of John Dewey's *Ethics*, he includes five short chapters in which he explores the ethics of economics and business.[2] I think he's forward-thinking in his consideration of the tensions between family and work life, artisanship and mass production, capitalism and socialism, training and education, etc., Dewey appears to bridge public-private tensions by arguing for something along the lines of economic justice—basic social security for all. He does so in typical form: laying out the opposing sides of, say, excessive concentrations of wealth on the one hand and abject poverty on the other. He dislikes monopolies and appears nostalgic for craft guilds and artistic communities. This dislike of corporate control is why I'm combining ethics with business and economics. Dewey sees a direct link between our economic system and the way we live in society and learn in schools. Some people have a lot. Some people have nothing. Is that fair? Is it just? Dewey says no. Here's why: there are at least four economic options for culture and society: (1) everyone earns what they can (earning); (2) everyone earns what they can, but some earn more than others because of who they know, not what they know (merit); (3) everyone should get an equal share (communism); or (4) everyone should have a basic living wage and, above that, everyone earns what they can. Dewey rejects the first three as follows: (1) the complexity of production and distribution makes "earning" so unclear as to be unworkable; (2); "merit" suffers a similar fate, nonetheless operating via meta-narratives of hard work and competition but concentrating wealth for a few at the expense of the many; and (3) communism undermines pluralist democratic community.[3]

---

2 John Dewey, *Ethics* (1932), in *John Dewey: The Later Works, 1925–1953*, vol. 7, ed. Jo Ann Boydston (Carbondale: Southern Illinois University Press, 1981). For an explication of Dewey's early works on ethics, see Welchman, *Dewey's Ethical Thought*. This chapter is limited to five of the last chapters of Dewey's 1932 *Ethics* dealing with business and economics.

3 Dewey, *Ethics*, 407-411.

Dewey claims that the fourth principle is the best option because it "would abandon, in part at least, the attempt to distribute justly on the basis of giving to each man [*sic*] a precise equivalent for his contribution, or of giving him an equal share on the basis of the assumed equality of all human beings, or on the basis of what he can get in the market."[4] Instead, the fourth option requires "a regard for the public good."[5] Dewey notes that the fourth option "asks what is a good condition of society, and what standard of living is necessary or conducive to a good society."[6] Such a project is an ethical one and requires not only understanding ethics, but demonstrating and enacting ethics, as well. The link to public education is the opportunity to formally consider the ethics of economics within a pluralist space for solving social problems and demonstrating the public good. The public good is a phrase that, for Dewey, captures the interrelationships between individuals and groups with one significant qualification: democratic community.

> Only when we start from a community as a fact, grasp the fact in thought so as to clarify and enhance its constituent elements, can we reach an idea of democracy which is not utopian. The conceptions and shibboleths which are traditionally associated with the idea of democracy take on a veridical and directive meaning only when they are construed as marks and traits of an association which realizes the defining characteristics of a community. Fraternity, liberty, and equality isolated from communal life are hopeless abstractions.[7]

Schools are central to this project only if they demonstrate, in word *and* deed, the factual engagement to which Dewey refers. The engaged thinking Dewey expects of schooling requires diverse students investigating and solving various social problems, including economic ones. The processes of investigation are communal—public—and require students and teachers to engage in imaginative, critical inquiry.

---

4   Ibid., 410.

5   Ibid.

6   Ibid.

7   John Dewey, *The Public and Its Problems* (New York: Henry Holt, 1927), 149. See, also, Joseph Grange, "The Disappearance of the Public Good: Confucius, Dewey, Rorty," *Philosophy East and West* 46, no. 3 (July, 1996): 351-366.

Remember the point of this chapter: it considers the primary arguments Dewey offers regarding ethics, but specifically business ethics. It explores whether his optimism is a bridge between economics and education and whether his view is too positive for contemporary times. Is Dewey's view of ethical economics opposed to his otherwise functional, pragmatist philosophy of education? That is, does Dewey's view of basic economic justice run counter to how public schooling operates in the US in 2020? I proceed with three sections so you can see how the argument is laid out: (1) a brief overview of the main claims Dewey makes toward the end of *Ethics*; (2) an exploration of structural differences in Dewey's view of economics of his time and current fiscal contexts in relation to schooling in the US; and (3) an analysis of Dewey's hopeful view that schools as democratic, public spheres can contain the worst ethical lapses of business fundamentals and still provide positive economic options for contemporary life. The ultimate point of this chapter is to turn the tables on businesses; to use their exploitation of teachers, students, and schools as object lessons for understanding and action. To do so, I begin by situating Dewey's business ethics in educational contexts to reconsider whether his hopeful vision still holds.

Overview of Dewey's Business Ethics

In *Ethics*, Dewey provides five chapters with the following titles: "Ethical Problems of the Economic Life," "Collective Bargaining and the Labor Union," "Moral Problems of Business," "Social Control of Business and Industry," and "Toward the Future."[8] I begin where Dewey ends and then tease out key elements from these chapters to show what arguments he makes and what might follow from them for current society and schools. Dewey concludes that if economic considerations are the driving force in our lives, something is tragically wrong. His worry is that the finer things of life, like love, joy, reflection, happiness, etc., will be distorted by an unrelenting focus on materialism, commercialism, and economic domination. Here's Dewey's summation:

> If the economic dominates life—and if the economic order relies chiefly upon the profit motive as distinguished from the motive of professional excellence, i.e., craftsmanship [sic], and from the func-

---

8   Dewey, *Ethics*, 371-437.

tional motive of giving a fair return for what is received—there is
danger that a part of life, which should be subordinate or at most
coordinate with other interests and values, may become supreme.[9]

Dewey's caution is informed by historical symbols. He begins his analysis
of economic life by pointing to architecture and how, in important periods
of history, buildings symbolized what society valued most. For Athens, it
was the temples on the Acropolis. For Rome, it was the forums and temples to government. Medieval cities had cathedrals towering above the mar-
ketplace. But the modern city, Dewey complains, is filled with corporate
basilicas, sprawling manufacturing plants, and banks. "Government is less
prominent;" he writes, "the churches follow the residences into the suburbs;
business reigns."[10] Dewey's concern is that nearly "half our citizens neglect
to vote; at least as many abstain from the services of the churches; but business and industry admit no absence."[11] We don't escape commercialism and
consumerism.

Dewey then lays out how we arrived at the current condition of business
dominating society. He highlights the rise of industrialism, machinery, and
resulting factory work. Importantly, he straddles the progressive benefits of
industrialization while also raising serious questions about the consequences
of that same industrialization. He notes, for example, that earnings increased
from the nineteenth to the twentieth centuries, but not without struggles over
horrible working conditions. People may have had more money to spend, but
Dewey questions the meaningfulness of lives that endure repetitive motions
within environments that increase risks of physical injury and mental monotony. Think sweat shops. Nike factories. With earnings from such work,

---

9   Ibid., 436.

10   Ibid., 373. An argument could easily be made that churches have become businesses,
but that point is for another time. Dewey's point is that traditional communitarian spaces
are displaced by businesses. Shopping malls, for instance, became substitute spaces of public
gathering, but subsumed under commerce. After 9/11, George W. Bush clarified this point
when he encouraged Americans to show their patriotism by shopping. Now malls are facing a challenge even to the idea that they are public gathering spaces. With Amazon drones
delivering consumer goods to houses, we no longer even have to leave home and interact
with others. Banks automate tellers, grocery stores install automatic check-out counters,
and we become increasingly isolated. In the Covid-19 era, Zoom meetings and Facebook
Live try to ease such isolation, but I wonder if these platforms only reinforce separation.

11   Ibid.

what are those wages used for? In some cases, workers' housing was rented from the factory and food had to be purchased from company stores. Wages were cycled back to industry in a commercial loop of corporate-self-interest. Where is the public good in this example? More will be made of this point in the next section but note how schools conform to a similar cyclical function: perpetual preparation and training of future workers to compete in a global economy reinforces the idea that public schools exist primarily for private enterprise. This is a problem because public schools should not be exploited by market forces. Why? Because fads and tastes change quickly. Dewey was interested in long-term, stable democratic life that embraced innovation, not fads. Active inquiry and scientific advancement? Yes. Fads to make a lot of money? No. Cell phones may be great, but if Apple designs them to be obsolete every five years, they control us.

In chapter 18 of *Ethics*, "Ethical Problems of the Economic Life," Dewey provides a broad outline of the rise of industrialization in the US and some of the consequences that followed. The conditions of work altered significantly such that the economic realities redefined priorities and individual power. Importantly, Dewey isn't arguing against the industrial revolution, per se, nor arguing that feudal life was egalitarian and happy. He is arguing against the effects of the way the industrial revolution was carried out: not only were monopolies funneling enormous wealth to a very small number of industrialists, but the social and collective interaction of communities was fundamentally and reductively changed. Again, it didn't change from utopia to dystopia, but, as Dewey notes, "it makes a difference whether [our] relations with [our] fellow workers or employers are of a family or neighborly or friendly character, or whether the relation is purely impersonal and the motive for work is the acquisition of money in some form as wage or salary or profits."[12] Here Dewey returns to a vision of human being that is not encased in materialist drudgery. His point is that the more materialist our lives become, the less likely we are to enjoy what it means to be more fully human. Note the qualifiers. Dewey is not arguing against work or jobs or making a decent (i.e., beyond subsistence) wage. He's arguing for a society that's communal, fair, and filled with the kinds of artful serendipity and generative expertise that make us laugh and appreciate existing (remember chapter 2). What makes this view *not* utopian is the functional anchoring

---

12   Ibid., 375.

that comes with democratic socialism. Problems still exist. Chores must still be done. Threats persist. Addressing these realities is best done, though not perfectly so, by a democratic socialist ethos tethered to a pragmatic vision of the world. In place of Adam Smith's elevation of individuals, Dewey sees individuals interested in more than self-preservation or, worse, self-promotion. There simply *must* be more to life than Tik Tok and YouTube videos and the "influencers" they promote.

Dewey distinguishes between functional and acquisitive societies as follows: functional societies have individuals performing their own parts or roles, where these parts and roles are inseparable from the total society and its growth and security; acquisitive societies have individuals performing their own parts or roles, where these parts and roles are the focus at the expense of a greater good. Functional societies require interpersonal collaboration. Acquisitive societies pit individuals against one another to secure financial superiority in constant competition and comparison to others. Functional societies require altruism. Acquisitive societies promote selfishness at the same time as they play on the trope of meritocracy.[13]

How does a functional society come about, then? The answer, for Dewey, is partly through a public schooling process that bridges inquiry and content not divorced from the social and economic realities students (and teachers) already embody in schools. Beyond cliché, schools as embryonic communities are not separate from the publics in which they reside. Social, political, and economic factors *already* color what school does and what school means. An unreflective stance yields schools continuing to reinforce order, control, and a view of preparation that narrowly ties the purpose of schooling (and the purpose of living) to job skills, training, testing and employment. Dewey challenges this view by arguing that the problems of classism and income inequality should become part of the curriculum. Students should not be taught that there are "free markets," when the markets operate in constant mediation of political and regulatory fluctuations to the continued advantage of the rich and at the expense of everyone else.[14] The system is rigged, in other words. Corporations are gaming the system

---

13   Ibid., 410-411.

14   Twenty-six of the richest people in the world have more money than 3.8 *billion* of the rest of the world. See https://www.marketwatch.com/story/worlds-wealthiest-saw-their-fortunes-increase-by-25-billion-a-day-in-2018-oxfam-2019-01-21.

to their advantage and are exploiting schools, teachers, and students in the process. Dewey sees corporations using schools, teachers, and students as unethical. So should you.

Bridging Structural Differences in Economics and Education: Dewey in 2020 and Beyond?

Remember that Dewey's *Ethics* was first written as a textbook with James Hayden Tufts in 1908. It was updated, and expanded, in 1932. Given World War I and the Great Depression in the intervening years, not to mention over-looked-but-significant court cases like *Adair v. U.S.* and *Coppage v. Kansas*,[15] are there significant structural differences between the economics of Dewey's time and the economics of the present? The short answer is yes, but there are also some important similarities that are striking. For instance, in chapter 21 of *Ethics* ("Social Control of Business and Industry"), Dewey writes about the Great Depression, but seems prescient regarding the 2007-8 start of the Great Recession and the 2020 Covid-19 pandemic. He writes that a

> . . . complete change in economic conditions is slowly compelling recognition of the fact that men [*sic*] are likely to be thrown out of work by a general business depression without the least fault or possibility of escape on their part. It is also apparent that, in so far as labor is regarded as a commodity to be bought in the cheap-est market and scrapped like a machine when it is no longer at its maximum efficiency, the older protections against poverty and old age—which existed when the employer had a personal interest in his workmen [*sic*]—no longer exists. A society which claims to be just, to say nothing of being humane, must take account of these changed conditions and make provision, either through the indus-tries themselves, or through government administration, against those contingencies which the present development of industry has brought about. The old maxim was, "Where the tree falls, there let it lie." The modern conscience believes that a society which makes

---

15   *Adair v. U.S.* was the Supreme Court case overturning a 1898 law barring employers from firing employees because they joined a union. See https://supreme.justia.com/cases/federal/us/208/161/; and *Coppage v. Kansas* was a state case arguing the same point. Employees lost in both cases, securing business rights over workers' rights. See https://supreme.justia.com/cases/federal/us/236/1/.

any pretense to understand what it is about should prevent trees from falling—or when this is not possible should at least prevent the fall from crushing the helpless members of the commonwealth.[16]

Dewey is arguing against *laisse faire* libertarianism (think Koch brothers, Ayn Rand, etc.) and for an economic system that safeguards basic work *and* living conditions. While it might be argued, in 2020 and beyond, that democratic socialism is enjoying a resurgence in public discourse, thanks to Alexandria Ocasio-Cortez, Elizabeth Warren, and Bernie Sanders (among others), it faces the same kind of negative reaction and negative stereotypes that existed in Dewey's time. As he noted in the chapter "Toward the Future," it "is absurd to object to a national plan for mitigating suffering and injustice on the ground that it was first tried in Europe. The argument that social insurance is 'paternalistic' or 'socialistic' or 'German' is convenient hokum."[17] "Convenient hokum" means bullshit.

The structural differences between economics and education are few. Given Frederick Taylor's time-and-motion studies merging manufacturing plants and schools, the rise of David Snedden's social-efficiency advocacy in early 20th century debates about the purposes of schooling, and the increased conceptual substitution of education for training, schools operate far more like factories than communities of learners.[18] This point goes beyond bell schedules and the curriculum. The point is that nearly 70 percent of adults in the US believe that schools should focus more on career and technical skills-based classes than on more honors and advanced academic courses.[19] Such preferences indicate the success of a century-old effort to see schools as vocational, even if the majority of schools are not, strictly speaking, named technical and vocational institutions. At least two historical points are worth considering here in order to build the philosophical bridge from Dewey's time to today: The Smith-Hughes Act and globalization after World War II.

Briefly, the Smith-Hughes Act was one of the first times federal money

---

16   Dewey, *Ethics*, 414.

17   Ibid., 433.

18   See Herbert Kliebard, *The Struggle for the American Curriculum, 1893-1958* (New York: Routledge, 2004); and Arthur G. Wirth, *John Dewey as Educator: His Design for Work in Education (1894-1904)* (Malabar, FL: Krieger Publishing Co., 1979).

19   http://neatoday.org/2016/08/29/the-purpose-of-education-pdk-poll/

was spent on state schooling. In 1905, Massachusetts studied the need for vocational training and a national discussion followed concerning agriculture, industry, and home economics. The Smith-Hughes Act embodied "social determinist theory" to identify those unable to do academic work but who were identified as future workers for industry. This simply means that tracking (some call it "ability grouping") was alive and well in 1917. The debate then, as now, was between technocratic indoctrination or humane development of community.[20] As Emery Hislop-Margison notes:

> The debate between Snedden and Dewey . . . reflects many of the arguments . . . on both sides of the vocational education divide. Snedden considered specific skill training an essential educational element to meet existing labor force demands, enhance national competitiveness, and promote economic progress. Advancing an *argumentum ad populum* to support his position, he suggested if Americans were forced to choose between social efficiency and democracy as the basis for public education, they would invariably select the former. Not unlike current social efficiency advocates, then, Snedden equated vocational education with providing students the skills, values and attitudes required by industry. From Dewey's perspective, however, vocational education should be designed to meet student instead of corporate needs and prepare the former for the various challenges of social life rather than for specific occupational roles.[21]

Then, as now, arguments in favor of job preparation saturated media. Promoted by groups like the National Association of Manufacturers, patriotism became synonymous with industrialism. Citizenship narrowed to workforce preparation and jobs became the primary focus of family support. With

---

20   Arthur G. Wirth, "Philosophical Issues in the Vocational-Liberal Studies Controversy (1900-1917): John Dewey vs. The Social Efficiency Philosophers," *Studies in Philosophy of Education* 8, no. 3 (September 1974): 169–182. For an overview of the odd coalition supporting Smith-Hughes, see John Hillison, "The Coalition that Supported the Smith-Hughes Act or a Case for Strange Bedfellows," *Journal of Vocational and Technical Education* 11, no. 2 (Spring 1995): 4-11. See, also, Emery J. Hyslop-Margison, "An Assessment of the Historical Arguments in Vocational Education Reform," Eric Document, no. 435 825 (Washington, DC: ERIC, 1999): 1-14, https://files.eric.ed.gov/fulltext/ED435825. pdf; and Joseph K. Hart, *Education and the Humane Community* (New York: Harper and Brothers, 1951).

21   Hyslop-Margison, 8-9.

World War II, a shift to national defense further reinforced the idea that national interests centered around manufacturing. The military-industrial complex became entrenched and schools were further regarded as sites to produce future workers.[22]

After World War II, economists associated with the Mont Pèlerin Society (MPS) exploited post-war Europe in a strategic effort to expand classical, monetarist economic thought.[23] Milton Friedman, Friedrich von Hayek, and Ludwig von Mises were leading members of the MPS who argued vigorously against government intervention into "free markets," championing instead a vision of capitalism that promoted individualism and competition. Where John Maynard Keynes argued for government expenditures, the MPS essentially argued, and Friedman specifically did, that profit is the only purpose of business.[24] Dewey, though not perfectly aligned with Keynes, viewed business with deep suspicion. In writing about the havoc wrought by the cycles of surplus-recession-depression associated with MPS-like capitalism, Dewey laments that "it is doubtful whether there will be any escape from the cycle so long as business and industry are left to the unlimited control of the profit motive."[25] The consequences, according to Dewey, reinforce a bizarre reality. "Business wants to be left alone by government, but at the same time it virtually admits that it has no plan, except to make as large profits as possible in times of prosperity, and when depression comes to throw the burden of unemployment upon charity"[26] or the very government it appears to hate. Corporations don't want to pay taxes, but they are first in line for "their share" of the trillions of dollars the US government was forced to offer in light of Covid-19. This point is another way to understand how schools are exploited by corporations.

Schools as Democratic, Public Spheres to Critique Business Ethics?

Schools find themselves in a double bind insofar as state governments lure

---

22   Sputnik and the resulting National Defense Education Act of 1958 only reinforced this movement.

23   See Philip Mirowski and Dieter Plehwe, *The Road from Mont Pèlerin: The Making of the Neoliberal Thought Collective* (Cambridge, MA: Harvard University Press, 2015).

24   There were differences between neoliberals and ordoliberals within MPS, to be sure, but the society is staunchly monetarist and exclusionary of state intervention, at least in theory. See Mirowski and Plehwe, 88-123.

25   Dewey, *Ethics*, 383.

26   Ibid.

companies to headquarter or relocate to their area by offering significant tax incentives. Amazon is a recent example, but only because it was so large. Many smaller "deals" are constantly made as part of the globalization/ MPS-approach to trade. As Tyler Mac Innis and Juan Carlos Ordóñez note, using Oregon to illustrate the issues facing all states:

> Over the decades, the Oregon corporate income tax has declined dramatically as a source of revenue. This is evident from several perspectives. First, as a share of the state's economy, corporate tax contributions have shrunk by more than half since the late 1970s. Second, as a share of all income taxes collected in Oregon, corporate income taxes have also contracted. Third, corporate income taxes have eroded to such an extent that the Oregon Lottery now brings in more revenue than the corporate income tax. And fourth, in recent years many profitable corporations have paid nothing or next-to-nothing in income taxes.[27]

The result is that schools are structurally underfunded and, *because of that underfunding*, are then used in school-business partnerships where companies call attention to their generosity. I call this false philanthropy. Dewey called it charity. He also found it ethically dubious when he argued that "to resort to charity to remedy a situation which ought to be prevented by the economic system is a confession of weakness. For charity places the burden not on those who are able, nor on those who have profited most from previous prosperity, but on those who are willing."[28] Partnerships can be terminated and grants to schools from corporations can be withdrawn. Budgets can be cut, too, of course, but tax revenue is far more reliable than donations.[29] Oprah Winfrey, Ellen DeGeneres, and Tyler Perry can donate checks

---

27   Tyler Mac Innis and Juan Carlos Ordóñez, "The Gaming and Decline of Oregon Corporate Taxes," Oregon Center for Public Policy (Portland, OR: OCPP, 2016), 2. https://www.ocpp.org/media/uploads/pdf/2016/06/rpt20160629-corporate-tax-shift _fnl_.pdf

28   Dewey, *Ethics*, 382.

29   I don't have the space to delve into other elements associated with this situation, like wealthy schools versus poorer schools and the fact that wealthy public schools continually "out-raise" other schools or how millage rates (property tax rates) in wealthy areas are significantly *lower* than in depressed or poorer areas, but yield substantially *more* revenue. These issues will have to be for another time. See, however, Jean Anyon, *Radical Possibilities: Public Policy, Urban Education, and A New Social Movement* (New York: Routledge, 2014).

to teachers and schools. We applaud them. We thank them. We appreciate their generosity. That's fine. But we don't seem to realize that celebrities should *not* have to donate to schools in the first place. Schools shouldn't need to sell candles, wrapping paper, or chocolates to take school trips. Teachers shouldn't have to beg for school supplies, either.

The reason we appreciate celebrity donations is because they have become necessary because *public schools are structurally and intentionally underfunded*. Schools as charities are certainly not what Dewey had in mind when he argued for embryonic, democratic communities where students and teachers engage in imaginatively solving social problems. Using corporate tax subsidies and school funding as projects for inquiry and critique is much more in keeping with Dewey's view. Why? Because they take a real-world problem and subject it to questioning. They are not concerned that what they are doing is in some way "political" because they realize that schooling is political. Teaching is political. Learning, too, *is* political. We don't hide behind that fact. We face it. We take up the challenge to avoid partisanship, but we can't divorce inquiry from politics. It's impossible to make that kind of separation, though most traditional teachers sweep the political realities under the rug and side-step the point altogether. This move is a big mistake because it hides or covers over opportunities for learning.

By studying economics as a contested field, Dewey was rejecting the nineteenth century effort to view economics as akin to physics.[30] Part of Dewey's point is that capitalism did not appear out of thin air. Free markets do not naturally occur. They are social vestiges of value: moral commitments that are made and re-made for purposes of power and control. When students understand that economics is not an objective science, they challenge what is otherwise accepted as an "all-knowing" specialization. Belief in objective, *a priori* market ideals masquerading as a physics-like science is arguably part of the reason economists are interviewed and quoted so much, even though they are wrong much of the time.[31] Learning that economics is debatable, ideological, and value-laden means taking the field down from its constructed "perch" and democratizing the thinking about the function of economics in a democratic sphere. Accordingly, learning communities

---

30   William Jevons made this link in 1871.

31   Marion Fourcade, Etienne Ollion, and Yann Algan, "The Superiority of Economists," *Journal of Economic Perspectives* 29, no.1 (Winter 2015): 89–114.

and schools, too, are made and constructed and are never pure and wholly good. They are like nature, for Dewey—evolving contexts requiring constant checks and revisions for the purpose of justice beyond liberty (remember chapter 4).

For a society to advance economic justice, the law and political institutions will need to re-think the purpose of economic policy and practice. For Dewey, there must also be a rethinking of the purpose of education such that economics is tested and rethought by students and teachers in schools. Note this point. Economic policy and practice are not divorced from the purpose of education, but they aren't the sole determination of them, either. In the *Ethics* chapter, "Toward the Future," Dewey stipulates the five central problems to be taken up by schools re-evaluating economics for justice: (1) production and waste; (2) security; (3) worker protections; (4) elevating understanding and taste on the part of consumers; and (5) "problems of a juster [*sic*] distribution of the enormous gains in economic processes—juster both as measured by service to the community, and as measured by the requirements of a functional society."[32] Perhaps this point is the one Dewey advocates most in *Ethics*: functional societies utilize ethics in determining a good life. Regarding economics and ethics, I return to the central question of this chapter. Does Dewey's view of basic economic justice run counter to how public schooling operates in the United States? Yes. It does.

Dewey's view is one in which schools are laboratories for critique, investigation, and critical inquiry, including—as stipulated in this chapter—economics as a field and as a subject. Current schools teach economics largely from one view, i.e., MPS-like neoliberalism: "free markets." So, like other content areas, teaching is essentially telling students "the way the world is." When the Texas state board of education voted not too long ago to get rid of the term "capitalism" in the state's economics curriculum, it was so epithets could not be attached (think "capitalist pig").[33] The phrase that replaced the term was "free market economics" and might represent what Nancy MacLean identifies as "intentional design."[34] Coordinating

---

32 Dewey, *Ethics*, 430.

33 See https://www.washingtonpost.com/outlook/2018/09/21/once-again-texass-board-education-exposed-how-poorly-we-teach-history/.

34 Nancy MacLean, *Democracy in Chains: The Deep History of the Radical Right's Stealth Plan for America* (New York; Penguin Books, 2017), 217.

efforts between the American Legislative Exchange Council (ALEC), the Charles Koch-funded State Policy Network, the Cato Institute, the Foundation for Economic Education, and the Independent Institute has meant a tidal wave of misinformation about climate change, taxes, and the role of public schools in society.[35] If the role and function of public education is to advance a largely one-sided view of job preparation, individualism, competition, and selfishness, then Dewey's view of economic justice has been overtaken by an ethics of business that sees society as merely a grouping of consumers. Gregory Pappas, a Dewey scholar I quoted at the beginning of this chapter, puts it this way: "Even in societies with a political democracy there is growing concern about the deterioration of public discourse and of communal bonds, and the transformation of citizens into apathetic consumers."[36] As Dewey noted, the "point . . . is that exclusive reliance upon the profit motive and upon the supreme importance of wealth tends to distort the proper perspective for life as a whole."[37] Schools subvert this goal of the public good by celebrating and promoting individualist competition tied almost exclusively to job training and future employment. To challenge such a reality requires changing what it means to teach and to learn from acceptance to imaginative critique. It also requires reimagining the function of schools to be places where ethics become central to various fields of inquiry. Otherwise, the public good is merely a phrase for a bumper sticker or a refrigerator magnet.

It's here where we link the background argument and the ultimate point to a case study that starts the next chapter. In the next section, I pick up on an earlier Deweyan point: that businesses exploit schools, teachers, and students for private gain. I explain why corporate exploitation of schools is bad and how teachers might use object lessons to challenge the corporate narrative imposed on themselves, students, and schools.

The Exploiting Business

Exploit (eks-ploit) *n.* [ME. & OFr. *esploit* < L. *explicitum*, neut. pp. of *explicare*: see EXPLICATE] an act remarkable for brilliance

---

35   Ibid., 207*ff.*

36   Pappas, *John Dewey's Ethics*, 10. See, also, Jack Conrad Willers, "Ethics in Educational Policy Analysis," *Philosophical Studies in Education* 17 (1986): 1-11.

37   Dewey, *Ethics*, 437.

or daring; bold deed *–vt.* **1.** to make use of; turn to account; utilize productively **2.** to make unethical use of for one's own advantage or profit; specif., to make profit from the labor of (others).[38]

My claim is this: that school-business partnerships exploit schools in the sense that they make unethical use of schools for their own advantage or profit. School-business partnerships promote consumer materialism, thwart criticality, and negatively alter what it means to be a teacher, student, and citizen. The intention of this section of the chapter is to champion the first definition of "exploit" in order "to make use of, turn to account, [and] utilize productively" school-business partnerships and corporate influence as object lessons for your critical analysis. One way to overcome the negative influence of business partnerships utilizes the partnerships themselves. This part of the chapter shows why exploiting business partnerships is as important to do as it is difficult to achieve. To understand why, let's look at two key concepts: consumer materialism and critical transitivity.

Consumer materialism is the focus only or primarily on goods and ends. Perhaps best characterized by you wanting to know how little you have to do in order to "get" a passing grade or whether you're going to "get" your "money's worth" for a course, consumer materialism evades process in favor of product. Consumer materialism is also the valuing of easy answers over difficult investigation. Linked to convenience, consumer materialism manifests itself in schools via business partnerships when the ends or goods (like exclusive cola contracts, "free" pizza, trips to amusement parks, rewards for promoting "partner" logos, etc.) become the focus. It's also seen when such a focus isn't analyzed or investigated. Said differently, consumer materialism commodifies our existence by reducing searching, being, and thinking. For schooling, it means, in part, that students see their roles as seeking "right" answers to questions instead of searching for meaning by questioning and inquiring. Similarly, teachers see their roles as seeking procedures that will allow the efficient transfer of information from them (or the

---

38   David B. Guralnik, ed., *Webster's New World Dictionary* (New York: Simon and Schuster, 1982), 494.

adopted texts/curriculum) to their students.[39] Recall "banking education" from chapter 2. Teachers demonstrate consumer materialism when they participate in school-business partnerships without questioning and analyzing the ideological, symbolic, and practical consequences of partnering with the private sector in overtly commercial ways.

Critical transitivity is best understood when compared to two other levels of awareness–intransitivity and semi-transitivity. The phrases come from Paulo Freire and intransitivity means "noncritical (in)action." Freire clarifies that intransitivity denies the power of individuals to change their lives when, for example, teachers claim "I can't speak out about school-business partnerships because my school might lose funding . . . that's the 'real world' and I can't do anything about it."[40] Semi-transitivity is characterized by individuals who see the world as changeable, but see the world in unrelated segments such that semi-transitivity is two-dimensional and short term. Business groups may donate money, time, or materials, for example, but teachers do not ask whether businesses are getting tax credits, free advertising, or other "perks."[41] While intransitivity and semi-transitivity are visible in schools, Freire's ultimate goal—critical transitivity—is rarely seen. Critical transitivity is demonstrated when individuals make, according to Ira Shor, "broad connections between individual experience and social issues . . . In education, critically [transitive] teachers and students synthesize personal and social meanings with a specific theme, text, or issue."[42] Students and teachers who critique school-business partnerships rather than seek them out and/or participate in them without question, are demonstrating, in a small way, what critical transitivity means.

My point of connecting consumer materialism and critical transitivity in relation to school-business partnerships is to engage teachers and students

---

39   Peter McLaren uses a similar phrase, "consumer capitalist culture," to make a connection between what he calls postmodern pathologies and the constitution of the body/subject. See Peter McLaren, *Critical Pedagogy and Predatory Culture: Oppositional Politics in a Postmodern Era* (New York: Routledge, 1995). See, also, Deron Boyles, *American Education and Corporations: The Free Market Goes to School* (New York: Taylor and Francis, 2000), 33*ff.*

40   See Paulo Freire, *Education for Critical Consciousness* (New York: Seabury, 1973); and Ira Shor, *Empowering Education* (Chicago: University of Chicago Press, 1992), 127-128. The quotation marks indicate an illustrative hypothetical question, not a direct quote.

41   Freire and Shor, ibid.

42   Shor, *Empowering Education*, 87.

in debates and arguments over the motives for business involvement in schools, the benefits from partnerships for schools versus the benefits for businesses, and what is gained and lost in specific partnerships. Are businesses altruistic in their "support"? How much time and money is spent by school districts in "human hours" securing and maintaining partnerships? If businesses paid non-reduced taxes, would the dollar amount of their "contributions" to schools be greater or smaller than what they would have paid if they had not received a tax break? These are the kinds of questions that critical transitivity requires and are also questions that, by virtue of their being formed and asked, challenge consumer materialist assumptions regarding easy answers and convenient, simple conclusions. Dewey's vision of imaginative teaching requires critical transitivity.

Critical transitivity utilizes processes of investigation that do not accept the rigid realities that Maxine Greene calls the "givens" of an imposed "real world."[43] In this sense, teachers and students would be better off being Deweyan philosophers of education: questioning their own schooling at the very time they are engaged in it. Unfortunately, formal opportunities for questioning are limited as testing-, grading-, and preparation for future life-oriented curricula (i.e., pro consumerism, job and workforce preparation, skills-oriented approaches) are more than plentiful. My concern here is that business partnerships inherently inhibit questioning and instead help develop uncritical consumers rather than critically transitive citizens. Accepted by schools and reinforced in society, business assumptions including consumer materialism and *in*transitivity become beyond question. Unwilling or unable to raise questions out fear of losing their jobs teachers and school leaders often demonstrate for their students what it means to agree to the given of commercialism and consumer materialism. Think "Coca-Cola Day," advertisement-heavy school apps, candy and candle sales, etc. One result is that schools promote non-criticality and confer diplomas to students who are unable to raise questions about motive, meaning, and the consequences of supporting business influences on and in schools. Another cycle is established where business expectations for schools beget schools that push products, provide free advertising, and produce future consumers who, in turn, favor and support business interests and corporate involvement in public

---

43 See Maxine Greene, *The Dialectic of Freedom* (New York: Teachers College Press, 1988), 22 *ff*.

schooling. Some call this a "win-win" situation, but who wins what? Who wins how much? Who wins in the long run?

While I think a compelling case can be made to get rid of school-business partnerships altogether, this part of the chapter (a) assumes school-business partnerships are not going away; and (b) argues that, therefore, schools should exploit their partnerships by engaging in critically transitive investigations of the partnerships themselves. Doing so would demonstrate, in part, what Dewey means by imaginative teaching and learning.

Commercial Intrusion, Profit Margins, and Opportunities for Critique

Schools are so saturated by business partnerships and corporate logic that examples are everywhere. In virtually every neighborhood grocery store, you'll find a program where a percentage of sales will be "donated" to local schools. In Michigan, Glen's Markets has a "Save-Share 2000" plan. The store, like most others, provides a loyalty card and customers swipe their card at the register. From the total bill, one percent or so will be donated to a school the shopper designates, typically in the surrounding community. Interestingly, the store does not keep track of the individual contributions so that those who shop at the store have no idea whether their contribution was made.[44] Harris Teeter has a similar, long-standing program. They boasted, as long ago as 1998, in a letter to River Eves Elementary School (Roswell, GA), that they "gave away $500,000 to 1,955 schools."[45] Each school, in other words, received $255.75. Like Glen's (and Kroger, Publix, Acme, Bruno's, Stop-n-Shop, etc.), Harris Teeter uses schools as no-cost marketing tools for their stores. In the letter to River Eves Elementary, Harris Teeter informed the school that it had only $8.78 earmarked for its school. Since the company will not cut a check for an amount less than $250 (but keeps the interest accrued on such funds?), the school was sent a list of ideas "to increase [their] dollars earned." The suggestions included posting the Harris Teeter account number on the school's marquee as well as in sight of the carpool line. The suggestions also included advertising the program in the school newsletter, announcing the program at school events and PTA meetings, and copying reminder cards to be distributed to parents. For $250,

---

44   Glen's Market flyer, "This Year, We Plan to Share," August 30, 2000.

45   Carol Trout to Eve Neumeister, letter dated 27 October 1999, in author's possession. See also, https://www.harristeeter.com/assets/images/TIE_OfficialRules_17-18.pdf

DEWEY'S ETHICS APPLIED TO SCHOOLS

Harris Teeter gets free advertising in a variety of ways (the school marquee, newsletters, handouts, and announcements) and the school spends money and time on paper, printing, and "human hours" devoted to advertising. The "River Eves Eagles Newsletter" did, indeed, include a "front page" headline proclaiming, "Hooray for River Eves Business Partners."[46]

Lakeside High School, in Atlanta, Georgia, participated in a program that many other schools also adopted. They had "The Student Planner," which was a calendar for students. Distributed by the American Student Activity Planner, LLC, 1,650,000 copies were handed out nationwide. The copies were free because sponsors underwrite the cost of the calendar by including advertisements throughout the document. Sixteen pages–out of one hundred and sixty pages—were for Lakeside's listing of policies, phone numbers, the alma mater, discipline code, etc. The rest of the spiral booklet had calendars on the right page, while the left side had full page advertisements. One hundred and forty-two pages (out of 160) included some form of advertisement. Advertisers included Paramount Pictures, AT&T, Barra-Quda.com, Roxy Watches, OTB ("One Tough Brand" for "young men & boys," "One Tuff Babe" for "juniors and girls"), DKNY Jeans, SeanJohn. com, PacSun, Muddjeans.com, Gellyroll pens, Toyota, Best Buy, T.J.Maxx, U.S. Coast Guard, and Quicksilver. Each page showed weekly dates and times and had at the top of each page a smaller advertisement. Certain dates within the weekly calendar listing encouraged students to "Let Madame Clizia predict your future @ Muddjeans.com."[47] SAT and ACT registration deadlines and test dates were noted, as is the promise to "Win Cool Prizes– Today Only @ www.gellyroll.com."[48] One advertisement by PNB Nation (a clothing web site) explained its initials: "PNB nation stands for 'post no bills.' The term [sic] 'post no bills' means, 'do not put up advertisements.' We have used this term as a metaphor for individuals to not put up false images of themselves, but to represent whoever they are . . ."[49] The irony of

---

46   "River Eves Elementary School Newsletter," November 5, 1999, 1.

47   "2000-2001 Student Planner," Lakeside High School, Atlanta, Georgia, 70. An updated version of this problem can be found at https://techwiser.com/homework-planner-apps-for-students/. As with many student technology initiatives, not only is advertising a concern, but also student privacy and the tracking that is done by online programs and apps.

48   Ibid., 97.

49   Ibid., 146.

this advertisement is at least two-fold: (1) "post no bills" is not a term, but a phrase; and (2) the claim is self-refuting of the advertisement itself.

Coca-Cola has a summer "economics" institute program to promote competitive business practices. Nissan automobile dealerships participate in "automotive services apprenticeships." CiCi's Pizza sets aside one night per month when students and parents from participating schools come to the restaurant. A percentage of the net sales (not gross) is "donated" to the school—a point I explain later in terms of Chick-fil-A. Subway provides "free" subs to a local school and a representative from the store, in order to make an "educational" link, comes to the school as a guest speaker on "health occupations." McDonald's secures itself as part of a cafeteria "choice" program in a Colorado school and offers business credit to students who "intern" as cooks and servers. In August 2000, National Public Radio reported the case of a father in Ohio who sued his local school to stop the school from giving student information to local banks who contact students about setting up savings accounts. The principal of the school, demonstrating either intransitivity or semitransitivity, interpreted the suit as a nuisance and he defended the bank as being a "friend to the school." Twenty years later and there are multiple lawsuits concerning student data being sold or hacked.[50]

The General Accounting Office (GAO) wrote a report warning of the increase in commercialization in schools. As noted in a *New York Times* article:

> The G.A.O. report cites textbook covers distributed by Clairol, Ralph Lauren, and Philip Morris with company names and logos fully displayed. In New York City, the Board of Education is considering a plan that would provide computers for all of its students, starting in the fourth grade. The computers might carry ads and possibly encourage shopping on a particular Web site.[51]

---

50   See https://www.washingtonpost.com/education/2019/09/11/is-new-york-state-about-gut-its-student-data-privacy-law/; https://edscoop.com/college-board-student-data-lawsuit/; and https://corpwatch.org/article/lawsuit-against-google-highlights-mining-student-data.

51   Constance L. Hays, "Commercialism in U.S. Schools is Examined in New Report," *The New York Times* (14 September 2000): C1 and C25, C1.

Those concerns have already become reality. In the past twenty years, student data has become a prime target for corporations and marketers.[52] Far from being limited to dated supermarket programs, school-business partnerships are increasing in number and variety and arguably represent a larger, exploitative agenda. The agenda is a pro-business, pro-capitalist, pro-careerist one that excludes questions about whether businesses exploit workers and consumers, whether capitalism is the only or best economic theory, and whether elementary school students should be forced to consider their future based *not* on "What do you want to *be* when you grow up?" questions, but "What do you want to *do* when you grow up?" questions.[53]

Typical of the agenda identified above, the Cobb County (GA) Chamber of Commerce lists the benefits of school-business partnerships as follows: "Present firsthand requirements, satisfactions, and expectations of the business world . . . Alert teachers to the job skills applicants need and help them find ways to develop these skills . . . Help develop career awareness geared to specific local job-market needs both now and in the future . . . Gain understanding of the school systems, whose health is vital to the economic wellbeing of the community . . . Become known as a community involved company which adds to your public relations efforts."[54] Note the slant. The benefits are for businesses, but schools are referred to in ways that assume them to be beneficiaries as well. It does not follow that the benefits for the schools are anything more than residual. The benefits also appear linked to the kind of fiscal policies that primarily favor businesses. Teachers are supposed to teach their students what businesses desire in terms of "job skills."

---

52   See, for example, https://www.politico.com/story/2014/05/data-mining-your-children-106676; https://www.brookings.edu/wp-content/uploads/2016/06/04-education-technology-west.pdf, and http://www.columbia.edu/~rsb2162/Encyclopedia%20Chapter%20Draft%20v10%20-fw.pdf.

53   To be clear, capitalism *may* be the best economic theory ("at least compared to all the rest," as the phrase is usually stated), but my point is not to have the assumption accepted without Deweyan investigation.

54   "Benefits of School Partnerships to the Business and School," Cobb Chamber of Commerce (Education Department), 3. For a detailed treatment of a state-wide business initiative (Michigan) to reform schools, see John W. Sipple, "Institutional Constraints on Business Involvement in K-12 Education Policy," *American Educational Research Journal* 36, no. 3 (Fall, 1999): 447-488. There are plenty of recent examples, too. See https://www.uschamberfoundation.org/event/career-readiness-business-led-approach-supporting-k-12-schools; and the Campaign for a Commercial- Free Childhood, https://commercialfreechildhood.org/.

Businesses benefit from learning more about schools, but for the purpose of the "economic well-being of the community." To the possible question "why should my business get involved," the chamber of commerce already provides the answer: so your business will be *perceived* as being involved in the community, "which adds to your public relations efforts."

Schools are faced with programs connecting them with businesses while also having other outside forces further the idea that schools and businesses should become even more closely aligned.[55] The problem with this is that students and teachers become subsumed in a market logic that, in part because of its pervasiveness, seems above critique.[56] Fortunately, there are examples of those working to thwart further corporate encroachment. In university communications departments, students study media for their symbolism, hidden messages, overt messages, aesthetics, etc. Guided by experts in the field, the meanings of ads are identified, revealed, and debated. Much like in textual analysis, literary criticism, and studies of pop culture, the ads become examples to investigate. School-business partnerships offer the same opportunity. Consider one example.

After studying school-business partnerships, critical transitivity, and a variety of other related topics during a university summer term, a middle school music teacher returned to her classroom for the fall semester. Her intention was to explore the possibility that her fifth grade students might alter the climate of their classroom by questioning the school-business partnership program she operated to fund set production for school musicals. Relating her experiences, the student wrote the following to me:

---

55   See Alex Molnar, *Giving Kids the Business: The Commercialization of America's Schools* (Boulder, CO: Westview, 1996), 166-184; Deron Boyles, ed., *The Corporate Assault on Youth: Commercialism, Exploitation, and the End of Innocence* (New York: Peter Lang, 2008); Tal Gilead, "Education and the Logic of Economic Progress," *Journal of Philosophy of Education* 46, 1 (2012): 113-131; and Kenneth J. Saltman, *Scripted Bodies: Corporate Power, Smart Technologies, and the Undoing of Public Education* (New York: Routledge, 2016).

56   See Pam Bettis, "Corporate Discourses in School: Adapting to the Prevailing Economic Climate," *Educational Foundations* (Winter, 2000): 23-49; Abe Feuerstein, "Selling Our Schools? Principals' Views on Schoolhouse Commercialism and School Business Interactions," paper presented to the American Educational Studies Association, November 1-5, 2000, Vancouver, British Columbia, Canada; Trevor Norris, *Consuming Schools: Commercialism and the End of Politics* (Toronto: University of Toronto Press, 2011); and Catherine Gidney, *Captive Audience: How Corporations Invaded our Schools* (Toronto: Between the Lines Publishing, 2019).

> I had to let you know about several classroom conversations today.
> . . . I introduced my fifth graders to a new concept–critical transi-
> tivity! I shared with them my dilemma regarding the "Box Tops
> for Education" [General Mills initiative whereby tops from cereal
> boxes are collected for money] fund raiser for the coming year. We
> talked about the large profit margin for General Mills and the free
> advertising I'd provided for the past two years. I then asked them
> why General Mills would want to "help" schools like this. After a
> brief silence, one little boy said, "They want to control schools."
> Another little girl corrected him and said, "they want to manipu-
> late schools!" I almost fell over in amazement. From the mouths
> of babes! "We" decided, collectively, not to continue the Box Tops
> campaign.[57]

Only anecdotal evidence, and only in one classroom, the example nonetheless gives us a glimpse of the challenge. Forget for the moment that the
teacher considered the change a success. One might, for example, wonder
whether the teacher is accurate in her assessment that the students learned
or demonstrate critical transitivity. They might have been led to the conclusion the teacher wanted and thus void the larger claim. Yet, there might be
enough of a glimpse in what the teacher wrote to suggest that she really did
demonstrated the larger point being made here. Including the students in the
inquiry is vital, even though the set-up was suggested (that the teacher had a
dilemma regarding the "Box Tops for Education" program). Their respons-
es, little cynics though they may appear, indicate a level of sophistication
and understanding that, should schools provide the opportunity for their
development, would go a long way toward developing critical consumers
and more discriminating citizens in line with Dewey's imaginative vision of
teaching and learning.

Getting the teacher to consider a critical stance regarding school-business partnerships was not an easy process, however. This teacher was not
initially willing to consider that the business she courted could be seen as
anything other than helpful. It took a variety of examples and lots of conversation to move the student from intransitivity to critical transitivity.

---

57 Shelly Hall to author, e-mail dated 17 August 2000, in author's possession.

Indeed, the revelation and refutation of her pre-existing beliefs resulted in her proclaiming, as though she just realize she had been "had" or "taken," that she had been a "Cap'n Crunch pimp" for years.

To look at school-business partnerships differently, some guiding questions might help:

1. What is the primary reason for entering into the school-business partnership?

2. Whose interests are being served? Who benefits? Who benefits most? Who benefits in the long run?

3. How much time is given to the business part of the school-business partnership? What amount, in terms of teacher (or administrator) salary, does the time equal on an hourly basis?

4. What is learned as a result of the partnership? In addition to the claims associated with specific projects, what is the larger message or meaning being conveyed to students?

5. Are business partners willing to share financial information with teachers and students regarding their benefits from the partnership? Is independent auditing an option?

6. Can individual teachers or classes opt out of partnership programs?

These and other questions might form the basis of an initial critique of school-business partnerships. The student in the example asked at least some of these and used them to guide her actions. My point is not, however, to impose the questions as though the list is complete or exhaustive.

My point is to illustrate how using school-business partnerships as object lessons goes toward critical transitivity and critical consumerism. The teacher noted, in fact, that "one small effort has been made in developing critical transitivity."[58] It is not a complete package to be "had" just because one program was challenged. What other programs, inside or outside the specific school in the example, might also offer opportunities for further critique? Such a question goes to the Deweyan point that problems solved only

---

58   Ibid.

reveal other problems to be solved in such a way that habits of the mind are formed from educative experiences. The example is not yet educative in the sense that we do not know whether further learning and further educative experiences followed. Still, Dewey would have to be pleased that students were engaged, actions were taken, and a problem was identified and temporarily solved.

One caution to repeat is that teachers have plenty of curriculum mandates to keep them busy with objectives, goals, and testable material. Adding to the curriculum isn't my intention. Instead, the point is to take what is already a part of school life–and an increasing part of school life–and raise questions about it. The not-so-covert intention here is to reveal how school-business partnerships are pushing uncritical consumerism into what businesses no longer consider schools, but markets.[59] For such a viewpoint to go unchallenged will mean giving over to businesses the markets they so eagerly crave. Businesses exist to make money. Public schools don't. By carefully examining school-business partnerships, such distinctions may help to reveal larger ethical and social concerns, namely, the concentration of power by the wealthiest businesspeople. As Dewey wrote in *Reconstruction in Philosophy*:

> In spite of its interest in a thoroughly social aim, utilitarianism fostered a new class interest, that of the capitalistic property-owning interests, provided only property was obtained through free competition and not by governmental favor. The stress that [Jeremy] Bentham put on security tended to consecrate the legal institution of private property provided only certain legal abuses in connection with its acquisition and transfer were abolished . . . provided possessions had been obtained in accord with the rules of the competitive game–without, that is, extraneous favors from government. Thus utilitarianism gave intellectual confirmation to all those tendencies which make "business" not a means of social service and

---

59 See Michael Engel, *The Struggle for Control of Public Education: Market Ideology vs. Democratic Values* (Philadelphia: Temple University Press, 2000); See, also, Richard Brosio, *A Radical Democratic Critique of Capitalist Education* (New York: Peter Lang, 1994); and and Daniel P. Liston, *Capitalist Schools: Explanation and Ethics in Radical Studies of Schooling* (New York: Routledge, 1988).

an opportunity for personal growth in creative power but a way of accumulating the means of private enjoyments.[60]

Schools, as extensions of government, are being delivered to corporations just like Dewey notes. The "social service" and "personal growth in creative power" that schools *can* offer is consistently under attack by commercial interests. This, again, is the second definition of "exploit" from above–"to make unethical use of for one's own profit; specifically, to make profit from the labor of (others)." Combating the second definition is the first definition: "to make use of; to turn to account; utilize productively." In terms of school-business partnerships, teachers and students should demonstrate the first definition by investigating—in critically transitive and imaginative ways—the influence and effect school-business partnerships have on their classroom, school, and lives outside of school. This is ethics in the real world. This is Dewey's vision of imaginative teaching.

Also in the real world are more and more lesson plans being supplied to teachers and schools by businesses and other organizations.[61] I turn, in the next chapter, to a case study of one such curriculum mandate. It's based on the perceived need that schools teach character. Dewey was fine with this idea, writing in *Democracy and Education* that "manners are but minor morals."[62] What's not ok with Dewey, however, is the imposition of a curriculum developed by a fast-food chain that was headed by an avowed fundamentalist Christian. I'll unpack several problems in the case study and link it to the important topic of diversity but note one obvious problem: the lesson wasn't written by teachers and the point of the lesson might undermine its own stated goals.

---

60 John Dewey, *Reconstruction in Philosophy* (Boston: Beacon Press, 1920), 182-183.

61 And other teachers. The websites TeachersPayTeachers and WeAreTeachers are example of the consumer mentality Dewey's criticizing. See https://www.teacherspay teachers.com/and https://www.weareteachers.com/.

62 John Dewey, *Democracy and Education* (New York: The Free Press, 1916), 22.

References

Adair v. United States. 208. U.S. 161 (1908). https://supreme.justia.com/cases/federal/us/208/161/

Altman, Andrew. "John Dewey and Contemporary Normative Ethics." *Metaphilosophy* 13 (2) 1982: 149–60.

Anyon, Jean. *Radical Possibilities: Public Policy, Urban Education, and a New Social Movement.* New York: Routledge, 2014.

Baker, Ryan. (Forthcoming). "Data Mining for Education." In *International Encyclopedia of Education,* 3rd ed., edited by Barry McGaw, Penelope Peterson, and Eva Baker. Oxford: Elsevier. http://www.columbia.edu/~rsb2162/Encyclopedia%20Chapter%20Draft%20v10%20-fw.pdf.

Bettis, Pam. "Corporate Discourses in School: Adapting to the Prevailing Economic Climate." *Educational Foundations* (1) 2000: 23–49.

Boyles, Deron. *American Education and Corporations: The Free Market Goes to School.* New York: Taylor & Francis, 2000.

Boyles, Deron, ed. *The Corporate Assault on Youth: Commercialism, Exploitation, and the End of Innocence.* New York: Peter Lang, 2008.

Brosio, Richard. *A Radical Democratic Critique of Capitalist Education.* New York: Peter Lang, 1994.

Campaign for a Commercial-Free Childhood. 2020. https://commercialfreechildhood.org/.

Campbell, James. *Understanding John Dewey.* Chicago: Open Court Publishing, 1995.

Cobb Chamber of Commerce, Education Department. (2001). Benefits of School Partnerships to the Business and School. https://www.cobbchamber.org/member-services/education-programs.aspx.

Coppage v. Kansas. 236 U.S. 1 (1915). https://supreme.justia.com/cases/federal/us/236/1/

Dewey, John. *Reconstruction in Philosophy.* New York: Henry Holt, 1920.

Dewey, John. *The Public and its Problems.* New York: Henry Holt, 1927.

Dewey, John. *Ethics* (1932). In *The Later Works of John Dewey, 1925–1953: Volume 7. 1932: Ethics,* edited by Jo Ann Boydston. Carbondale: Southern Illinois University Press, 1981.

Engel, Michael. *The Struggle for Control of Public Education: Market Ideology vs. Democratic Values.* Philadelphia: Temple University Press, 2000.

Feuerstein, Abe. "Selling our Schools? Principals' Views on Schoolhouse Commercialism and School Business Interactions." Paper presented to the *American Educational Studies Association,* Vancouver, British Columbia, Canada, November 1–5, 2000.

Foresman, Betsy. "College Board Sold Student Data for 47 Cents Each, Lawsuit Claims." *edScoop,* December 16, 2016. https://edscoop.com/college-board-student-data-lawsuit/.

Fourcade, Marion, Etienne Ollion, and Yann Algan. "The Superiority of Economists." *Journal of Economic Perspectives* 29 (1) 2015: 89–114.

Freire, Paulo. *Education for Critical Consciousness.* New York: Seabury, 1973.

Gidney, Catherine. *Captive Audience: How Corporations Invaded our Schools.* Toronto: Between the Lines Publishing, 2019.

Gilead, Tal. "Education and the Logic of Economic Progress." *Journal of Philosophy of Education* 46 (1) 2012: 113–31.

Grange, Joseph. "The Disappearance of the Public Good: Confucius, Dewey, Rorty." *Philosophy East and West* 46 (3) 1996: 351–66.

Greene, Maxine. *The Dialectic of Freedom.* New York: Teachers College Press, 1988.

Guralnik, David B., ed. *Webster's New World Dictionary.* New York: Simon and Schuster, 1982.

Hart, Joseph K. *Education and the Humane Community.* New York: Harper and Brothers, 1951.

Hays, Constance L. "Commercialism in U.S. Schools Is Examined in New Report. *The New York Times,* September 14, 2000, C1, C25.

Hillison, John. "The Coalition that Supported the Smith-Hughes Act or a Case for Strange Bedfellows." *Journal of Vocational and Technical Education* 11 (2) 1995: 4–11.

Honneth, Axel. "Between Proceduralism and Teleology: An Unresolved Conflict in Dewey's Moral Theory." *Transactions of the Charles S. Peirce Society* 34 (3) 1998: 689–711.

Hyslop-Margison, Emery J. "An Assessment of the Historical Arguments in Vocational Education Reform" (ED435825). Washington, DC: ERIC, 1999.

Kliebard, Herbert. *The Struggle for the American Curriculum, 1893–1958.* New York: Routledge, 1995.

Kollmeyer, Barbara. "World's Wealthiest Saw their Fortunes Increase by $2.5 Billion a Day in 2018: Oxfam." *Market Watch,* January 21, 2019. https://www.marketwatch.com/story/worlds-wealthiest-saw-their-fortunes-increase-by-25-billion-a-day-in-2018-oxfam-2019-01-21.

Liston, Daniel P. *Capitalist Schools: Explanation and Ethics in Radical Studies of Schooling.* New York: Routledge, 1988.

Mac Innis, Tyler, and Juan Carlos Ordóñez. "The Gaming and Decline of Oregon Corporate Taxes." Portland: Oregon Center for Public Policy. 2016. https://www.ocpp.org/media/uploads/pdf/2016/06/rpt20160629-corporate-tax-shift_fnl_.pdf.

MacLean, Nancy. *Democracy in Chains: The Deep History of the Radical Right's Stealth Plan for America.* New York: Penguin Books, 2017.

McLaren, Peter. *Critical Pedagogy and Predatory Culture: Oppositional Politics in a Postmodern Era.* New York: Routledge, 1995.

Mirowski, Philip, and Dieter Plehwe. *The Road from Mont Pèlerin: The Making of the Neoliberal Thought Collective.* Cambridge, MA: Harvard University Press, 2015.

Molnar, Alex. *Giving Kids the Business: The Commercialization of America's Schools.* Boulder, CO: Westview, 1996.

Norris, Trevor. *Consuming Schools: Commercialism and the End of Politics.* Toronto: University of Toronto Press, 2011.

Pappas, Gregory. *John Dewey's Ethics: Democracy as Experience.* Bloomington: Indiana University Press, 2008.

Perillo, Jonna. "Once Again, Texas's Board of Education Exposed How Poorly We Teach." *The Washington Post,* September 21, 2018. https://www.washington

post.com/outlook/2018/09/21/once-again-texass-board-education-exposed-how-poorly-we-teach-history/.

Putnam, Hilary. *Renewing Philosophy.* Cambridge, MA: Harvard University Press, 1992.

Saltman, Kenneth J. *Scripted Bodies: Corporate Power, Smart Technologies, and the Undoing of Public Education.* New York: Routledge, 2016.

Shor, Ira. *Empowering Education.* Chicago: University of Chicago Press, 1992.

Simons, Stephanie. "The Big Biz of Spying on Little Kids." *Politico,* May 5, 2014. https://www.politico.com/story/2014/05/data-mining-your-children-106676.

Sipple, John W. "Institutional Constraints on Business Involvement in K–12 Education Policy." *American Educational Research Journal* 36 (3) 1999: 447–88.

Strauss, Valerie. "Is New York State about to Gut its Student Data Privacy Law." *The Washington Post,* September 11, 2019. https://www.washingtonpost.com/education/2019/09/11/is-new-york-state-about-gut-its-student-data-privacy-law/.

Telbis, Rozali. Lawsuit against Google Highlights Mining of Student Data. *Corp-Watch: Holding Corporations Accountable,* May 26, 2014. https://corpwatch.org/article/lawsuit-against-google-highlights-mining-student-data.

Tiles, J. E. *Dewey.* New York: Routledge, 1988.

US Chamber of Commerce Foundation. "U.S. Chamber of Commerce Foundation Youth Employment Series. Career Readiness: A Business Led Approach for Supporting K-12 Schools." September 19, 2016. https://www.uschamberfoundation.org/event/career-readiness-business-led-approach-supporting-k-12-schools.

Walker, Tim. "What's the Purpose of Education? Public Doesn't Agree on the Answer." *neaToday,* August 29, 2016. http://neatoday.org/2016/08/29/the-purpose-of-education-pdk-poll/.

Welchman, Jennifer. *Dewey's Ethical Thought.* Ithaca, NY: Cornell University Press, 1995.

West, Darryl. *Big Data for Education: Data Mining, Data Analytics, and WEB Dashboards.* Governance Studies at Brookings. Washington, DC: Brookings Institution, 2012. https://www.brookings.edu/wp-content/uploads/2016/06/04-education-technology-west.pdf.

Willers, Jack Conrad. "Ethics in Educational Policy Analysis," *Philosophical Studies in Education* 17 (i) 1986: 1–11.

Wirth, Arthur G. "Philosophical Issues in the Vocational-Liberal Studies Controversy (1900-1917): John Dewey vs. the Social Efficiency Philosophers." *Studies in Philosophy of Education* 8 (3) 1974: 169–82.

Wirth, Arthur G. *John Dewey as Educator: His Design for Work in Education (1894–1904).* Malabar, FL: Krieger Publishing, 1979.

CHAPTER SIX

DEWEY AND DIVERSITY

IN THIS FINAL CHAPTER, I address issues of diversity and the relationship between diversity and Dewey's view of imaginative teaching. I do so in what might seem like an odd way: I primarily focus on religious diversity. I begin this chapter with a case study that involves curriculum, character, diversity, and teacher autonomy. Each of these topics is rethought in light of religion, specifically fundamentalist Christianity. But the topic of religious fundamentalism in the case study is also representative of the struggle between standardized expectations for teaching and learning that marginalize difference in other ways, too. The critical way I approach the case study might also be helpful in showing how criticism can be used to reveal otherwise hidden meaning and power. The goal is to show where and how teacher and student power is subsumed under ideological and market forces—in this case with religion as the cover for character education.

I then move to another, more personal illustration of Dewey's philosophy of education in practice that also raises further questions about diversity. I retell my experience as a fifth grader and the Deweyan project we undertook involving Thanksgiving. I also problematize elements of my experience with the benefit of hindsight that does not regress or lessen itself to the kind of woke presentism I also question at the end of the chapter. I close the chapter by highlighting debates about whether Dewey was a racist, a sexist, and an ethnocentrist. He wasn't any of these things, but I'd be wrong not to share with you some of the work that makes such charges. I don't engage the complexity of every aspect of diversity, but I provide sources that can be read to figure out for yourselves what you think Dewey's view of diversity was. I note work that calls Dewey's appreciation of diversity into question, but I don't spend a lot of time dealing with their concerns. Still, this chapter highlights the importance of diversity and how Dewey's philosophical and theoretical concerns influence practical realities in classrooms. In all, this chapter draws on the previous chapters to close out the book in what should be typical Deweyan fashion: messy questions and continuing inquiry. First, some historical background on character education, then the actual details of a curriculum mandate that raises questions about ethics, diversity, and imaginative teaching.

Character Education: History and Case Study

"Character education" represents a long-standing staple of U.S. schools. From the "Old Deluder Satan" Law of 1647 to *The New England Primer* in the eighteenth century to McGuffey Readers from the late 1830s (and well into the 1920s), the idea of transmitting core values to the young is so deeply rooted in the history of schooling that morality is often assumed to be a given.[1] Over time, various social and religious concerns merged into a taken-for-granted assumption that schools should play a major role in transmitting "good character" and fostering character development. In current schools, state curricula include character education and a series of groups have been established to advance the idea that character education is fundamental to schooling the United States.

National programs that currently exist include, among others, "Character Counts!" from the Josephson Institute and "A 12-Point Comprehensive Approach to Character Education" from The Center for the 4th and 5th Rs (respect and responsibility). Other national and international organizations

---

1   See, for example, Richard Mosier, *Making the American Mind: Social and Moral Ideas in the McGuffey Readers* (New York: Russell & Russell, 1965); Carl F. Kaestle, *Pillars of the Republic: Common Schools and American Society, 1780-1860* (New York: Hill and Wang, 1983); Joel Spring, *The American School, 1642-2004* (Boston: McGraw-Hill, 2005); Thomas Lickona, *Character Matters: How to Help Our Children Develop Good Judgement, Integrity, and Other Essential Virtues* (New York: Simon and Schuster, 2004); Ernest J. Zarra, "Pinning Down Character Education," *Kappa Delta Pi Record* 36, no. 4 (Summer 2000): 154-157; and Mary M. Williams, "Models of Character Education: Perspectives and Development Issues," *Journal of Humanistic Counseling, Education and Development* 39, no. 1 (September 2000): 32-40. See, also, Martin E. Marty and R. Scott Appleby, eds., *Fundamentalism and Society: Reclaiming the Science, the Family, and Education* (Chicago: The University of Chicago Press, 1997).

include the Character Education Partnership (CEP) and The Institute for Global Ethics.[2] These groups proclaim themselves to be non-partisan and each identifies universal values that should be adopted, though the number of values varies. Michael Josephson developed "Character Counts!" the most widely used character education program in the US. Josephson retired from careers in law, business, and education to run the Joseph and Edna Josephson Institute, named for his parents. He serves the organization without a salary and all proceeds from speaking engagements and written work are stated as going directly back into the non-profit institute.[3] The Center for the 4th and 5th Rs is led by Thomas Lickona, a professor of educational psychology at the State University of New York-Cortland. The Center for the 4th and 5th Rs is a university bureau committed to "building a moral society and developing schools which are civil and caring communities."[4] Lickona is a widely published author who also serves on the board of the CEP. Josephson and Lickona, however, are not the only ones influencing character education programs. Truett Cathy also continues to influence character education curriculum in the US.

Cathy was the founder and CEO of Chick-fil-A, the fast food restaurant headquartered in Georgia. Cathy was also an avowed Christian fundamentalist.[5] He donated an "age-appropriate" (protestant) Bible to every school library in the state of Georgia in 2003. He was also the financial resource behind the national Core Essentials character education initiative based in Georgia and through his financing, Chick-fil-A sponsors the teacher's guides sent to each school.[6] In addition, Cathy teamed with William Bennett to

---

2   See, for example, http://www.character.org, http://www.charactercounts.org, and http://www.cortland.edu/c4n5rs/.

3   See http://www.charactercounts.org. See also, Michael Josephson, "Character Education is Back in Our Public Schools," *The State Education Standard* (Autumn 2002): 41-45; and https://whatwillmatter.com/2011/10/what-will-matter-745-3/.

4   http://www2.cortland.edu/centers/character/. See, also, Thomas Lickona, *Character Matters: How to Help Our Children Develop Good Judgment, Integrity, and Other Essential Virtues* (New York: Simon and Schuster, 2004).

5   See S. Truett Cathy, *Eat MOR Chikin: Inspire More People Doing Business the Chick-fil-A Way* (Nashville: Cumberland House Publishing, 2002); S. Truett Cathy, *It's Easier to Succeed Than Fail* (Nashville: Thomas Nelson Publishers, 1989); and Ken Blanchard and S. Truett Cathy, *The Generosity Factor* (Grand Rapids, MI: Zondervan, 2002). Both Thomas Nelson and Zondervan are Christian publishing houses.

6   Core Essentials, *Core Essentials: A Strategy for Teaching Character* (Alpharetta, GA: Core Essentials, Inc., 2001). See, also, https://coreessentials.org/.

offer wrist bands as part of "kid's meals" at various Chick-fil-A stores. The
wrist bands tout such values as "respect," "courage," and "honesty." This
part of the chapter explores three main lines of inquiry: 1) the specifics
of "Core Essentials" as a strategy for teaching character; 2) the role, and
ironies, of private businesses influencing public school curricula; and 3) the
assumptions inherent in the kind of teaching of character outlined by Core
Essentials. Like the overall point of this book, we're looking at influences
that restrict Dewey's notion of imaginative teaching. At risk of repeating
myself, I just want to be clear: this is a case study about the problematic
enterprise of teaching character, itself, as if it's an unquestionable topic. As
noted earlier, the case study comes at the question of diversity in a slightly
different way than diversity is usually discussed. That is, diversity is usually
understood in terms of race, gender, class, and sexuality. I will address those
elements toward the end of the chapter, but I begin with a case that highlights how religion and business are used in public schools to limit diversity.
I also use Theodore Brameld's *Ends and Means in Education*, John Dewey's
Moral Principles in Education, and Pierre Bourdieu's *Acts of Resistance* and
Firing Back to tie together ethical theory from chapter 5 to diversity issues
in this chapter.[7]

Since Truett Cathy was a fundamentalist Christian as well as private
businessman, I question why then-Georgia State Superintendent of Schools,
Kathy Cox, in a July 1, 2003 letter to Georgia school principals, accepted
Cathy's donated Bibles, as noted above. She wrote that Truett Cathy was
"a pioneering businessman" whose "generosity" allowed for an "age-appropriate Bible" to be placed in every school library in the state. She also
wrote that Truett Cathy's "initiative has been completely funded by Mr.
Cathy. No state funds have been used to supply this book to your school.
Mr. Cathy has a passion for helping children, and he sees this as another
way to encourage the youth of our great state."[8] What does the distinction between state and private funds for Bible purchases and placement

---

7   Theodore Brameld, *Means and Ends in Education: A Midcentury Appraisal* (New
York: Harper and Row Publishers, 1950); John Dewey, *Moral Principles in Education*
(Carbondale, IL: Southern Illinois University Press, 1909); Pierre Bourdieu, *Acts of Re-
sistance: Against the Tyranny of the Market* (New York: The New Press, 1998), trans.
Richard Nice; and Pierre Bourdieu, *Firing Back: Against the Tyranny of the Market 2*
(New York: The New Press, 2003), trans., Loïc Wacquant.

8   Kathy Cox, letter to school principals, July 1, 2003.

mean for diversity? Does the fact that a Christian fundamentalist funded a character education program represent any challenges or concerns for, say, students who are Jewish or Agnostic or Muslim? Is there any connection between Kathy Cox's endorsement of Cathy and Cox's claim that the term "evolution" is a "buzzword" that should be replaced in the state curriculum of Georgia?[9] If Truett Cathy was interested in the welfare of children, why would he promote unhealthy fast food as part of a character education program that touts "honesty" as a virtue? Indeed, what assumptions are made by Cathy, furthered by the state, and pushed into the hands of teachers by the private, non-profit Core Essentials organization that Cathy's profits from Chick-fil-A support?

The Program Itself: An Overview of Various Aspects

The Chick-fil-A website reveals an interesting point. On the page displaying information regarding Chick-fil-A's support of Core Essentials, the company also notes the following:

> Amid our nation's growing concern for children's character development, Chick-fil-A has found a way to help. Since 2000 we've been a national sponsor of Core Essentials, an educational program that gives teachers and parents tools for imparting key values to elementary-age boys and girls. By teaching inner beliefs and attitudes such as honesty, patience, respect, orderliness and courage, Core Essentials helps children treat others right, make smart decisions, and maximize their potential. The entire program teaches 27 values over a three-year period. To learn more about Core Essentials, contact a Chick-fil-A franchisee in your area.[10]

The website also notes that there are "tools" and "free stuff" for teachers to help in the teaching of character. The curriculum is separated into four areas: seedlings, core, reconnect, and canopy.[11]

---

9   See Mary MacDonald, "Georgia May Shun 'Evolution' in Schools: Revised Curriculum Plan Outrages Science Teachers," *The Atlanta Journal-Constitution* (29 January 2004): A1.

10   https://coreessentials.org/cfa_partners.

11   https://coreessentials.org/#cev-section-home-curriculum-seedlings

My analysis is of *Core Essentials: A Strategy for Teaching Character*, the lesson plans supplied to teachers. The first page of the teachers' guide outlines three main elements of the program: Identifying Basic Components, Preparation, and Establishing a Routine. Each of the three main elements has sub-headings identifying key features that characterize the main elements as well as the overall intent of the larger program. Under "Identify the Basic Components," exists "teacher's guide, bookmarks/ tablecards, value-able card, and posters." The teacher's guide is the booklet and tells teachers what to do, when to do it, and how to do it. The sub-section that explains elements in the teacher's guide notes that "each month you have age-appropriate materials at two academic levels, K-2 and 3-5. Included in the guide are literature and video suggestions which may be displayed in the library by the media specialist."[12] For the bookmarks/tablecards, the booklet instructs that "the bookmark is perforated and should be separated from the tablecard, which is designed to be folded and placed in a convenient location at home (kitchen counter or table). The parents of each child may then use this tool to emphasize the value through family discussions and activities." For the value-able card, importantly, the booklet reveals that the

> . . . card is a key component which leads to successful implemen-
> tation of the program. It is designed as the incentive for children
> who are caught [*sic*] displaying the value. Each month you will see
> suggestions in the Teacher's Guide for 'Catching Kids.' Use these
> ideas to help you choose students who show they understand the
> value. The card rewards them with a FREE Chick-fil-A Kid's Meal.
> *Ideally, you should have enough cards to reward each student every*
> *month (if earned).*[13]

Remember the highlighted sentence. It'll come back shortly when reconsidering the primary motives behind the Core Essentials program as a whole.

Good, Old-Fashioned Character

With this overview, consider what happens to the students in classes that adopt the Core Essentials program. I outline the specific instructions that

---

12   *Core Essentials*, 1.

13   Ibid. Italics in the original.

are included in the teacher's guide and highlight the elements that make this character education plan a restrictive and troubling approach to teaching children. You can argue that a traditional approach to character education is what is needed. Core Essentials relies heavily on the idea that values are to be "imparted," reinforcing a banking approach to teaching and learning where the teacher deposits data into the students' "empty vaults" (or minds).[14] As I did earlier in this book, however, my goal is to problematize the banking approach and show that there are underlying ironies related to diversity that make the program highly questionable. There are also elements of hypocrisy that make the whole program suspect.

There is a different value for each month of the year represented by the guidelines in question. They include, beginning in September and ending in May: initiative, respect, uniqueness, peace, orderliness, kindness, courage, joy, and patience. For each month, the teacher's guide begins with the exact same formula: a definition of the term, a list of suggested books that represent the value, a list of quotes, a story about an animal that illustrates the value, and directions for teachers. Consider the directions for October. The value is "respect" and the teacher is given the definition: "responding with words and actions that show others they are important."[15] One of the "famous person" quotes given in the booklet is "Always respect your parents . . . Do whatever your parents say. They are your best friends in life." Aside from the obvious parallel to one of the Ten Commandments (Honor thy father and mother), there is also an irony in having the quote signify "respect." The quote is attributed to George Steinbrenner, the notorious baseball owner whose fights with managers and team members were legendary.

For December, the value is peace and is defined as "proving that you care more about each other than winning an argument." The booklet also indicates that "the first step toward living peaceably is one made quietly inside ourselves. We must decide that other people are worth more to us than our own selfish desires, and that the value of agreement is greater than the satisfaction of defeating an opponent."[16] While the moralistic sentiment sounds nice, I wonder about a possible hidden agenda. Much like the

---

14   See Paulo Freire, *Pedagogy of the Oppressed* (New York: Continuum, 1970).

15   *Core Essentials*, 5.

16   Ibid., 11.

"always respect your parents . . . do whatever they say" quote from the October lesson, I wonder whether students are being treated as too naïve. As though a sexually abusive parent's directions are always to be followed, the underbelly of universalism reveals itself with careful analysis. That a corporate fast-food chain arguably interested in increasing market share via competition supports a program that appears to want to produce docile, unquestioning students goes to the heart of the school-business intersection as well. Go back to an earlier question. Are schools about producing unquestioning consumers via a character education program that appears to elevate passivity and dogma? This concern not only applies to the students subjected to the program, however. Teachers, too, are under a formula that subjugates and marginalizes their expertise and professionalism via preordained scripts.

Each week in December, for example, has a corresponding paragraph that begins "Our value this month is peace. The definition of peace is 'proving that you care more about each other than winning an argument.'"[17] Forget that the vast majority of schools are not in session for four weeks in December, the four-week script nevertheless reflects a kind of de-skilling of teaching at the same time that it seems to mimic catechism-like recitations from Christian churches. For the "bulletin board" aspect of the teacher's guide for December, teachers are told to "design a bulletin board with a chimney made of craft paper. Give each child a stocking made out of construction paper. On the stocking, have the students write how they care for other people. The children may decorate their stockings afterwards. Hang their stockings on the chimney that you have made." The title given to the bulletin board assignment is "The Stockings Were Hung By the Chimney with Peace." Aside from the overly prescriptive directions that devalue teachers' autonomy and professionalism, stockings are typically hung by chimneys in Christian homes, not Jewish, Muslim, or Atheist homes. Furthermore, if stockings are hung in homes for the Christmas holidays, is the point of young children hanging the stockings to "care for other people," or to receive presents? I don't mean to be snarky. I mean to critique the limiting of diversity.

A Christian theme is discerned in other parts of the Core Essentials handbook as well. For January, orderliness is the value and while the

---

17   Ibid., 12.

paragraph begins with "a study of nature," the teacher is supposed to explain to the students that "the constellations are a beautiful example of the order which exists in the skies."[18] Given the controversy in Georgia concerning Kathy Cox and evolution, the "order in the skies" reference sounds eerily like creationist "grand design" assertions.[19] For February, the value is kindness and the teacher is supposed to explain that a wise saying is "do to others as you would have them do to you."[20] Fine as far as it goes, the *un*hidden "Golden Rule" taken together with other religious themes raises concerns about diversity of thought. Should elementary students hassle their parents into taking them to Chick-fil-A for their "free" meal during the month of X, they would receive a bracelet/watch-type band that has a compartment to hold more information from the Core Essentials program. For "responsibility" the plastic holder on the wrist band is a sheep dog and the insert of stickers includes statements like "guard sheep dogs are responsible for protecting sheep" and "shepherds trust their sheep dogs to do what is expected of them." While I don't want to make too much of these points, it does seem to me to be another Christian theme. Sheep? Shepherds? Further, married with the religious and overwhelmingly Christian themes are themes about work and capitalism. For the month of April, for example, students read quotes from Dale Carnegie and Henry Ford. Carnegie's quote is "when fate hands you a lemon, make lemonade" and Ford's is "there is joy in work."[21]

What these and other quotes within the curriculum indicate is a mixture of Christianity and capitalism that limits diversity. By weaving a language of accommodation with a language of economics, contrived optimism becomes an unquestioned foundation for docile, naïve workers. The merger results in a confused nationalist mythology that takes Christian values for granted while accommodating the lauding of individualism and pretenses of participating in a democracy. The myth that "anyone can be anything they want" given "free markets," "hard work," and entrepreneurialism, masks the reality faced by increasing numbers of workers. As Bourdieu points out,

---

18 Ibid., 14.

19 See Mary MacDonald, "Evolution Furor Heats Up," *The Atlanta Journal-Constitution* (31 January 2004): A1.

20 *Core Essentials*, 17.

21 Ibid., 23.

there are more and more low-level service jobs that are underpaid and low-productivity, unskilled or underskilled (based on hasty on-the-job training), with no career prospects—in short, the *throwaway jobs* of what André Gorz calls a "society of servants." According to economist Jean Gadrey, quoting an American study, of the thirty jobs that will grow fastest in the next decade, seventeen require no skills and only eight require higher education and qualification. At the other end of social space, the *dominated dominant*, that is, the managers, are experiencing a new form of alienation. They occupy an ambiguous position, equivalent to that of the petty bourgeois at another historical stage in the structure, which leads to forms of organized self-exploitation.[22]

Part of the historical stage to which Bourdieu refers was outlined in 1926 by Richard Henry Tawney. In his classic text, *Religion and the Rise of Capitalism,* Tawney noted that "rightly or wrongly, with wisdom or its opposite, not only in England but on the Continent and in America, not in one denomination but among Roman Catholics, Anglicans, and Nonconformists, an attempt is being made to restate the practical implications of the social ethics of the Christian faith, in a form sufficiently comprehensive to provide a standard by which to judge the collective actions and institutions of mankind [sic], in the sphere both of international politics and of social organizations."[23] What happens to diversity, then?

The scenario goes something like this: instill the youngest and most impressionable with externally contrived religious values and increasingly mold the docile congregation of followers into workers who honor authority. In the process, remove opportunities for critique and questioning by championing ideals like consensus and the status quo. Where there is consensus and a status quo, there is limited diversity. According to Charles Lindblom, corporations are intimately tied to this very process and set up the intersection between capitalism and Christian moral codes at the expense of diverse public debate and authentic democratic governance. He notes the key features in business terms and calls them "the grand issues of politico-economic organization: private enterprise, a high degree of corporate autonomy, protection

---

22   Bourdieu, *Firing Back*, 31. Italics in original.

23   Richard Henry Tawney, *Religion and the Rise of Capitalism* (New York: Harcourt, Brace, and Company, 1926), 5.

of the status quo on distribution of income and wealth, close consultation between business and government, and restriction of union demands to those consistent with business profitability . . . They try, through indoctrination, to keep all these issues from coming to the agenda of government."[24] For the parallel to schools, I'm reminded of Theodore Brameld's discussion of indoctrination when he was attempting to defend the notion of diversity in schools in his *Ends and Means in Education.*[25]

Brameld defined indoctrination as a "method of learning by communication which proceeds primarily in one direction . . . for the purpose of inculcating in the mind and behavior of the latter a firm acceptance of some one doctrine or systematic body of beliefs—a doctrine assumed in advance by its exponents to be so supremely true, so good, or so beautiful as to justify no need for critical, scrupulous, thoroughgoing comparison with alternative doctrines."[26] Brameld's concern was that schools practiced indoctrination at the expense of a diverse society. For the purpose of this chapter, however, he went even further. He indicted "the Church" for establishing the very conditions that promoted learning of the kind he deplored (and this book challenges). "For many centuries," Brameld wrote, "the Church has deliberately and frankly inculcated its own doctrine as alone true and good, its chief indoctrinators being priests vested with authority to communicate its tenets to receptive minds . . . this kind of education flourishes oftener than not: inculcation of moral codes or social folklore, and especially of attitudes and programs identified with the traditional economic-political system, simply means that public schools, far more often than most of their personnel themselves realize, are under the heavy influence of the dominant ideology."[27] What happens to diversity, if Brameld is correct?

When specifically looking carefully at the text of the Core Essentials teacher's guide, to link and illustrate Brameld's point, questions should be asked. When, in March, the theme is courage, teachers are told that "courage is the foundation of our democracy. Discover the courage of the young citizens in your class by using a few of these ideas: Watch for students who do the right thing even when it has consequences; Observe students who

---

24   Charles E. Lindblom, *Politics and Markets: The World's Political-Economic Systems* (New York: Basic Books, 1977), 205.

25   Brameld, *Means and Ends in Education*, 65*ff.*

26   Ibid., 66.

27   Ibid., 67.

stand up for their beliefs; Notice those students who do not give in to peer pressure; and Let students write or discuss what courage means to them. Allow them to make a pledge about their courage and watch to see who lives up to that pledge."[28] Given the preceding months that privileged meekness and obedience to authority, what should be "discovered" about the "young citizens" in the class? If citizenship has been crafted in a hierarchical and externally imposed fashion, with the teacher at the center—or more accurately, the Core Essentials program at the center—how serious are teachers supposed to take the task laid out for them? In terms of power, if the teachers are the ones "allowing" students to make a pledge and "letting" students write and discuss what courage means to them, the idea of students as diverse, courageous citizens is further suppressed under the power and authority of the teacher via the Core Essentials curriculum.

Values and the Drive-Thru?

Throughout the Core Essentials teacher's guide there are sections called "Catching Kids." These sections are intended to "catch" children "doing good," to turn the idea of "catching" a student doing something into a positive rather than a negative action. Unique to the Core Essentials program, however, is that, because the program is underwritten by Chick-fil-A, the "Catching Kids" sections have "value-able cards." These cards are considered rewards by the program and when given out by the teacher to the student to enable the student to get a free kid's meal at Chick-fil-A. Remember, too, that the cards are sent home with students so their parents can reinforce that Chick-fil-A is a treat, goal, reward.

A couple of issues converge around this point. First, the students who earn the reward are specifically within Grades K through 2 and 3 through 5. What we have are the youngest and most impressionable students in schools being bribed to act in particular ways in order to get a meal that is unhealthy. As Carolyn Vander Schee has pointed out, childhood obesity is a concern that has direct links schools and programs they sponsor (both via in-school food services and out-of-school connections like Core Essentials).[29] Other

---

28   *Core Essentials*, 20.

29   See Carolyn Vander Schee, "Food Services and Schooling," in *Schools or Markets?: Commercialism, Privatization, and School-Business Partnerships*, ed., Deron Boyles (Mahwah, NJ: LEA, 2004), 1*ff*.

studies also conclude that fast food intake among school children is part of a growing obesity epidemic.[30]

By using an unhealthy meal as a reward for complying with a "character education" program, you should wonder about the hypocrisy. Where in the program, for example, are students instructed to demonstrate courage by questioning the corporate underwriting of the program itself? When are the students encouraged to consider the fact that in order for them to redeem their "kid's meal" voucher they will have to be accompanied by an adult who most likely will purchase food and provide profit for Chick-fil-A? Indeed, recall the direct quote from the teacher's guide noted toward the beginning of this section. The guide encourages teachers to "use these ideas to help . . . choose students who show they understand the value . . . *Ideally, you should have enough cards to reward each student every month (if earned)*." The point may not to be to reward students for good character, even if we could agree on what good character means. The point is to get as many children from Grades K through 5 into a fast food chain to eat greasy food with their parents. Can we imagine that the marketing department at Chick-fil-A has not figured out the amount of business they would generate over a three-year period? Perhaps the most extreme evidence of Chick-fil-A's hypocritical approach to the issue of caloric intake and nutrition is their stance that eating plenty of their fast food is not really the problem. The problem is lack of exercise. Indeed, and incredibly, Chick-fil-A offers a "Chick-fil-A 10-Second Tip" in the Children's Hospital's (Knoxville, TN) "Healthy Kids" newsletter. The tip is, "Rather than only focusing on decreasing a big eater's intake, try to increase activity and exercise."[31]

---

30   Shanthy A. Bowman, Steven L. Gortmaker, Cara B. Ebbeling, Mark A. Pereira, and David S. Ludwig, "Effects of Fast-Food Consumption on Energy Intake and Diet Quality Among Children in a National Household Survey," *Pediatrics* 113, no. 1 (January, 2004): 112-118; Richard J. Deckelbaum and Christine A. Williams, "Childhood Obesity: The Health Issue," *Obesity Research* 9, suppl. 4 (November, 2001): 239S-243S; David S. Ludwig, Karen E. Peterson, and Steven Gortmaker, "Relation between Consumption of Sugar-Sweetened Drinks and Childhood Obesity: A Prospective, Observational Analysis," *The Lancet* 357 (17 February 2001): 505-508. See, also, Marion Nestle, *Food Politics: How the Food Industry Influences Nutrition and Health* (Berkeley, CA: University of California Press, 2003); and Michael Gard and Carolyn Pluim, *Schools and Public Health: Past, Present, Future* (New York: Lexington, 2014).

31   "Chick-fil-A 10-Second Tip," *Children's Hospital's Healthy Kids: A Quarterly Publication for Parents Preschoolers* [sic] (Knoxville, TN), volume IX (Winter, 2003): 3. That the hospital condones (and promotes) this kind of logic is for another book.

To illustrate the link between the previous claims concerning the problems with externally imposed ideology and health issues associated with fast-food intake, consider that students in the Core Essentials program are structurally inhibited from exploring the issue of healthy eating. The subject doesn't fall under any of the categories that are preordained for and imposed on teachers. Teachers are told that the program will "only take 15 minutes," so when would teachers find the time to go beyond the pre-packaged approach anyway? Missing here is the kind of Deweyan approach developed by those critical of fast-food exploitation.[32] There should be a general structure through which students can answer the question "Can you 'eat healthy' by frequenting fast food restaurants?" Investigating food pyramids and food facts in the face of fast-food chain propaganda seems like a no-brainer. But corporate money is powerful and the influence corporations wield is enormous. The Core Essentials program does not foster critical inquiry. Its primary concern is with making money for Chick-fil-A, and long-term customers, through the external imposition of preordained assumptions about character.

I wonder what it would be like if, during the month of October (when "respect" is the value of the month), students would be encouraged to ask whether they, as a diverse group, are actually being shown "respect" via the very program touting the value. Said differently, when is respect for the diversity of children shown by the teachers, Core Essentials executives, and Truett Cathy? What role did they have in determining whether they should be subjected to the overtly Christian themes embedded in the program? I also wonder whether the lessons being taught—regardless of whether they are ultimately valid—are also being demonstrated by the people who are promoting the program? How patient would Chick-fil-A be of students demonstrating against their stores? How respectful of students would authorities be if they refused to engage in surveillance of one another as the "catching kids" section of the program encourages?

Implications and Further Considerations

One point, then, is to discern the ironies and to tease out the inconsistencies related to the Core Essentials program. We have, in short, a program funded

32   https://www.washingtonpost.com/news/wonk/wp/2015/10/29/how-mcdonalds-is-using-schools-to-try-to-change-what-kids-eat/

by a fundamentalist Christian whose company uses "kid's meals" as a bribe for behaving in docile, disempowered, uncritical, non-diverse ways. Is this the motive for the program? That is, might it be the case that imposing hierarchy, developing non-questioning students, and privileging Christian-corporate values are intentional acts perpetrated by those wishing to maintain and increase their power, even at the expense of the very diverse students to which they preach equality and kindness? To have Core Essentials and Chick-fil-A work in tandem with William Bennett's *Book of Virtues* raises an obvious question about hypocrisy.[33] Bennett gambled away millions of dollars at the same time he was loudly proclaiming the importance of teaching virtues in schools. Is this a "do as I say, not as I do" problem? What does it mean that universalists like Bennett represent contextual realities that aren't easy to generalize? What does it mean when a State Superintendent of Schools wishes to delete "evolution" from the curriculum, but applauds Truett Cathy's donation of protestant versions of the Bible to all the public schools in the state?

Beyond critique of those in power and control of the program, we must consider the reality of classroom life. Teachers, in a perversely thankful way, simply don't have the time to spare to add the curriculum represented by Core Essentials. The state of Georgia, like every other state, already has a character education component. It also has a core curriculum that, given No Child Left Behind, Race to the Top, and Common Core, is increasing the amount of time teachers use to teach to end of year tests. Teachers simply don't have the time to alter their bulletin boards, monitor the Chick-fil-A vouchers, and "catch" students behaving in ways the authors of the program do not conduct themselves anyway. So, beyond exploiting the youngest students in schools, beyond the attempt to further de-skill teaching, beyond attempting to mold obedient and subservient future workers, and beyond the irony and hypocrisy, is there anything valuable about the values valued by Core Essentials? Maybe.

If "Core Essentials" would be used as an object lesson, itself, we might reveal a form of criticality that teaches about diversity while not imposing those values without critique. Diversity exists in schools. Students bring diversity to the classroom just like their teachers. The question is whether diversity is to be explored or whether it is to be subsumed. Dewey makes it

---

33 William Bennett, *Book of Virtues* (New York Simon and Schuster, 1996).

clear that "morals" are an important part of being a citizen (or any part of a group). He differs greatly from Core Essentials, though, in that he's not interested in externally imposed terms and themes spread out over three years as part of a preparation plan for future work or future citizenship. Education is a process of living and not a preparation for future living. In *Moral Principles in Education*, Dewey puts it this way: "We need to see that moral principles are not arbitrary, that they are not 'transcendental'; that the term 'moral' does not designate a special region or portion of life. We need to translate the moral into the conditions and forces of our community life, and into the impulses and habits of the individual. All the rest is mint, anise, and cumin."[34] In another passage, Dewey writes that "the emphasis then falls upon construction . . . rather than upon absorption and mere learning."[35] As though he is aware of Core Essentials and other such programs, Dewey argues that children are rarely emergent and constructive individuals in classroom settings. Their intellectual life and diversity are stunted by the proceduralism of traditional expectations and methods. So, too, says Dewey, of morals in schools.

> The child knows perfectly well that the teacher and all his fellow pupils have exactly the same facts and ideas before them that he [sic] has; he is not *giving* them anything at all. And it may be questioned whether the moral lack is not as great as the intellectual. The child is born with a natural desire to give out, to do, to serve. When this tendency is not used, when conditions are such that other motives are substituted, the accumulation of an influence working against the social spirit is much larger than we have any idea of –especially when the burden of work, week after week, and year after year, falls upon this side.[36]

Three years' worth of value-able kid's meal cards externally dangled for measly behaviorist results strikes me as the very thing Dewey would argue against. Importantly, Dewey's not arguing against morals. Instead, he's

---

34 Dewey, *Moral Principles in Education*, 58.

35 Ibid., 21.

36 Ibid., 22. See, also, Charles Anthony Earls, "John Dewey's Relational Concept of Character," *The Pluralist* 3, no. 3 (Fall 2008): 1-22.

arguing against morals "in the air . . . something set off by themselves . . . [morals] that are so *very* 'moral' that they have no working contact with the average affairs of everyday life."[37] As a pragmatist, the utility that various and diverse values might have get their worth in their organic growth and development in context. Dewey again:

> Here, then, is the moral standard, by which to test the work of the school upon the side of what it does directly for individuals . . . Does the school as a system . . . attach sufficient importance to the spontaneous instincts and impulses? Does it afford sufficient opportunity for these to assert themselves and work out their own results? Can we even say that the school in principle attaches itself . . . to the active constructive powers rather than to processes of absorption and learning?[38]

I submit that the answers to Dewey's questions are "no," "no," and "no." Far too often in far too many schools, far too many teachers fall back on methods of teaching that are comfortable and traditional. Students' natural tendencies to inquire become stifled in rooms that are organized (physically and in terms of curriculum) for convenience and regimented management.[39] While teachers are not primarily to blame for the external imposition of No Child Left Behind, Race to the Top, or Common Core mandates and high-stakes testing that structure their lives, the very frustration they often feel with such external imposition is not recognized by them when they, in turn, dump such expectations on their students. Core Essentials is simply another in a long line of impositions that teachers and students must navigate. The difference is the degree to which the program represents more corporate infiltration under the guise of character education and the lack of diversity it entails.

Extending Dewey, Bourdieu challenges the rhetoric of universalism that sets up the structures within which schools operate as stifling places for external imposition. For Bourdieu, "the effect of shared belief . . . removes

37 Ibid., 57.

38 Ibid., 53.

39 Herbert Kliebard, *The Struggle for the American Curriculum, 1893-1958* (New York: Routledge, 1995), 84, 162.

from discussion ideas which are perfectly worth discussing."[40] Bourdieu envisions a kind of collective intelligence that challenges deeply held beliefs. Long standing assumptions become the focus of renewed critique and action. He's specifically interested in examining the major power brokers in modern society. As he puts it, "the power of the agents and mechanisms that dominate the economic and social world today rests on the extraordinary concentration of all the species of capital—economic, political, military, cultural, scientific, and technological—as the foundation of a symbolic domination without precedent . . ."[41] This symbolic domination is difficult to critique, however, because of the power it has over members of society. For Bourdieu, students are also a direct target and engage in hegemonic practices that further subsume them under the influence of the market. He claims, for example,

> that the 'civilization' of jeans, Coca-Cola, and McDonald's [Chick-fil-A] has not only economic power on its side but also the symbolic power exerted through a seduction to which the victims themselves contribute. By taking as their chief targets children and adolescents, particularly those most shorn of specific immune defenses, with the support of advertising and the media which are both constrained and complicit, the big cultural production and distribution companies gain an extraordinary, unprecedented hold over all contemporary societies—societies that, as a result, find themselves virtually infantilized.[42]

Recall that Core Essentials is imposed on students in grades K-5. Bourdieu's suggestion that the larger society is infantilized by the hold corporate interests have over it is even more striking when we consider that the project of disempowerment literally begins with infants. Organic growth of student interests, for Dewey, paired with sociological critique of business influences, for Bourdieu, make for heady prospects when envisioning what schools—and their curricula—might look like if reformed. It will take, however, a sober reconsideration of the roles of students and teachers in schools to

---

40   Bourdieu, *Acts of Resistance*, 6.

41   Bourdieu, *Firing Back*, 39.

42   Ibid., 71.

engage in substantive reconstruction of schools. It will require a collective valuing of diversity and of various roles for teachers and students and, in order to do so, getting rid of corporate- and fundamentalist-sponsored, universalist edicts in the form of, among others, character education programs like Core Essentials.[43]

What's not being advocated is a substitution of one kind of pre-ordained morality for another. There shouldn't be, in other words, a revised script that suggests "The value of the month is criticality. Criticality is defined as . . ." This sort of "bait and switch" game has been played for too long in the history of curriculum. The function of indoctrination is the same, even though the forms may morph. Instead, students and teachers should develop their own imaginative versions of criticality as those versions emerge (and change) through the natural curiosity of students in Grades K through 5. In this way, a singular (Christian) view of character education is replaced with a pluralistic and diverse understanding of character. Teachers and students, taking a cue from Dewey, would utilize their instincts and impulses to explore that variety *with* one another and develop critical understanding and agency.

Looking Back to Look Forward

It's no secret that Dewey's lab school at the University of Chicago was a place for varying topics and diverse inquiries. The whole point of the experiment was to provide space and guidance for children to actualize their questioning so they could solve problems. Part of that process was in using a curriculum built around what we call "the basics" of reading, writing, and math, but these weren't discrete classes set apart from broader inquiries. Mayhew and Edwards make much of this point when they provide an overview of the curriculum in Dewey's lab school. As they tell it, most students in public and private schools at the time compartmentalized the students' day "without sufficient care for either social or intellectual relations."[44] They go on to restate how the lab school was located in a house in order that a "home" environment would be established and students' interests could be fostered.

---

43 See, also, Craig A. Cunningham, David Granger, Jane Fowler Morse, Barbara Stengel, and Terri Wilson, "Dewey, Women, and Weirdoes: or, the Potential Rewards for Scholars who Dialog across Difference," *Education & Culture* 23, no. 2 (2007): 27–62.

44 Katherine Camp Mayhew and Anna Camp Edwards, *The Dewey School: The Laboratory School of the University of Chicago, 1896-1903* (New York: J. Appleton-Century Company, Inc., 1936), 42.

"The materials about [the students] and the things that were being done
to and with them furnished the ideas for the initial start and choice of the
activities in the shop, laboratory, kitchen, and studios . . . [The materials]
started the child in his [*sic*] present, interested him to relive the past, and
in due time carried him on to future possibilities and achievements in an
ever developing experience. In brief, they furnished a thread of continuity
because they were concerned with the fundamental requisites of living."[45]
In these short sentences we can see three competing ideas that some have
taken to be a weakness or an inconsistency in Dewey's thought. Let's take
the issues one by one so we can clarify the problem and identify issues that
need to be addressed in order to understand Dewey's imaginative vision of
teaching in relation to diversity. The first point has to do with materials that
are furnished. The second point has to do with what's called "recapitulation
theory." The third point has to do with preparation. All these points have
implications for diversity. As I've tried to do consistently throughout this
book, let's take each of the points in turn.

A brief reading of Mayhew and Edwards might suggest that the teachers were the ones to furnish all the materials *for* students. That's only partially correct. For the youngest students, the home had related parts (like
the shop, lab, garden, etc.). A shop is a shop because it includes items like
hammers and screwdrivers. A lab is a lab because it includes microscopes
and Bunsen burners. A garden requires water hoses, trowels, and rakes. In
this way, yes, teachers (more accurately, the school administration) supplied materials. The uses to which those instruments were put are at least
partially influenced by the functional context. We hoe weeds so vegetables
will grow better. We saw wood to make a birdhouse. But the imaginative
work beyond these obvious functions is also an important point. Here's
how Mayhew and Edwards put it:

> In their constructive work the younger groups made their own jute-
> board pencil boxes, their own book covers, and other articles need-
> ed in school life. They selected the material for, measured, cut, and
> basted the dish towels for their laboratory kitchen. As they relived
> imaginatively the life and occupations of primitive man [sic] and
> reconstructed his environments and needs, they built into sand or

---

45 Ibid., 43.

clay or stone their ideas of the types of shelter used at this stage of life. They rediscovered the best kind of stone for making the weapons that he needed for protection from wild animals or the best kind of clay for many uses in the way of utensils. As a by-product, they learned many geological facts, the source of the clay from the silt of rivers, the different kinds of stone, and the reasons for their differences.[46]

In this passage we can see materials furnished and a theory of history, culture, and civilization represented. As I pointed out in the introduction and chapter 1, there is nothing wrong nor inconsistent in teachers furnishing raw materials or even lesson plans. The problems occur when those materials and lesson plans rigidly steer students to preordained goals unconnected to students' lives and open-ended inquiry. There may be a fine line between making learning fun and coercion, but the point Mayhew and Edwards are making is that utilizing various materials in inquiry yields a better understanding of history, the present, and future. That's why they point to continuity and integration. Mayhew and Edwards, again: "These ideas were chosen for study not alone because of their direct, clear, and explicit relationship to the child's own present environment and experience, but also because of their indirect, veiled, and implied relationship to the past out of which present conditions have developed and to the future which is dependent on the present."[47] This view is also a point of contention for several scholars.

Some people think the lab school curriculum followed a 19th-century view that "civilization" progressed in a natural set of stages that followed a specific linear path—and one that hierarchically valued Western civilization at the expense of other cultures. What's at issue here is what's known as recapitulation theory. Recapitulation theory dates to the 1820s and claimed that biology parallels culture in that animal embryos develop in phases that represent successive adult stages in the development of animal ancestors. The problem is that embryos develop differently, so the theory is flawed. Still, there were early anthropologists and psychologists who thought that child development was, essentially, a stage-like version of recapitulation theory. Dewey, however, rejected the formulaic and predeterminate elements of the

46 Ibid., 44-45.

47 Ibid., 43.

theory. His view of history "viewed the process of social and human development in organic, incorporative terms of process rather than conceiving it as abrupt shifts or stages represented by products of these eras."[48] The long quote from Mayhew and Edwards earlier illustrates the point. Still, the historical views assumed in Dewey's lab school *did* embrace a view of history that is similar, in some ways, to recapitulation theory. The difference, however, is the key. The difference is in the inquiry by students. Tools and materials may be supplied, and students may use those tool and materials in similar ways, but the goals and philosophy are different. Let me illustrate with a personal example.

History and Presentism: Why Woke Won't Work

When I was in fifth grade at William Henry Middle School in Dover, Delaware, our classes were set up in teams. We had math, science, history, and English classes, but in team-teaching fashion, our faculty members worked together so that themes, problems, and ideas were shared across the curriculum. We weren't unique at the time. Lots of schools had team teaching. We also weren't in a Dewey school. We were a public middle school. Our history teacher, James Orth, however, *was* Deweyan in his leading the team of teachers and the experiential project that came to characterize our lives that year. Simply put, we built a Puritan cabin and a Native American teepee in order to host our families for a Thanksgiving "feast." Set aside, for now, the many issues that such a project raises. Was the history accurate? Was it inclusive of alternate narratives of oppression? Was it at risk of caricature? I'll return to these important questions but set them aside for a minute and let's unpack what we, the students and teachers, experienced as part of the project.

Note, in keeping with some of Mayhew and Edwards' narrative, that the project didn't originate with the students. It's similar to the book donation at Chrysalis. However, the direction the overall project took *was* influenced by student inquiry and student direction of the experience. Somewhat like in Dewey's lab school, we integrated home economics with history. We had to prepare (at least part of) the meal. Parents, of course, were also involved. So were grandparents. The broader community made donations of everything

48   Thomas Fallace, "Repeating the Race Experience: John Dewey and the History Curriculum at the University of Chicago Laboratory School," *Curriculum Inquiry* 39, no. 3 (June 2009): 381-405, 398.

from lumber and fabric to canned yams. You get the picture. The point is that the action of making a village and providing a meal required investigation and connection with reality that represented, at least in part, the form of recapitulation theory Thomas Fallace identifies in Dewey's lab school.[49] We looked back to history to understand the present so we could move into the future with new knowledge and new experiences.

Hammering slats of wood together may have looked vocational, and in a way it was. But we didn't hammer to learn carpentry skills to get a job. We learned that hammering is connected to the larger project of building and that building is important for survival. Foundations must be level. Studs must be plumb. In these two examples, alone, we had to learn what a foundation was, what studs were, what level meant (and how to use a tool of the same name to prove the point), and why "plumb" was not a fruit. Further, we learned that if we wanted to keep rain out, the slats we were nailing to the sides of the structure also had to overlap. What geometry was involved in that part of the project? We didn't know the formula as much we understood the function of geometry (without calling it geometry, by the way). And, yes, some of us hit our thumbs instead of the nails and had to see the nurse. It's called life. Nobody sued anybody, though I'm sure parents had to fill out permission slips so we could engage in the experiment.

Furthermore, if we were going to serve turkey for the "feast," how many turkeys would be needed to feed x number of people? More math. But also cooking. How many birds and how long do they cook? And how many ovens do we have (not enough) and how long would all that take (too long for one home economics kitchen)? Oh, the planning! To link back to the beginning of the chapter, especially given the context of the project, would "grace" be said at the beginning of the meal? If so, would it be in the sense of a historical reenactment to avoid church-state separation? Would it represent reinforcing the very fundamentalist mythology we tend to teach in US culture?[50]

---

49   Ibid.

50   See Andrew L. Seidel, *The Founding Myth: Why Christian Nationalism Is Un-American* (New York: Sterling, 2019); Steven K. Green, *Inventing a Christian America: The Myth of the Religious Founding* (Oxford: Oxford University Press, 2015); Kevin M. Kruse, *One Nation Under God: How Corporate America Invented Christian America* (New York: Basic Books, 2015); and Michael W. Apple, *Educating the "Right" Way: Markets, Standards, God, and Inequality* (New York: Routledge, 2006).

Also consider the problem-solving that goes beyond merely the content subjects of math, science, history, and English. We learned sewing, too. And gardening, though the time of planting and time of harvest didn't fit our schedule for the final feast. Also, yes, some of us wore feathers on our heads and moccasins on our feet. Just like cultural epoch theory, as fifth graders we loved dressing up. Most (not all) kids enjoy any number of things when they are around *y* age. In our case, we were proud of our work.[51] We didn't make the picnic tables we used to eat the meal with our family members and broader community, but we ate together. And for a group of fifth graders who, in 1976, were one of the first racially integrated classes to attend what had been an all-black school, I think it's an important (though not unproblematic) point. That our parents found or made or were given the time to participate also features in questions about the role of economics and society. I'll get back to this idea in a minute, too.

When Thanksgiving came and our project ended, we engaged in reflection about what we had done, what we achieved, and what problems we encountered. Because we lived it, that is, engaged in the doing of the complex project of building a cabin, a teepee, and making a meal for about 100 people, we not only learned and solved problems, we better understood actual history (versus some of the caricature we performed). We *knew* it because we *did* it. What we did was varied: not everybody performed every task, though we did rotate from the cabin to the teepee to the kitchen, etc. Our engagement and our activity weren't trivial, even when some of our effort was ill-informed and might even be accused, in 2020, of being racist. I'll return to this point in a moment, as well.

For now, I simply want to highlight how the select elements I've pointed out (there are many more that could be identified) were consistent with Dewey's view of learning and also allowed a form of diversity that might be lost in my simple illustration. Even with the project set up and assigned by the teachers, students *still* modified the project and altered what plans had been drafted ahead of time. Since we built the village in a courtyard outside our classrooms, weather was an unplanned factor in our work and in our learning. Untreated lumber warps in the rain. Hammering is more difficult if

---

51 The "we" here is important, too. What was the makeup, what were the demographics, of our class? The specifics are less important than the point. Schools are still segregated and still function as sorting machines, so we shouldn't think that the makeup of the student body (or teaching ranks) are unimportant. See Joel Spring, *The Sorting Machine Revisited: National Educational Policy Since 1945* (Boston: Addison-Wesley, 1988).

it's cold outside and you need to wear gloves. These points may sound trite, but they indicate the very nuances of human learning that Dewey wants us to embrace, understand, and link. Recall that his theory of being and reality—his ontology—puts change at the center of everything. Without flexibility, there is no meaningful growth. We could have assembled the village, hypothetically anyway, from an IKEA box. Just like paint-by-numbers (recall chapter 2) is not the same thing as genuinely creating unique art, building a cabin and a teepee may have plans, but when you have a rotating number of fifth graders constructing them, you not only must understand flexibility but understand how valuable it is to learning and knowing. Our creation "fit" a broad vision held by the teachers but wasn't a cookie-cutter approach that all fifth graders would do by the third week of November. The project wasn't standardized, in other words. We couldn't be compared to other fifth graders to see who was #1 or "top ten" or whatever. What makes this view of teaching imaginative is at least partly structural. In the Thanksgiving project, teachers still gave directions. Students still followed them . . . except when the situation we were undergoing called for questioning and redirection.

Some things had to be scrapped because of time. Other things had to be reworked because of mistakes. I think it's in linking comparisons to the mistakes I just mentioned that we have more potential to better understand Dewey. In chapter 1, I talked about Dewey's *Democracy and Education*.[52] In that book he cautions us against comparing children to adults because such a comparison almost always favors adults and almost always puts children in an unfavorable light. If we understand childhood comparatively, children lose. Instead of comparing, Dewey wants us to see the value in doing and, yes, at times, failing. Where failing is making a mistake, we need to change the language so that "losing" and "failing" are revised. Some of the best learning comes from making a mistake. When we had to re-do the part of the teepee that was needed to hold the structure upright, it wasn't necessarily fun, but in re-doing it—in correcting it—we learned more than simply following the 1-2-3 steps in an instruction manual.

Part of making mistakes is also tied to questions that are central to this chapter and to which I alluded in the previous discussion about the village experiment. What historical mistakes were made? What history did we get wrong? Why does it matter? There are at least two ways to address these

---

52 Dewey, *Democracy and Education*, op. cit.

questions and I'll take them in the following order: 1) history; and 2) presentism. For 1), we fell prey to the cultural appropriation common to fifth graders at the time. We grew up watching television westerns, *The Three Stooges*, and *Looney Tunes*. *The Lone Ranger, Davey Crockett*, and *Bonanza* reinforced stereotypes just like lots of other shows and movies. Disney tends to whitewash disturbing elements of history and Hollywood tends to exploit caricatures of, say, Indigenous people. Our playing "Cowboys and Indians" reinforced tired tropes. It isn't good—and it isn't history. Learning this fact took time and was at least partially helped by the village-building experiment. Why? Because in the time-consuming process of making head dresses, big-buckled shoes, and teepees we learned by trial and error in ways that made us think. Wrap the teepee in butcher paper and we can be done early. Rain on the butcher paper covering the teepee and we have to start all over again. In that process, we were guided with questions toward reasoning in historical context. What *would* teepees consist of? What are buffalo? What are buffalo hides? You mean we'd have to kill and skin a massive animal? Ewww. But, also, aha! Learning. Understanding. Except . . .

We need to be careful not to make the same Disney-type mistake and think that the experiment was perfect. It wasn't. It was too easy to reinforce stereotypes, even when our teachers tried to correct us. Nobody, for instance, raised a question about why we were erecting a teepee in our village. It would have been more historically accurate to have built a wigwam instead of a teepee because the tribes in our geographic area of Delaware built and used wigwams, not teepees. Does it matter? Yes. It does. It also mattered to note that the ovens and refrigeration we used were obviously not even close to being historically accurate. I raise this point to note that the project did not have to be perfect to be educative. Further, that attention was called to such inconsistencies and inaccuracies is also part of learning. Rather than condemning the construction of the wrong native structure, we learned from it—more so because we got it wrong. But this also means we must be culturally aware and inclusive of difference. And I think Dewey would have specifically delighted in this point because, of all things, he was both a scientist and cultural pragmatist.[53] Investigations take us into unknown territory, by design. Embracing the unknown is part of human flourishing. Embracing diversity is, too.

---

53 On this specific point, he was also made sensitive to issues of Native Americans because his first father-in-law was an outspoken advocate for Indigenous peoples' rights.

To the degree that our understanding is informed by history books, we also need to be careful.[54] Historical work can be celebrationist (positive spins of history), revisionist (reinterpretations), critical (undermining previous ideas), etc. For schools, there is a long line of critique about what counts as history, who gets to write it, and what from history gets taught (and in what grades). For my purposes, I want to highlight the idea of *cultural presentism* to address the second point from above and close out the chapter and the book. Presentism is the general term historians use to criticize those who take a view or understanding from, say, 2020 and apply those views and understandings to, for instance, 1720. It's a mistake. We can't expect those of the past to know as much as we know. That doesn't mean figures from the past are pure. It doesn't mean they didn't make horrific decisions. But there is a disconnect between the relativists of the world and their selective application of presentism to history.

There are a few kinds of presentism: norms, hindsight bias, and survivorship bias are three that should help clarify my point. Norm presentism is when you use a standard or expectation (the norm) to evaluate historical people and events. There may be a consensus in 2020 about what, say, being a strong individual requires. In 1020 or 1620, however, a strong individual varied. Who "counted" as an individual also varied. Those committing the error of presentism disregard contexts by projecting an overgeneralization onto the past. Hindsight bias is similar in that we judge decisions made by figures in history as flawed (or brilliant), but based on our understanding of what counts as reasonable decision-making. Explorers were brave, when maybe they were lucky. Luddites were ignorant rubes, when maybe they understood the value of unionization. You get the point. Lastly, survivorship bias means that we give only credit to the successful exemplars from history and forget the thousands of people who failed at the task we credit the exemplar for. An athlete looks to an Olympic gold medalist for how to excel in a sport, forgetting that for every gold medalist, there are thousands of could-a, would-a, should-a athletes not on the podium. Dewey is sometimes criticized for being racist, sexist, and ethnocentrist. Frank Margonis'

---

54 Different textbooks are written for different states. Said more accurately, given the corporate logic I'm trying to challenge, different textbooks are written for different *markets*. See https://www.nytimes.com/interactive/2020/01/12/us/texas-vs-california-history-textbooks.html. See, also, Michael W. Apple, *Official Knowledge: Democratic Education in a Conservative Age* (New York: Routledge, 1999), and Christine Woyshner and Chara Haeussler Bohan, eds., *Histories of Social Studies and Race: 1865-2000* (New York: Palgrave Macmillan, 2012).

work is one example and has been widely cited.[55] Thomas Fallace has also
been critical of Dewey, though in an arguably more balanced way.[56] What
Fallace's work does, that Margonis' does not, is avoid the problem of presentism I outline above. I have no interest in going into the rabbit holes of
speculation that some would like. My interest is in pointing out how Dewey's imaginative vision of teaching is encompassing of students' interests, no
matter who the student is. For research and scholarly integrity, however, I
provide a fairly extensive note of some of the more important work critical
of Dewey regarding race, gender, class, etc. Read these sources and decide
for yourself.[57] But also read sources that examine the topic and come to very
different conclusions.[58]

---

55 Frank Margonis, "John Dewey's Racialized Visions of the Student and Classroom
Community," *Educational Theory* 59, no. 1 (2009): 17-39.

56 Thomas D. Fallace, *Dewey and the Dilemma of Race: An Intellectual History, 1895-
1922* (New York: Teachers College Press, 2010).

57 Shannon Sullivan, "From the Foreign to the Familiar: Confronting Dewey Confront-
ing Racial Prejudice," *Journal of Speculative Philosophy* 18, no. 3 (2004): 193-202; Kelly
Vaughan, "Progressive Education and Racial Justice: Examining the Work of John Dewey,"
Education & Culture 34, no. 2 (2018): 39-68; Walter Feinberg, "Progressive Education and
Social Planning," *Teachers College Record* 73 (May 1972): 485-505; Colin Greer, *The Great
School Legend* (New York: Basic Books, 1972); Charles A. Tesconi, Jr., and Van Cleve Mor-
ris, *The Anti-Man Culture: Bureau-Technocracy and the Schools* (Urbana, IL: University of
Illinois Press, 1972); and John Wesley Jones, "Dewey and Cultural Racism," (master's thesis,
University of Illinois, 2012).

58 See Sam F. Stack, Jr., "John Dewey and the Question of Race: The Fight for Odell
Waller," *Education & Culture* 25, no. 1 (2009): 17-35; J. Christopher Eisele, "John Dewey
and the Immigrants," *History of Education Quarterly* 15, no. 1 (1975): 67-85; Timothy Mc-
Cune, "Dewey's Dilemma: Eugenics, Education, and the Art of Living," *The Pluralist* 7, no. 3
(Fall 2012): 96-106; Charles F. Howlett and Audrey Cohan, "John Dewey and His Evolving
Perceptions of Race Issues in American Democracy," *Teaching Social Studies* 17, no. 1 (Win-
ter-Spring 2017): 16-22; Susan D. Carle, "John Dewey and the Early NAACP: Developing
a Progressive Discourse on Racial Injustice, 1909-1921," in John R. Shook and Paul Kurtz,
eds., *Dewey's Enduring Impact: Essays on America's Philosopher* (New York: Prometheus,
2011): 249-262; Daniel A. Morris, "Improvisation as Democratic Virtue: A Deweyan Possibility for African American Religion and Ethics," *Soundings: An Interdisciplinary Journal*
96, no. 4 (2013): 355-381; Connie Goddard, "Bordentown: Where Dewey's 'Learning to
Earn' Met Du Boisian [sic] Educational Priorities: The Unique Legacy of a Once Thriving but
Largely Forgotten School for Black Students," *Education & Culture* 35, no. 1 (2019): 49-70;
Charlene Haddock Siegfried, ed., *Feminist Interpretations of John Dewey* (University Park,
PA: Pennsylvania State University Press, 2001); Kory Spencer Sorrell, "Feminist Ethics and
Dewey's Moral Theory," *Transactions of the Charles S. Peirce Society* 35, no. 1 (1999): 89-
114; Gregory Fernando Pappas, "Dewey and Feminism: The Affective and Relationships in
Dewey's Ethics," *Hypatia* 8, no. 2 (Spring, 1993): 78-95; Ian T.E. Deweese-Boyd, "There are
No Schools in Utopia: John Dewey's Democratic Education," *Education & Culture* 31, no. 2
(2015): 69-80; and V. Denise James, "Theorizing Black Feminist Pragmatism: Forethoughts
on the Practice and Purpose of Philosophy as Envisioned by Black Feminists and John Dewey," *The Journal of Speculative Philosophy* 23, no. 2 (2009): 92-99.

To close the book, note that the practical implications that follow from embracing diversity are a logical and natural extension of Dewey's pragmatism and imaginative vision of teaching. Since US classrooms will only grow more diverse, hardening imposed curriculum expectations and national standards will not meet the needs of teachers and students. More corporate influence will only increase the technology and wealth gaps that have been increasing in the past fifty years. Dewey's commitment to diverse interests in service to solving social problems is one way to reimagine diversity and what teaching and learning mean for it. Dewey didn't write about lesbian, gay, bisexual, transgender, questioning, and intersex issues. That doesn't make him homophobic. It makes him old. We make a mistake, I think, in discarding the old in favor of the new and shiny. We risk overlooking some exceptional theorizing and practical experiments that could be updated and made more modern, if not post-modern. As we experienced at Chrysalis, the diversity of students was vital to expanding understanding, whether through community outreach, volunteering for after-school bilingual mentoring, or crossing generational and political divides regarding military service. The students directly interacted with others and did so with interest and excitement. Imaginative teaching and learning should be characterized by the continual inquiry represented by young people everywhere. We just need to set standardization, accountancy, and capitalist assumptions aside.

References

Apple, Michael W. *Official Knowledge: Democratic Education in a Conservative Age.* New York: Routledge, 1999.

Apple, Michael W. *Educating the "Right" Way: Markets, Standards, God, and Inequality.* New York: Routledge, 2006.

Blanchard, Ken, and S. Truett Cathy. *The Generosity Factor.* Grand Rapids, MI: Zondervan, 2002.

Bourdieu, Pierre. *Acts of Resistance: Against the Tyranny of the Market.* Translated by Richard Nice. New York: The New Press, 1998.

Bourdieu, Pierre. *Firing Back: Against the Tyranny of the Market 2.* Translated by Loïc Wacquant. New York: The New Press, 2003.

Bowman, Shanthy A., Steven L. Gortmaker, Cara B. Ebbeling, Mark A. Pereira, and David S. Ludwig. "Effects of Fast-Food Consumption on Energy Intake and Diet Quality among Children in a National Household Survey." *Pediatrics* 113 (1) 2004: 112–18.

Brameld, Theodore. *Means and Ends in Education: A Midcentury Appraisal.* New York: Harper and Row, 1950.

Carle, Susan D. "John Dewey and the Early NAACP: Developing a Progressive Discourse on Racial Injustice, 1909–1921." In *Dewey's Enduring Impact:*

Essays on America's Philosopher, edited by John R. Shook and Paul Kurtz, 249-262. New York: Prometheus, 2011.

Cathy, S. Truett. *It's Easier to Succeed than Fail*. Nashville, TN: Thomas Nelson, 1989.

Cathy, S. Truett. *Eat MOR Chikin: Inspire More People Doing Business the Chick-fil-A Way*. Nashville, TN: Cumberland House Publishing, 2002.

Chick-fil-A. Chick-fil-A 10-Second Tip. *Children's Hospital's Healthy Kids: A Quarterly Publication for Parents Preschoolers* 9 (Winter, 2003): 3.

Core Essentials. *Core Essentials: A Strategy for Teaching Character*. 2001. https://coreessentials.org/

Core Essential Values. n.d. "Character Education Curriculum." https://coreessentials.org/#cev-section-home-curriculum-seedlings

Core Essential Values. n.d. "Chick-fil-A Partners." https://coreessentials.org/cfa_partners

Cunningham, Craig A., David Granger, Jane Fowler Morse, Barbara Stengel, and Terri Wilson. "Dewey, Women, and Weirdos: Or, the Potential Rewards for Scholars who Dialog across Difference." *Education & Culture* 23 (2) 2007: 27–62.

Deckelbaum, Richard J., and Christine A. Williams. "Childhood Obesity: The Health Issue." *Obesity Research* 9 (Suppl. 4) 2001: 239S–43S.

Deweese-Boyd, Ian T. E. "There Are No Schools in Utopia: John Dewey's Democratic Education." *Education & Culture* 31 (2) 2015: 69–80.

Dewey, John. *Moral Principles in Education*. Carbondale: Southern Illinois University Press, 1909.

Earls, Charles Anthony. "John Dewey's Relational Concept of Character." *The Pluralist* 3 (3) 2008: 1–22.

Eisele, J. Christopher. "John Dewey and the Immigrants." *History of Education Quarterly* 15 (1) 1975: 67–85.

Fallace, Thomas. "Repeating the Race Experience: John Dewey and the History Curriculum at the University of Chicago Laboratory School." *Curriculum Inquiry* 39 (3) 2009: 381–405.

Fallace, Thomas D. *Dewey and the Dilemma of Race: An Intellectual History, 1895–1922*. New York: Teachers College Press, 2010.

Feinberg, Walter. "Progressive Education and Social Planning." *Teachers College Record* 73 (4) 1972: 485–505.

Ferdman, Roberto A. "The Controversial Thing Kids Are Being Taught about McDonald's at School." *The Washington Post*, October 9, 2015. https://www.washingtonpost.com/news/wonk/wp/2015/10/29/how-mcdonalds-is-using-schools-to-try-to-change-what-kids-eat/.

Freire, Paulo. *Pedagogy of the Oppressed*. New York: Continuum, 1970.

Gard, Michael, and Carolyn Pluim. *Schools and Public Health: Past, Present, Future*. New York: Lexington, 2014.

Goddard, Connie. "Bordentown: Where Dewey's 'Learning to Earn' Met Du Boisian Educational Priorities: The Unique Legacy of a Once Thriving but Largely Forgotten School for Black Students." *Education & Culture* 35 (1) 2019: 49–70.

Goldstein, Dana. "Two States. Eight Textbooks. Two American Stories." *The New York Times*, January 12, 2020. https://www.nytimes.com/interactive/2020/01/12/us/texas-vs-california-history-textbooks.html.

Green, Steven K. *Inventing a Christian America: The Myth of the Religious Founding*. Oxford: Oxford University Press, 2015.

Greer, Colin. *The Great School Legend*. New York: Basic Books, 1972.

Howlett, Charles F., and Audrey Cohan. "John Dewey and his Evolving Perceptions of Race Issues in American Democracy." *Teaching Social Studies* 17 (1) 2017: 16–22.

James, V. Denise. "Theorizing Black Feminist Pragmatism: Forethoughts on the Practice and Purpose of Philosophy as Envisioned by Black Feminists and John Dewey." *The Journal of Speculative Philosophy* 23 (2) 2009: 92–99.

Jones, John Wesley. "Dewey and Cultural Racism." Master's thesis, University of Illinois, 2012.

Josephson, Michael. "Character Education Is Back in our Public Schools." *The State Education Standard* Autumn, 2002: 41–45.

Josephson, Michael. "Poem 'What Will Matter.'" 2003. https://whatwillmatter.com/2011/10/what-will-matter-745-3/.

Kaestle, Carl F. *Pillars of the Republic: Common Schools and American Society, 1780–1860*. New York: Hill and Wang, 1983.

Kliebard, Herbert. *The Struggle for the American Curriculum, 1893–1958*. New York: Routledge, 1995.

Kruse, Kevin M. *One Nation under God: How Corporate America Invented Christian America*. New York: Basic Books, 2015.

Lickona, Thomas. *Character Matters: How to Help our Children Develop Good Judgment, Integrity, and Other Essential Virtues*. New York: Simon and Schuster, 2004.

Lindblom, Charles E. *Politics and Markets: The World's Political-Economic Systems*. New York: Basic Books, 1977.

Ludwig, David S., Karen E. Peterson, and Steven Gortmaker. "Relation between Consumption of Sugar-Sweetened Drinks and Childhood Obesity: A Prospective, Observational Analysis." *The Lancet* 357 (9255) 2001: 505–508.

MacDonald, Mary. "Georgia May Shun 'Evolution' in Schools: Revised Curriculum Plan Outrages Science Teachers." *The Atlanta Journal-Constitution*, January 29, 2004a, A1.

MacDonald, Mary. "Evolution Furor Heats Up." *The Atlanta Journal-Constitution*, January 31, 2004b, A1.

Margonis, Frank. "John Dewey's Racialized Visions of the Student and Classroom Community." *Educational Theory* 59 (1) 2009: 17–39.

Marty, Martin E., and R. Scott Appleby, eds. *Fundamentalism and Society: Reclaiming the Science, the Family, and Education*. Chicago: The University of Chicago Press, 1997.

Mayhew, Katherine Camp, and Anna Camp Edwards. *The Dewey School: The Laboratory School of the University of Chicago, 1896–1903*. New York: J. Appleton-Century, 1936.

McCune, Timothy. "Dewey's Dilemma: Eugenics, Education, and the Art of Living." *The Pluralist* 7 (3) 2012: 96–106.

Morris, Daniel A. "Improvisation as Democratic Virtue: A Deweyan Possibility for African American Religion and Ethics." *Soundings: An Interdisciplinary Journal* 96 (4) 2013: 355–81.

Mosier, Richard. *Making the American Mind: Social and Moral Ideas in the Mc-Guffey Readers*. New York: Russell & Russell, 1965.

Nestle, Marion. *Food Politics: How the Food Industry Influences Nutrition and Health*. Berkeley: University of California Press, 2003.

Pappas, Gregory Fernando. "Dewey and Feminism: The Affective and Relationships in Dewey's Ethics." *Hypatia* 8 (2) 1993: 78–95.

Seidel, Andrew L. *The Founding Myth: Why Christian Nationalism Is Un-American*. New York: Sterling, 2019.

Siegfried, Charlene Haddock, ed. *Feminist Interpretations of John Dewey*. University Park: Pennsylvania State University Press, 2001.

Sorrell, Kory Spencer. "Feminist Ethics and Dewey's Moral Theory." *Transactions of the Charles S. Peirce Society* 35 (1) 1999: 89–114.

Spring, Joel. *The Sorting Machine Revisited: National Educational Policy since 1945*. Boston: Addison-Wesley, 1988.

Spring, Joel. *The American School, 1642–2004*. Boston: McGraw-Hill, 2005.

Stack, Sam F., Jr. "John Dewey and the Question of Race: The Fight for Odell Waller." *Education & Culture* 25 (1) 2009: 17–35.

State University of New York College at Cortland. n.d. Center for the 4th and 5th R's. http://www.cortland.edu/c4n5rs/

Sullivan, Shannon. "From the Foreign to the Familiar: Confronting Dewey Confronting Racial Prejudice." *Journal of Speculative Philosophy* 18 (3) 2004: 193–202.

Tawney, Richard Henry. *Religion and the Rise of Capitalism*. New York: Harcourt, Brace, and Company, 1926.

Tesconi, Charles A., Jr., and Van Cleve Morris. *The Anti-Man Culture: Bureau-Technocracy and the Schools*. Urbana: University of Illinois Press, 1972.

VanderSchee, Carolyn. "Food Services and Schooling." In *Schools or Markets?: Commercialism, Privatization, and School-Business Partnerships*, edited by Deron Boyles, 1-26. Mahwah, NJ: Lawrence Erlbaum, 2004.

Vaughan, Kelly. "Progressive Education and Racial Justice: Examining the Work of John Dewey." *Education & Culture* 34 (2) 2018: 39–68.

Williams, Mary M. "Models of Character Education: Perspectives and Development Issues." *Journal of Humanistic Counseling, Education and Development* 39 (1) 2000: 32–40.

Woyshner, Christine, and Chara Haeussler Bohan, eds. *Histories of Social Studies and Race: 1865–2000*. New York: Palgrave Macmillan, 2012.

Zarra, Ernest J. "Pinning Down Character Education." *Kappa Delta Pi Record* 36 (4) 2000: 154–57.

Deron Boyles is Professor of Philosophy of Education in the Department of Educational Policy Studies at Georgia State University. His research interests include school commercialism, epistemology, ethics, pragmatism, and the philosophy of John Dewey. His work has been published in journals such as *Philosophy of Education*; *Social Epistemology*; the *Journal of Thought, Education & Culture*; *Philosophical Studies in Education*; *Dewey Studies*; the *Inter-American Journal of Philosophy*; *History of Education Quarterly*; *Educational Studies*; and *Educational Theory*. He is the author of *American Education and Corporations: The Free Market Goes to School* and the editor of *Schools or Markets?: Commercialism, Privatization, and School-Business Partnerships* and *The Corporate Assault on Youth: Commercialism, Exploitation, and the End of Innocence*. He is coauthor, with Benjamin Baez, of *The Politics of Inquiry: Education Research and the "Culture of Science"* and coauthor, with Kenneth J. Potts, of *From a Gadfly to a Hornet: Academic Freedom, Humane Education, and the Intellectual Life of Joseph Kinmont Hart*. Boyles is Past-President of the American Educational Studies Association and Past-President of the John Dewey Society.